SHEKHAR KAPUR'S
SNAKE WOMAN™

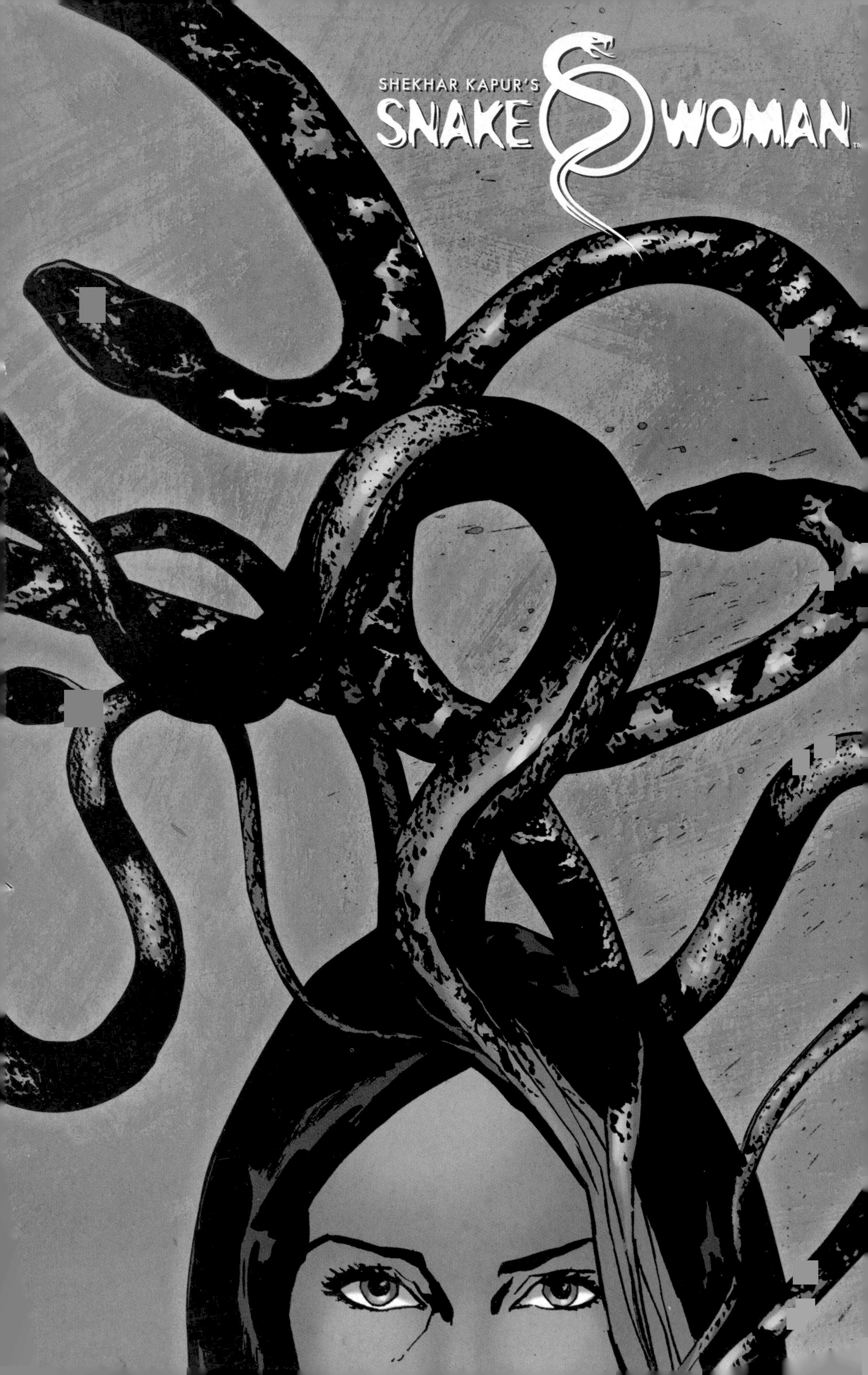
SHEKHAR KAPUR'S
SNAKE WOMAN

CREATED BY
SHEKHAR KAPUR

SCRIPT
ZEB WELLS

ART
DEAN HYRAPIET
VIVEK SHINDE &
MICHAEL GAYDOS

COVER ART
MICHAEL GAYDOS

ADDITIONAL COVER ART
GREG HORN
MUKESH SINGH
ADITYA CHARI
SATISH TAYADE
K. SAMPATH KUMAR

COLORS
A. SELVAN
I. JEYABALAN

LETTERS
B. S. RAVI KIRAN
NILESH S. MAHADIK
SUDHIR B. PISAL
JYOTSNA V. DOMSE
RAKESH B. MAHADIK

PROJECT MANAGER
REUBEN THOMAS

ASSISTANT EDITORS
MAHESH KAMATH
CHARLIE BECKERMAN
SANA AMANAT

EDITOR
MACKENZIE CADENHEAD

SHEKHAR KAPUR'S

SNAKE WOMAN™

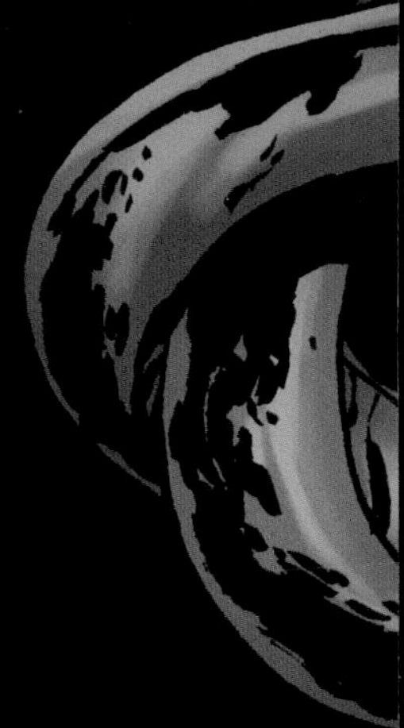

VIRGIN COMICS

Chief Executive Officer and Publisher
SHARAD DEVARAJAN

Chief Creative Officer
and Editor-in-Chief
GOTHAM CHOPRA

President and Studio Chief
SURESH SEETHARAMAN

Chief Marketing Officer
LARRY LIEBERMAN

SRVP - Studio
JEEVAN KANG

Head of Operations
ALAGAPPAN KANNAN

Director of Development
MACKENZIE CADENHEAD

Chief Visionaries
DEEPAK CHOPRA,
SHEKHAR KAPUR,
SIR RICHARD BRANSON

Special Thanks to:
FRANCES FARROW, DAN PORTER,
CHRISTOPHER LINEN, PETER FELDMAN,
RAJU PUTHUKARAI AND
MALLIKA CHOPRA

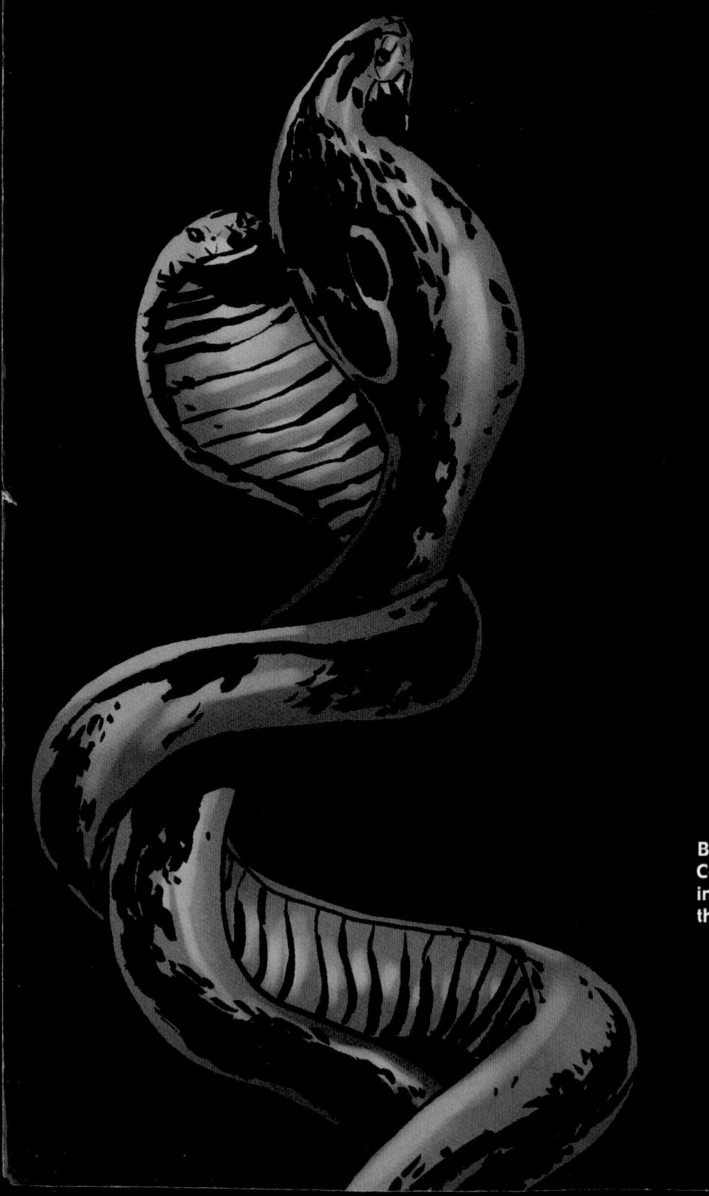

SNAKE WOMAN Vol. 2, September 2007 published by VIRGIN COMICS L.L.C. OFFICE OF PUBLICATION: 594 Broadway, New York, NY 10012.

Printed in Canada.
For advertising, licensing and sales info please contact: info@virgincomics.com or (212) 584-4040.
www.virgincomics.com

Introduction by
C.B. CEBULSKI

Superheroes seem to be everywhere these days, their adventures lighting up screens big and small, all over the world. Movies, TV shows and video games are all caught in the thrall of web-swingers, caped crusaders, and merry mutants. The geeks have spoken and have seized control of pop culture. Yes, comic book culture may now be international... but who's going to start bringing more international culture to comic books?

Virgin Comics, that's who!

Talk about a recipe for success... take a globally-recognized media mogul, combine one internationally renowned spiritual guru, mix them up with an award-winning Indian writer/director, and then add in two young globe-trotting visionaries with unbridled imaginations. The result is a creative collaborative the likes of which the comic book world has never seen. From the outset, the Virgin vision has been clear: take the myth and magic of India and open it up to an international audience using the comic book medium. Their mission statement was to bring their culture to ours; to use this ever-evolving form of sequential storytelling to open our eyes to the rich traditions of fantasy and folklore they grew up on. Some said it couldn't be done, but they're the ones being schooled now as Virgin's emergence has taught everyone a lesson or two along the way.

Shekhar Kapur's *Snake Woman,* the comic you now hold in your hands, is a textbook example of how to entertain and educate at the same time!

It's not often a comic company can boast they have a creator whose work has been nominated for an Academy Award, but Virgin sure can. Shekhar Kapur has been making critically acclaimed films for over twenty years now, so when he brings an idea for a comic book to the table, you listen. When that idea turns out to be one of the most original and inventive concepts to have come along in quite some time, you scour the globe for the top talent you can find to help turn those ideas into illustrated reality.

Virgin went after, and scored, Zeb Wells to write *Snake Woman,* which is inspired "casting" if you ask me. Better known for the humorous overtones in his writing thanks to projects like *Robot Chicken* and *New Warriors,* Zeb also has a dark side where he can tap into the secret lives of complicated characters and expose the underbelly of their seemingly normal existence. Zeb brings a grim and gritty depth to Jessica Peterson, the Snake Woman herself, as well as to her enemies, James Harker and The 68, that makes readers squirm in their seats, but keeps them turning the page, looking for what lurks around the next corner.

Then, in the spirit of true international cooperation, Virgin hired the best and brightest stars from India's exploding art scene to bring Shekhar and Zeb's vision to graphic light. The digital art of Dean Hyrapiet and Vivek Shinde, a modern mix of pencils and pixels, brings haunting realism to the world inside this comic. They make the characters move—or should I say slither—from panel to panel and page to page with an eerily ethereal ease to their storytelling.

Time-zones be damned, this rag-tag team of talents was able to seamlessly coordinate their efforts from different corners of the globe and take a story deeply rooted in Indian culture, mix it up and modernize it into something truly unique. With a flavor all its own, *Snake Woman* is leading Virgin's charge to break boundaries, smash stereotypes and show that culture is ready to be brought back to comics, now more than ever. By doing it with such stunning and spectacular sensibilities, this serpent has now succeeded in securing shelf space from the super heroes. I have a feeling *Snake Woman*'s aren't the only scales tipping in Virgin's favor....

C.B. Cebulski
Writer, ***Loners***
New York City
August 20th, 2007

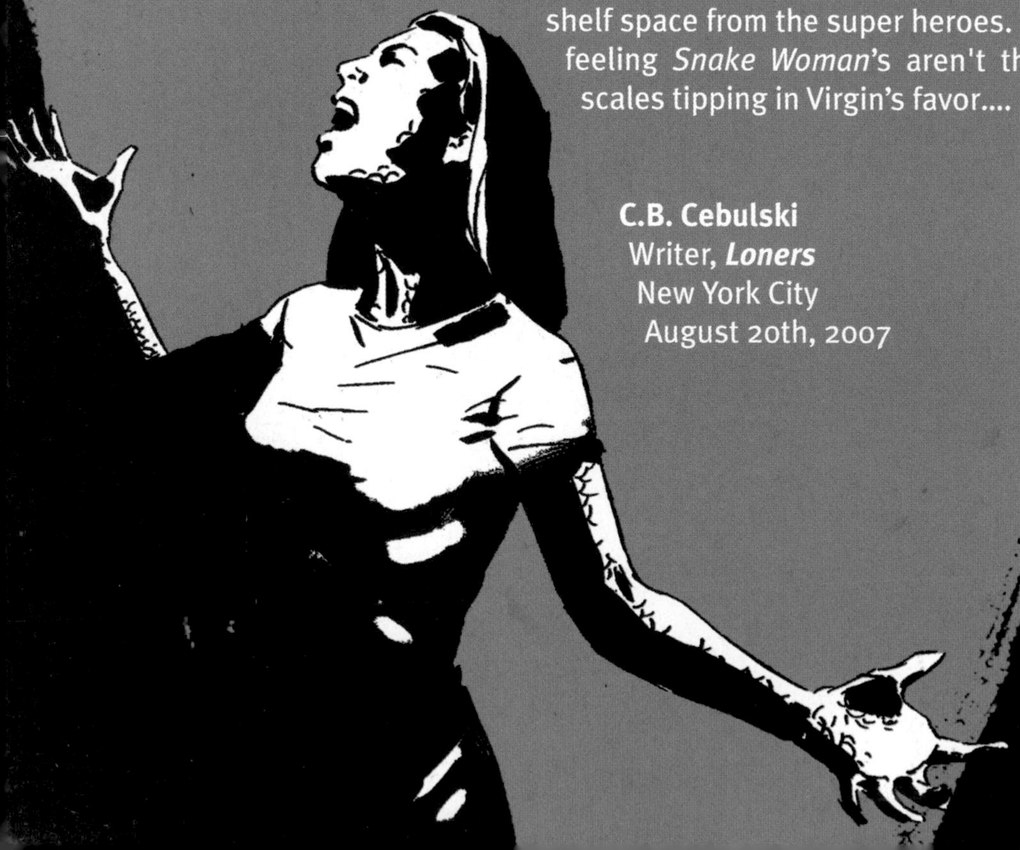

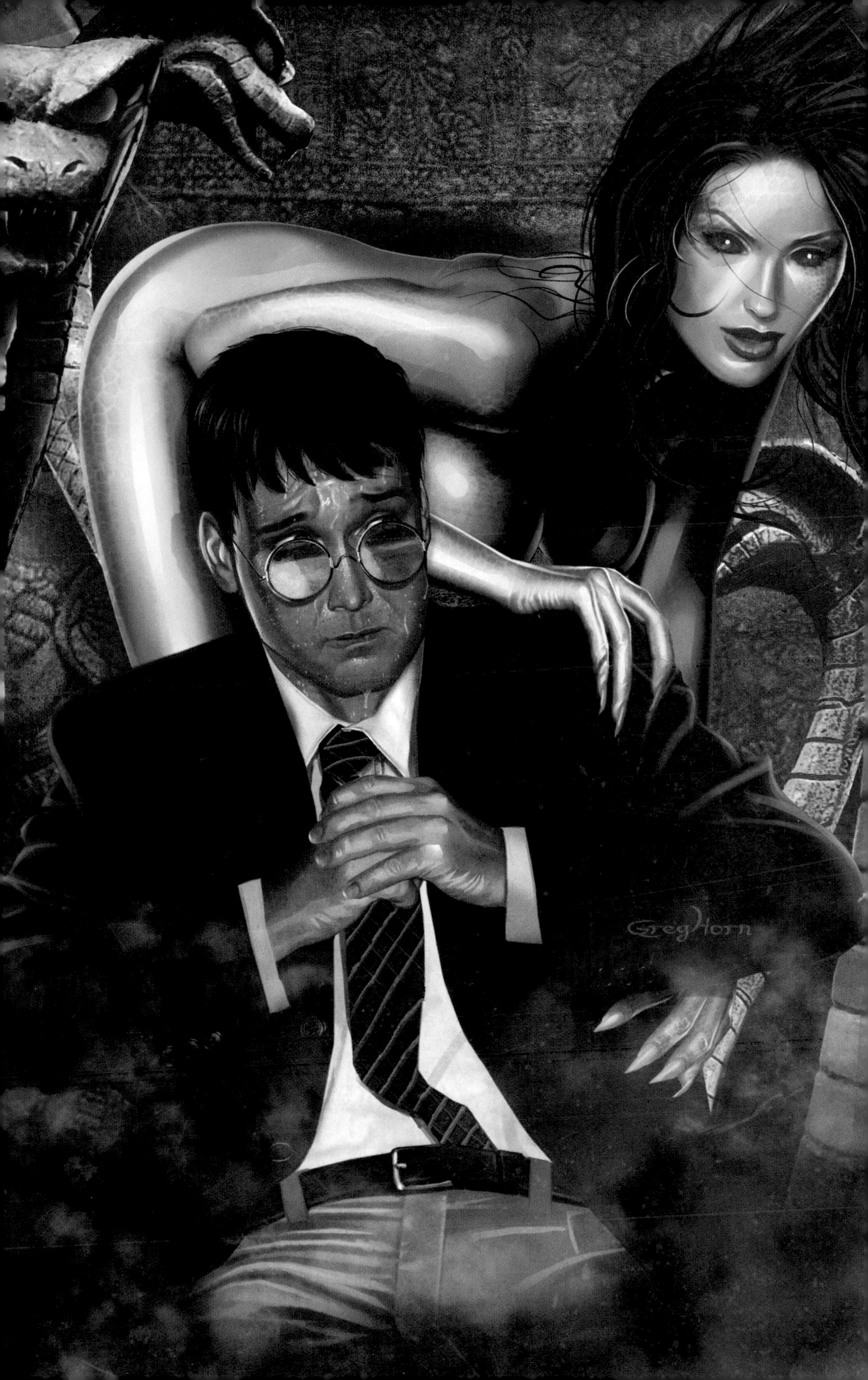
Greg Horn

In the early 18th century,
while exploring the vast Kabini Jungles of India,
a group of British explorers desecrate an ancient temple
erected to a Snake God. As a result, all sixty-eight
of them are destined to be reincarnated and
hunted by a woman, a woman imbued
with the powers of the Snake God.

As these men are reincarnated throughout
the decades in different lives and locations,
this Snake Woman's mission will only end when
all of the 68 are found and killed within a single lifetime.
If even one of the 68 survives to die of natural causes,
all are reborn to once again be hunted.
So has this cycle of death and rebirth
continued for centuries...

Now, in the 21st Century,
the 68 have become a powerful organization
led by a man called Harker. To be a member of
the 68 is to be hunted, but it is also to be rich
and powerful. Not all of them, however,
know who they are...

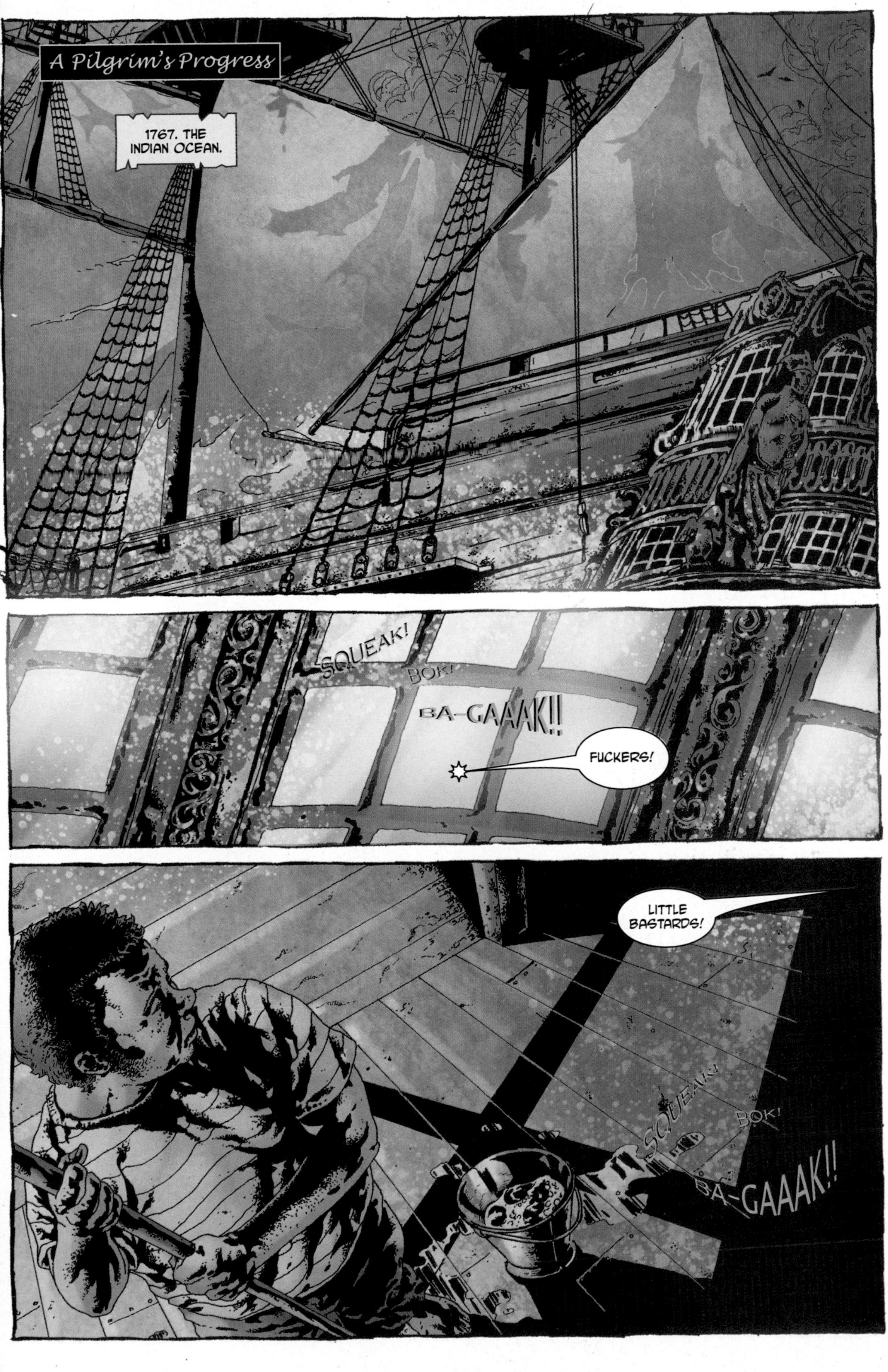
A Pilgrim's Progress
1767. THE INDIAN OCEAN.
SQUEAK!
BOK!
BA-GAAAK!!
FUCKERS!
LITTLE BASTARDS!
SQUEAK!
BOK!
BA-GAAAK!!

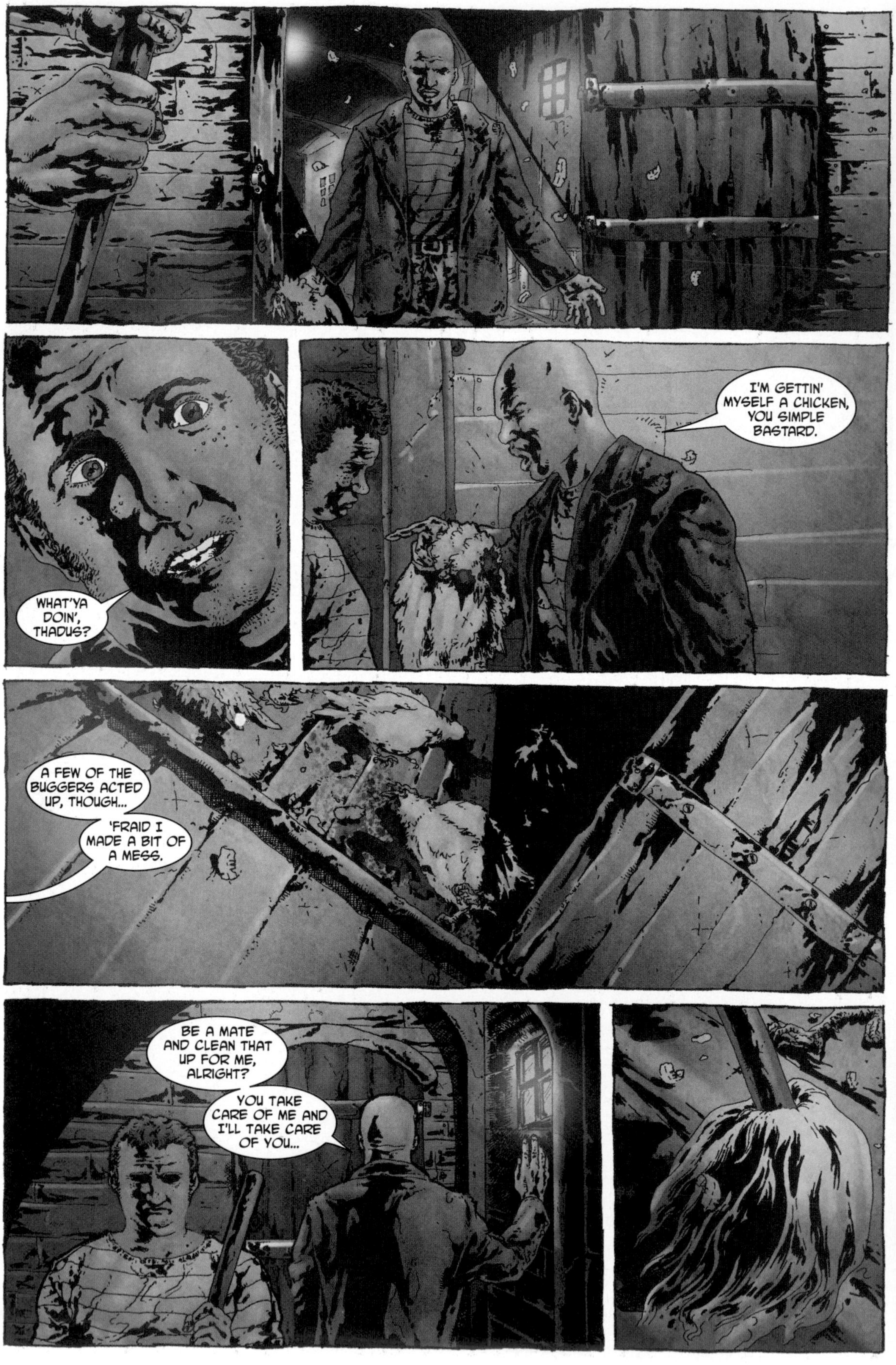
WHAT'YA DOIN', THADUS?
I'M GETTIN' MYSELF A CHICKEN, YOU SIMPLE BASTARD.
A FEW OF THE BUGGERS ACTED UP, THOUGH...
'FRAID I MADE A BIT OF A MESS.
BE A MATE AND CLEAN THAT UP FOR ME, ALRIGHT?
YOU TAKE CARE OF ME AND I'LL TAKE CARE OF YOU...

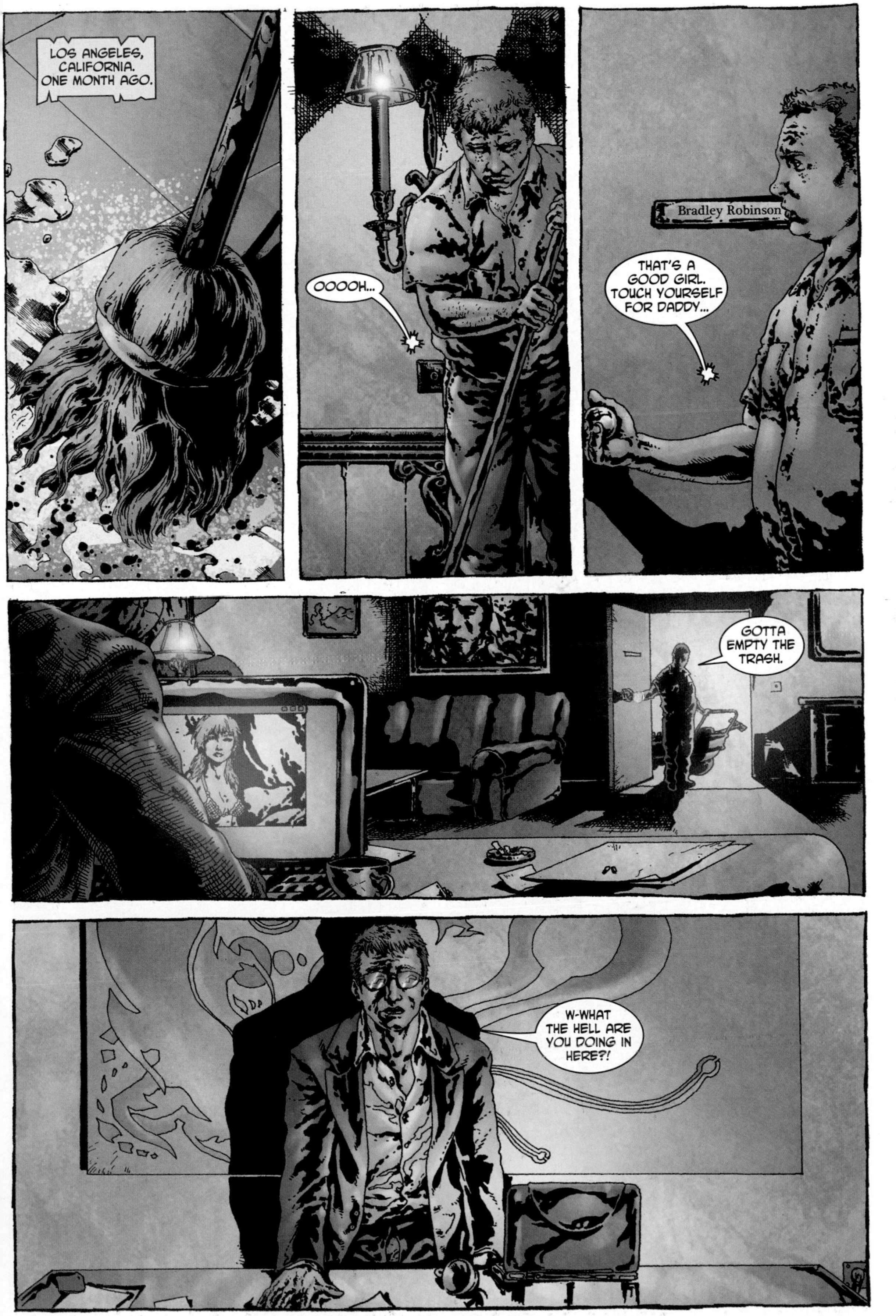
LOS ANGELES, CALIFORNIA. ONE MONTH AGO.
OOOOH...
Bradley Robinson
THAT'S A GOOD GIRL. TOUCH YOURSELF FOR DADDY...
GOTTA EMPTY THE TRASH.
W-WHAT THE HELL ARE YOU DOING IN HERE?!

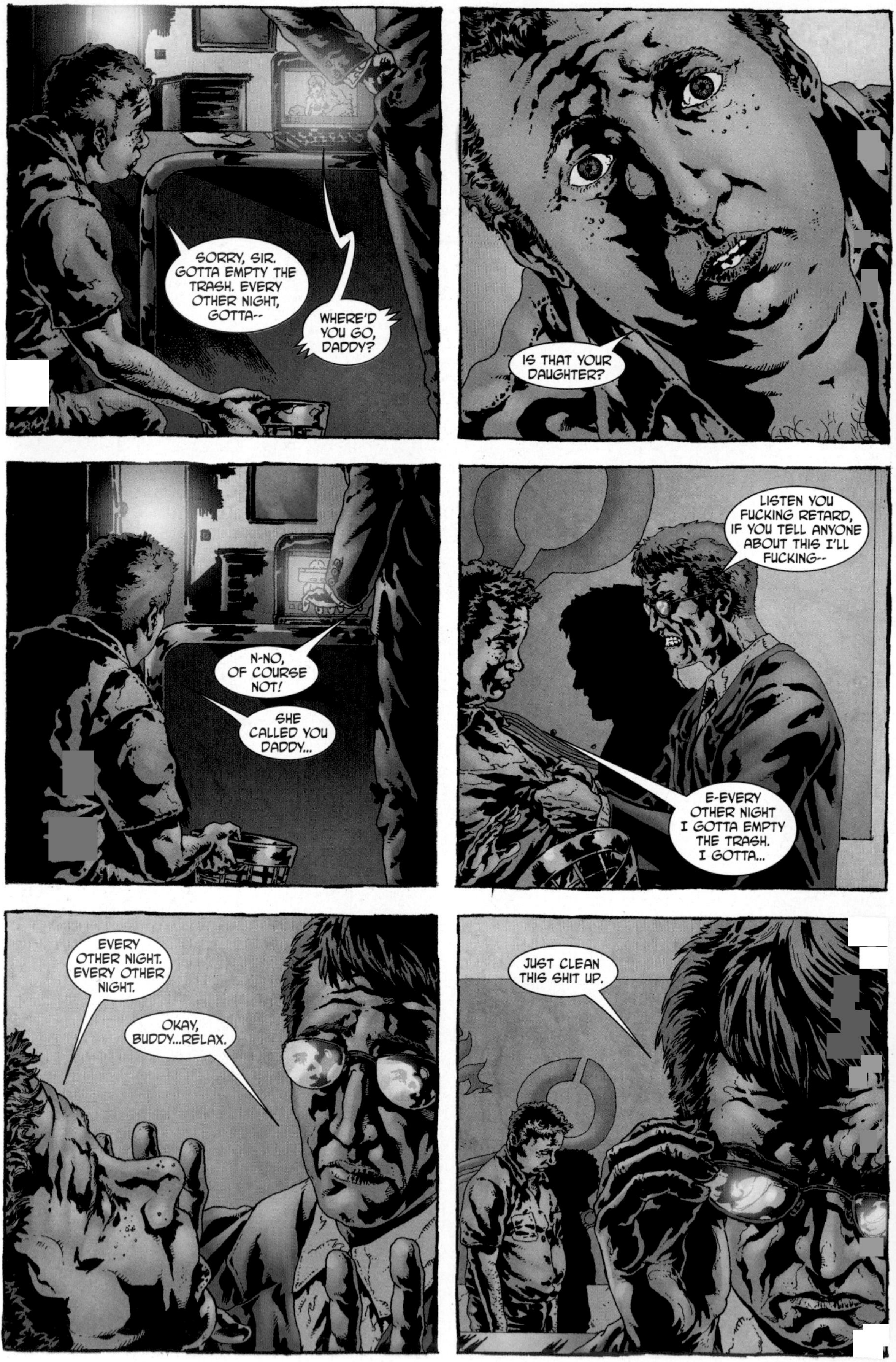
SORRY, SIR. GOTTA EMPTY THE TRASH. EVERY OTHER NIGHT, GOTTA--
WHERE'D YOU GO, DADDY?
IS THAT YOUR DAUGHTER?
N-NO, OF COURSE NOT!
SHE CALLED YOU DADDY...
LISTEN YOU FUCKING RETARD, IF YOU TELL ANYONE ABOUT THIS I'LL FUCKING--
E-EVERY OTHER NIGHT I GOTTA EMPTY THE TRASH. I GOTTA...
EVERY OTHER NIGHT. EVERY OTHER NIGHT.
OKAY, BUDDY...RELAX.
JUST CLEAN THIS SHIT UP.

MY NAME IS PAUL GILMORE. PEOPLE ARE ALWAYS TELLING ME TO CLEAN THINGS UP. BUT I DON'T MIND.

I'M A PRETTY GOOD CLEANER.

I GOT MY OWN PLACE SINCE MOMMA DIED. I KEEP THE PLACE SPICK AND SPAN.

THAT'S WHAT THE GAS MAN SAYS WHEN HE STOPS BY EVERY COUPLE OF MONTHS TO ASK FOR MONEY.

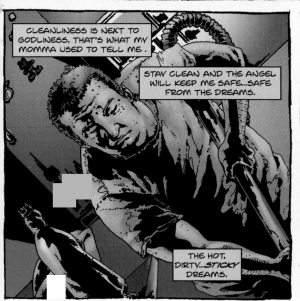

CLEANLINESS IS NEXT TO GODLINESS, THAT'S WHAT MY MOMMA USED TO TELL ME.

STAY CLEAN AND THE ANGEL WILL KEEP ME SAFE...SAFE FROM THE DREAMS.

THE HOT, DIRTY...*STICKY* DREAMS.

SOMETIMES I CAN FEEL THE DREAMS IN MY HEAD, TRYIN' TO GET OUT. THAT'S WHEN I KNOW I'VE GOT TO MAKE THE ANGEL HAPPY.

ELSE *HE'LL* COME FOR ME AGAIN...AND *HE'LL* MAKE ME CLEAN FOR *HIM*.

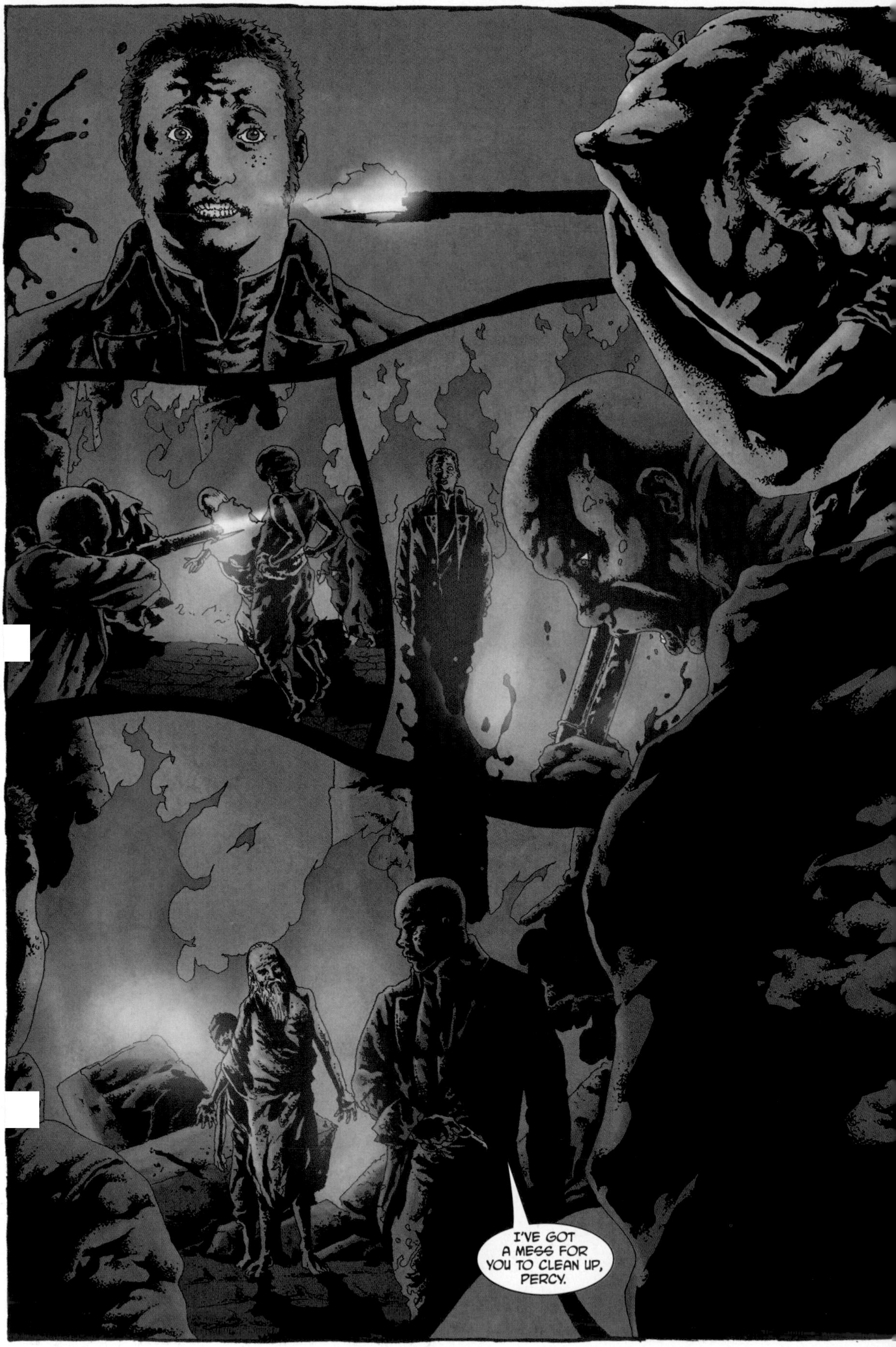
I'VE GOT A MESS FOR YOU TO CLEAN UP, PERCY.

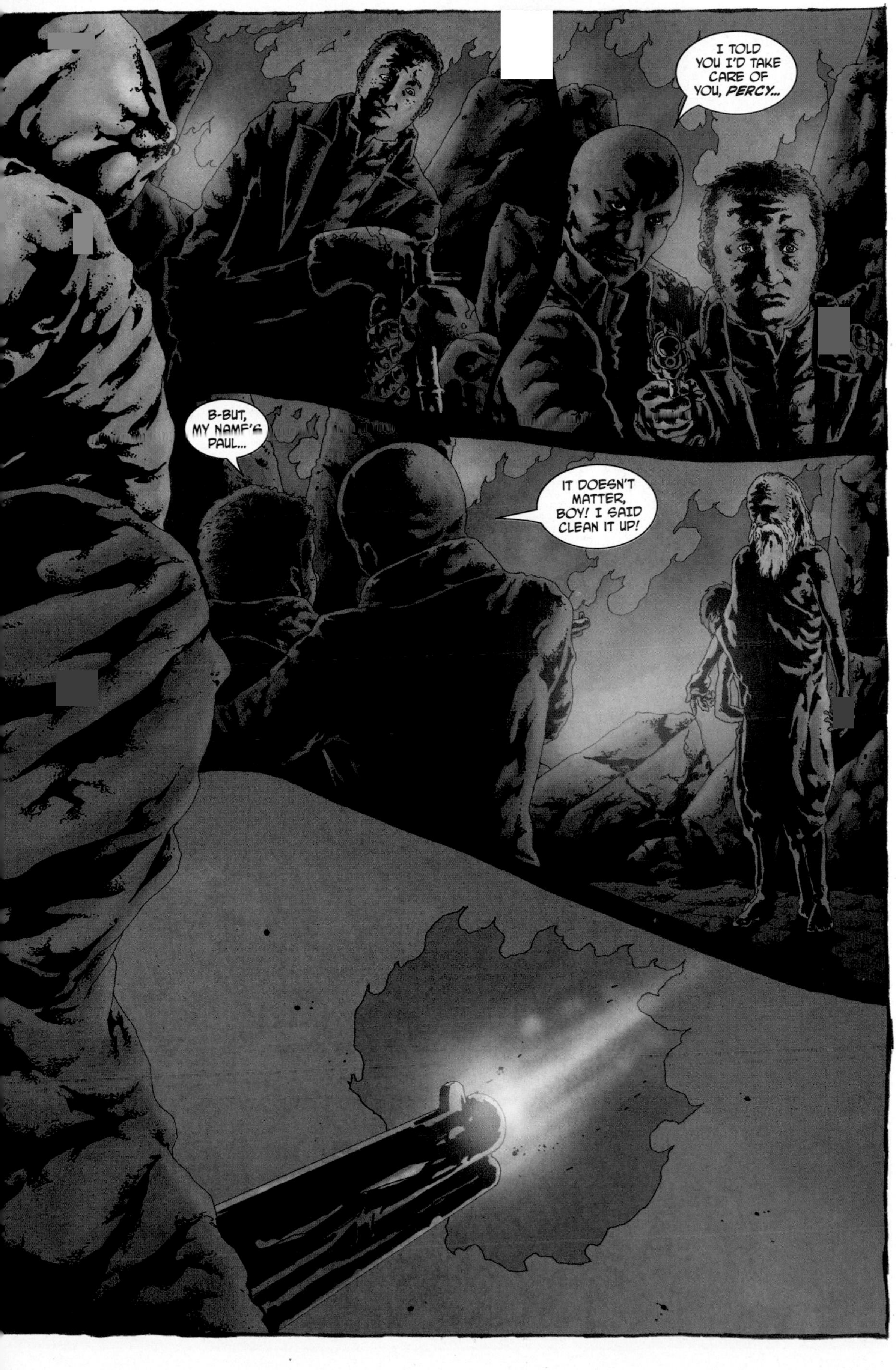
I TOLD YOU I'D TAKE CARE OF YOU, PERCY...
B-BUT, MY NAME'S PAUL...
IT DOESN'T MATTER, BOY! I SAID CLEAN IT UP!

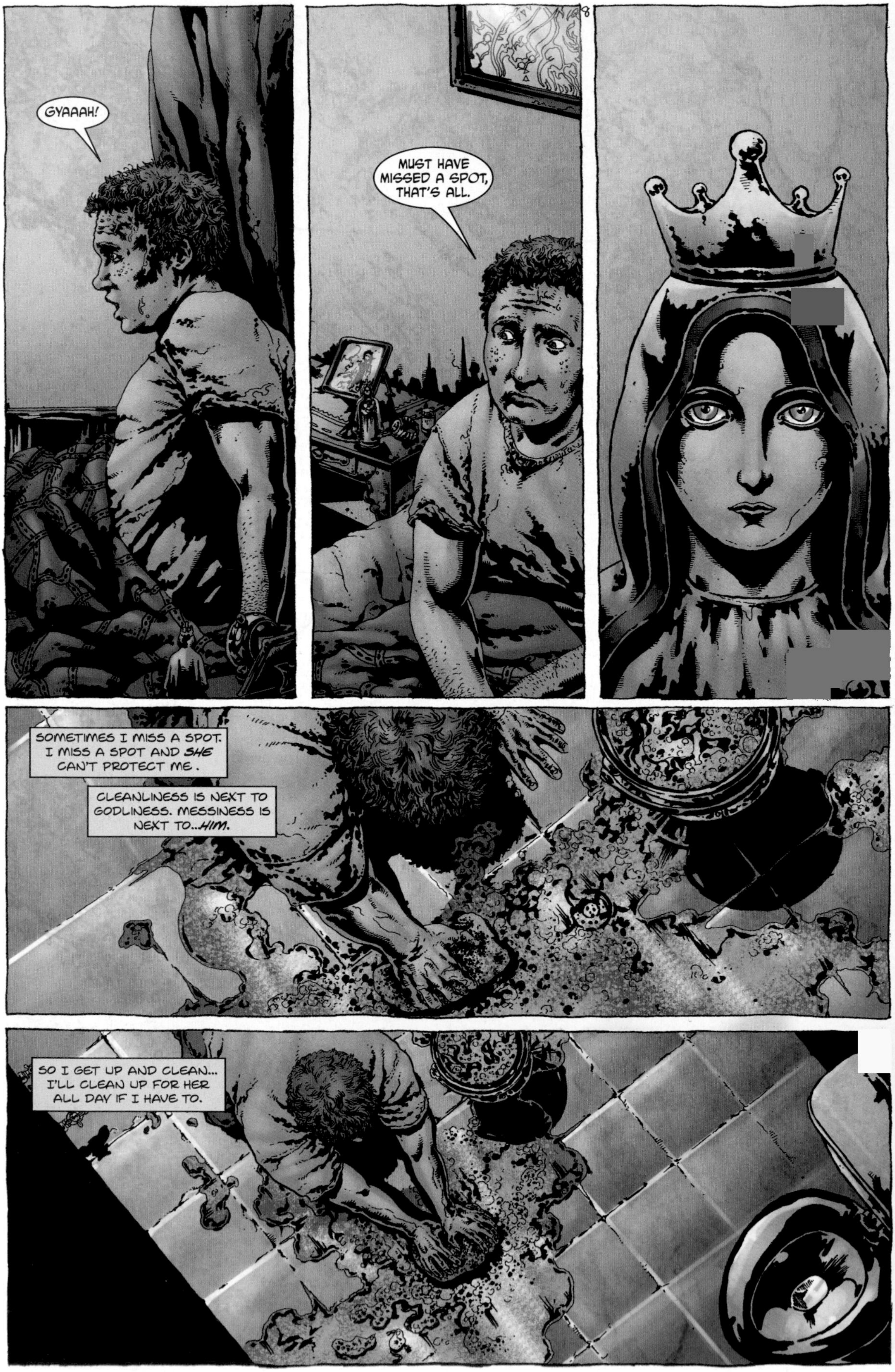
GYAAAH!
MUST HAVE MISSED A SPOT, THAT'S ALL.
SOMETIMES I MISS A SPOT. I MISS A SPOT AND SHE CAN'T PROTECT ME.
CLEANLINESS IS NEXT TO GODLINESS. MESSINESS IS NEXT TO...HIM.
SO I GET UP AND CLEAN... I'LL CLEAN UP FOR HER ALL DAY IF I HAVE TO.

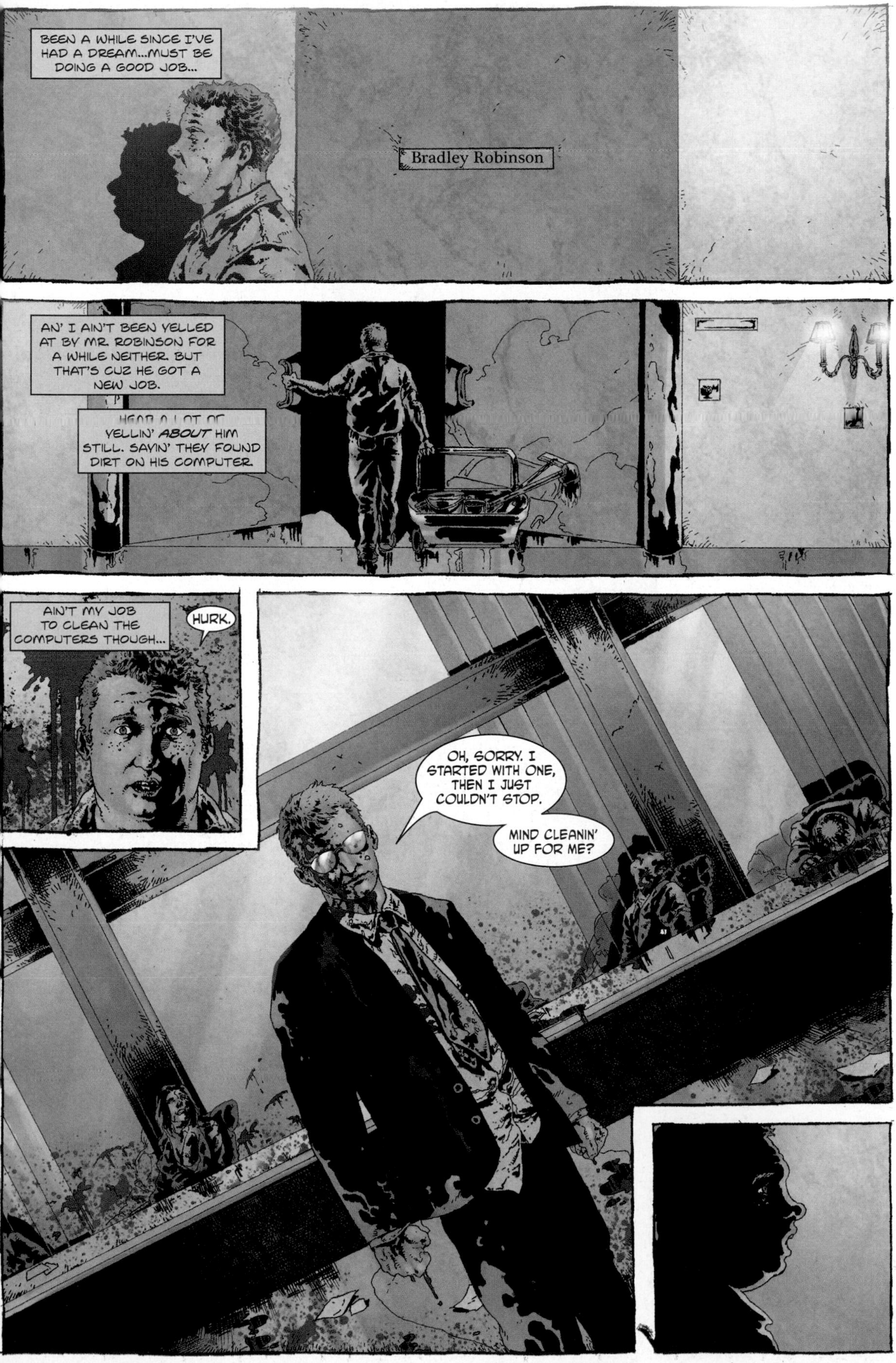
BEEN A WHILE SINCE I'VE HAD A DREAM...MUST BE DOING A GOOD JOB...
Bradley Robinson
AN' I AIN'T BEEN YELLED AT BY MR. ROBINSON FOR A WHILE NEITHER. BUT THAT'S CUZ HE GOT A NEW JOB.
HEAR A LOT OF YELLIN' ABOUT HIM STILL. SAYIN' THEY FOUND DIRT ON HIS COMPUTER.
AIN'T MY JOB TO CLEAN THE COMPUTERS THOUGH...
HURK.
OH, SORRY. I STARTED WITH ONE, THEN I JUST COULDN'T STOP.
MIND CLEANIN' UP FOR ME?

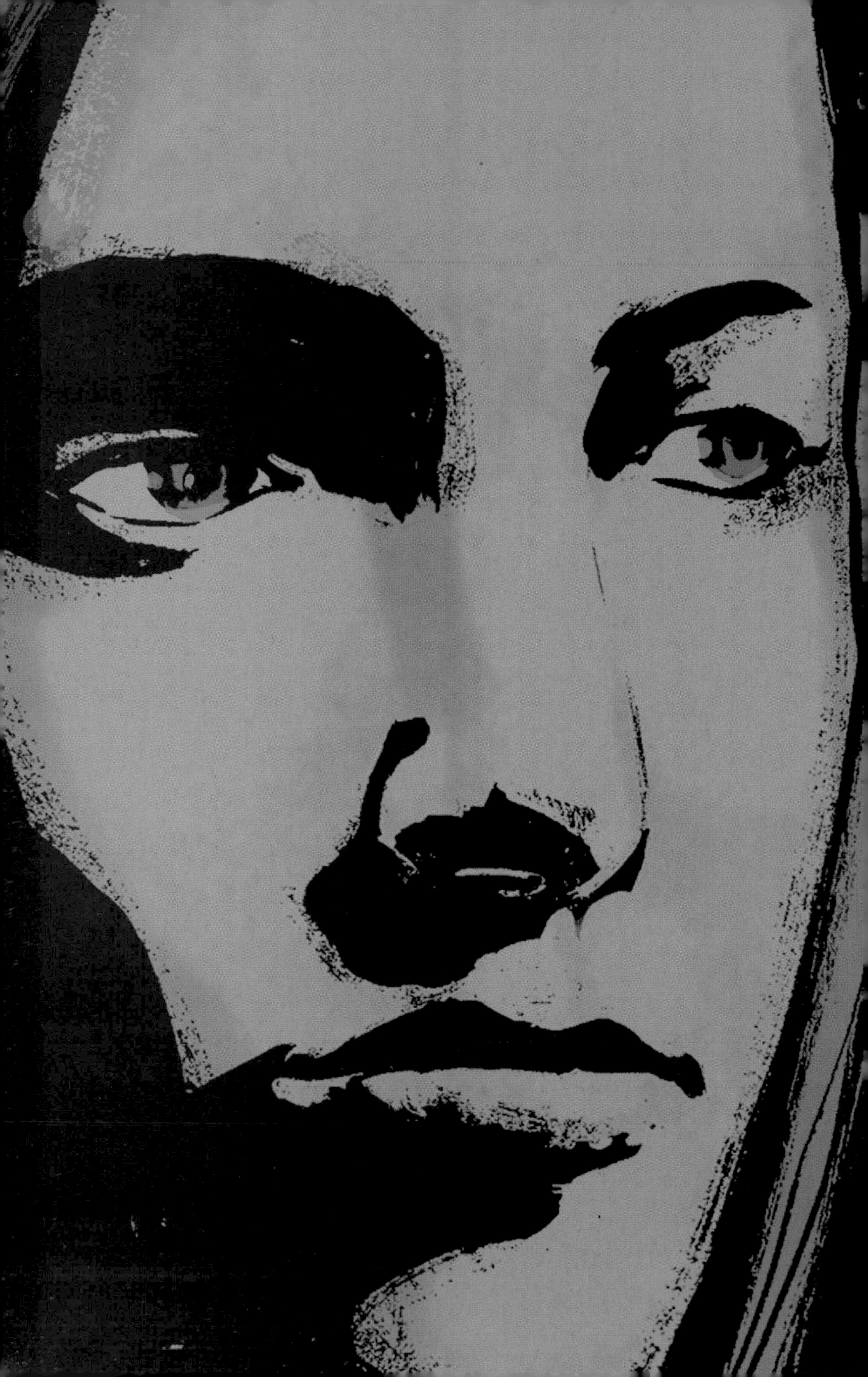

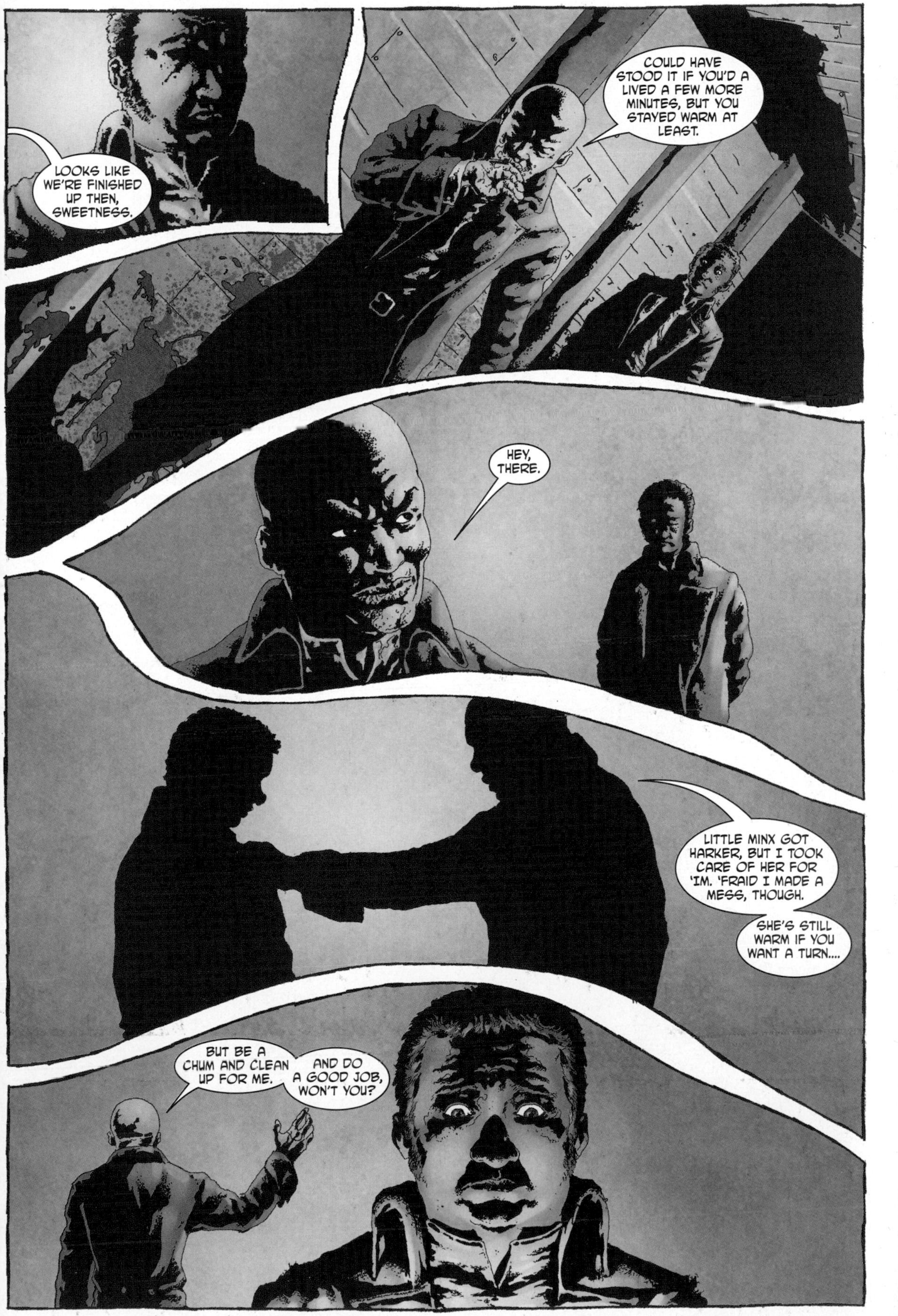
LOOKS LIKE WE'RE FINISHED UP THEN, SWEETNESS.
COULD HAVE STOOD IT IF YOU'D A LIVED A FEW MORE MINUTES, BUT YOU STAYED WARM AT LEAST.
HEY, THERE.
LITTLE MINX GOT HARKER, BUT I TOOK CARE OF HER FOR 'IM. 'FRAID I MADE A MESS, THOUGH.
SHE'S STILL WARM IF YOU WANT A TURN....
BUT BE A CHUM AND CLEAN UP FOR ME.
AND DO A GOOD JOB, WON'T YOU?

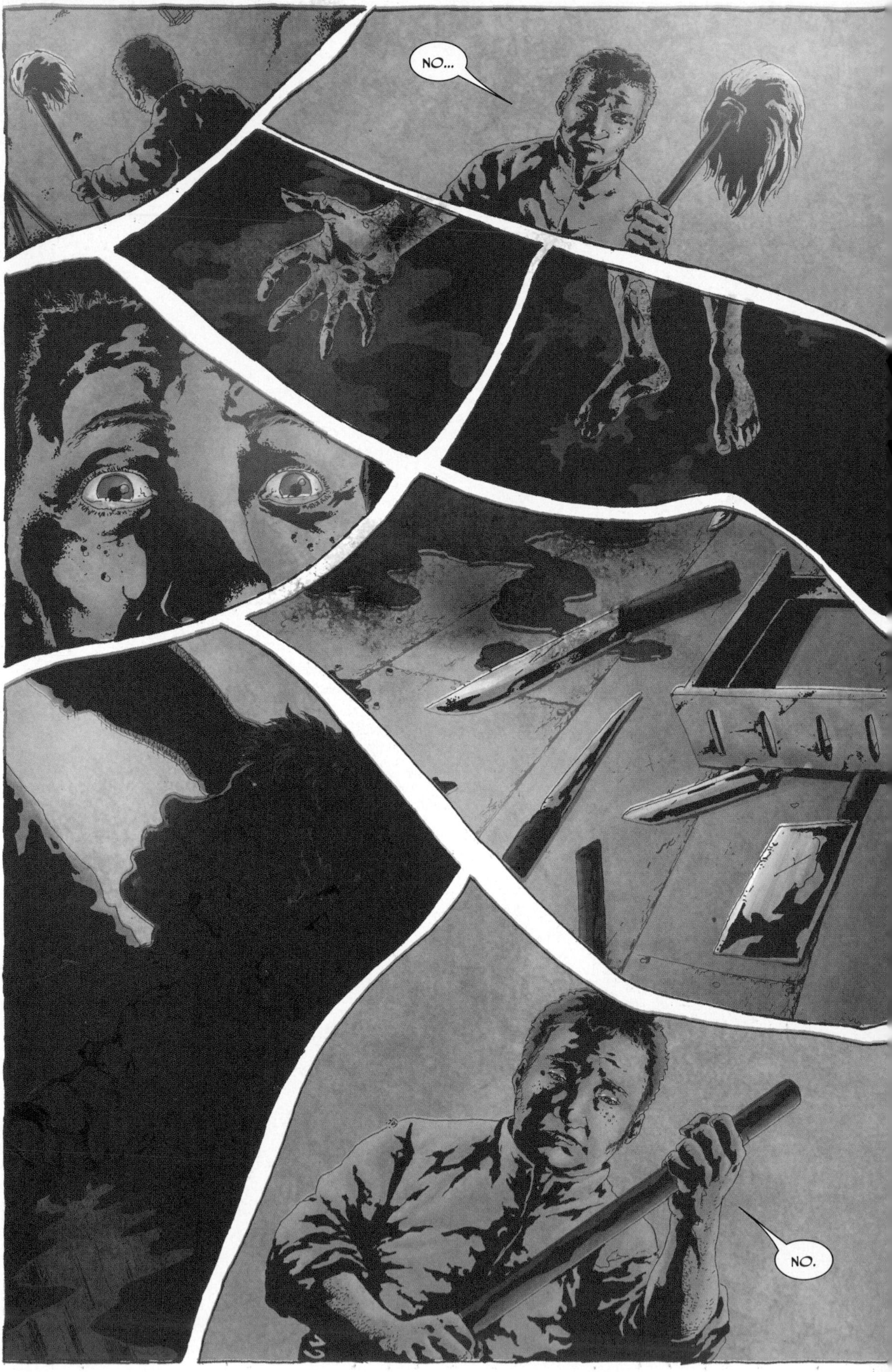
NO...
NO.

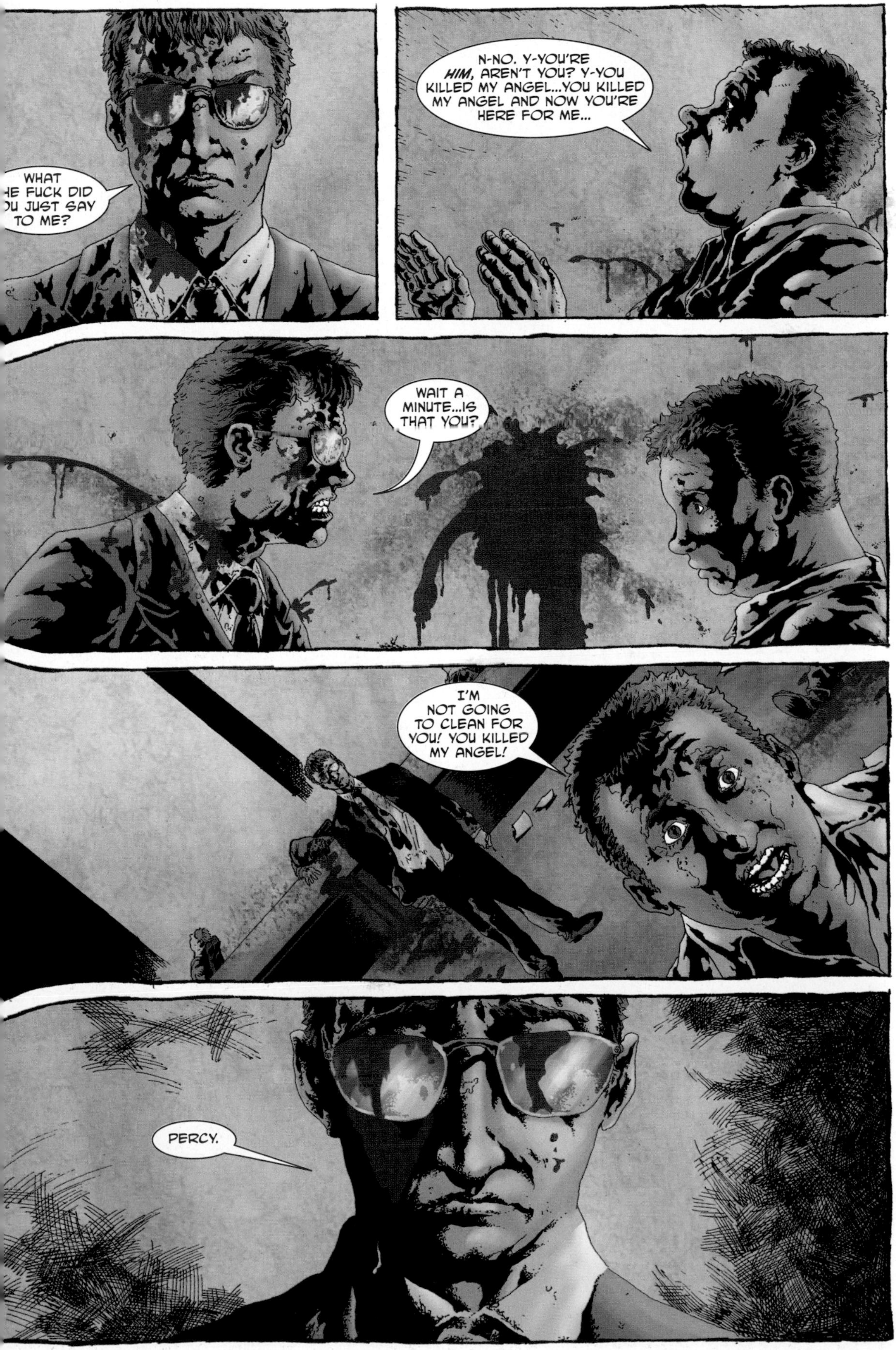
WHAT HE FUCK DID DU JUST SAY TO ME?
N-NO. Y-YOU'RE HIM, AREN'T YOU? Y-YOU KILLED MY ANGEL...YOU KILLED MY ANGEL AND NOW YOU'RE HERE FOR ME...
WAIT A MINUTE...IS THAT YOU?
I'M NOT GOING TO CLEAN FOR YOU! YOU KILLED MY ANGEL!
PERCY.

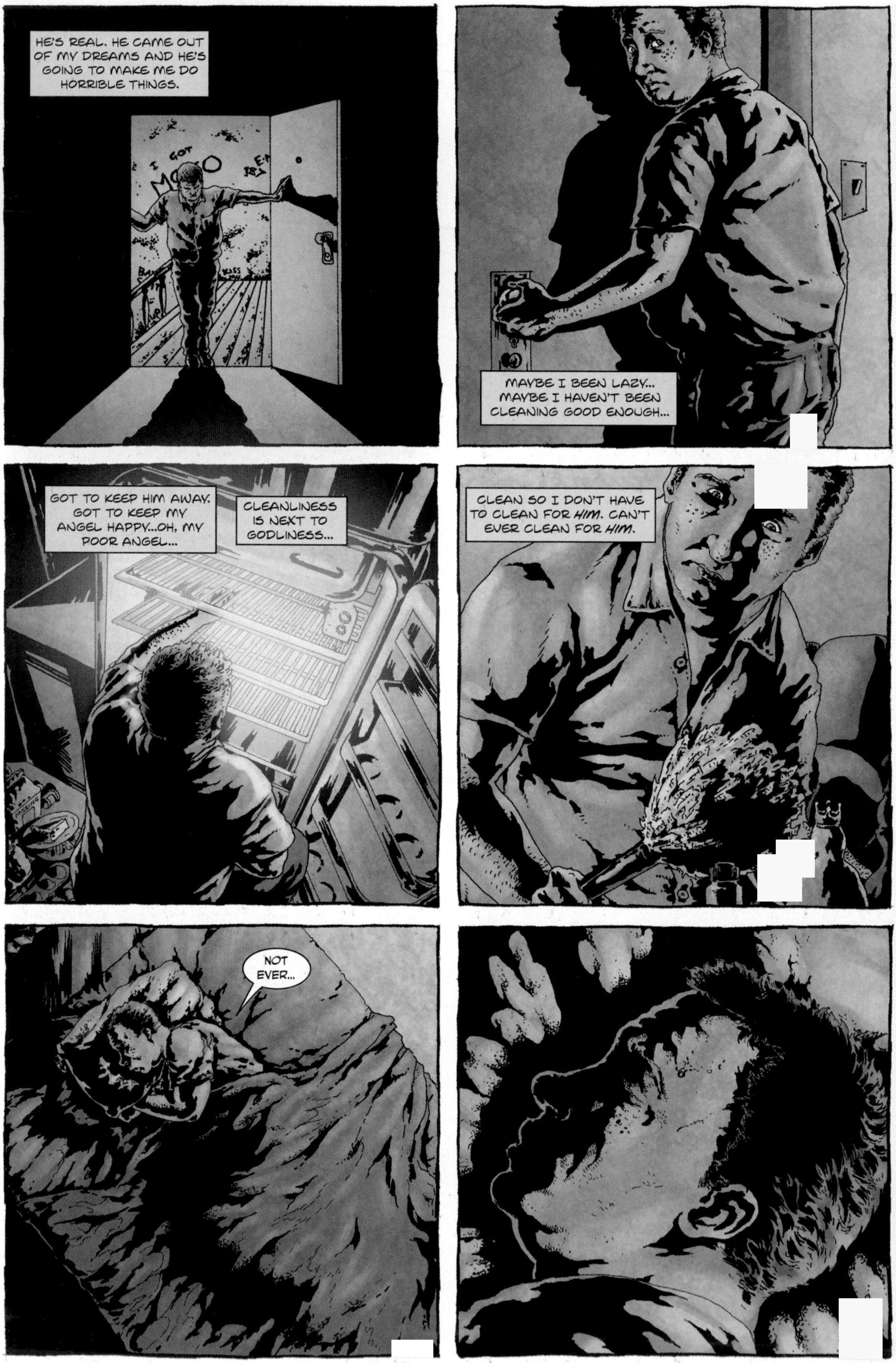

HE'S REAL. HE CAME OUT OF MY DREAMS AND HE'S GOING TO MAKE ME DO HORRIBLE THINGS.
MAYBE I BEEN LAZY... MAYBE I HAVEN'T BEEN CLEANING GOOD ENOUGH...
GOT TO KEEP HIM AWAY. GOT TO KEEP MY ANGEL HAPPY...OH, MY POOR ANGEL...
CLEANLINESS IS NEXT TO GODLINESS...
CLEAN SO I DON'T HAVE TO CLEAN FOR *HIM*. CAN'T EVER CLEAN FOR *HIM*.
NOT EVER...

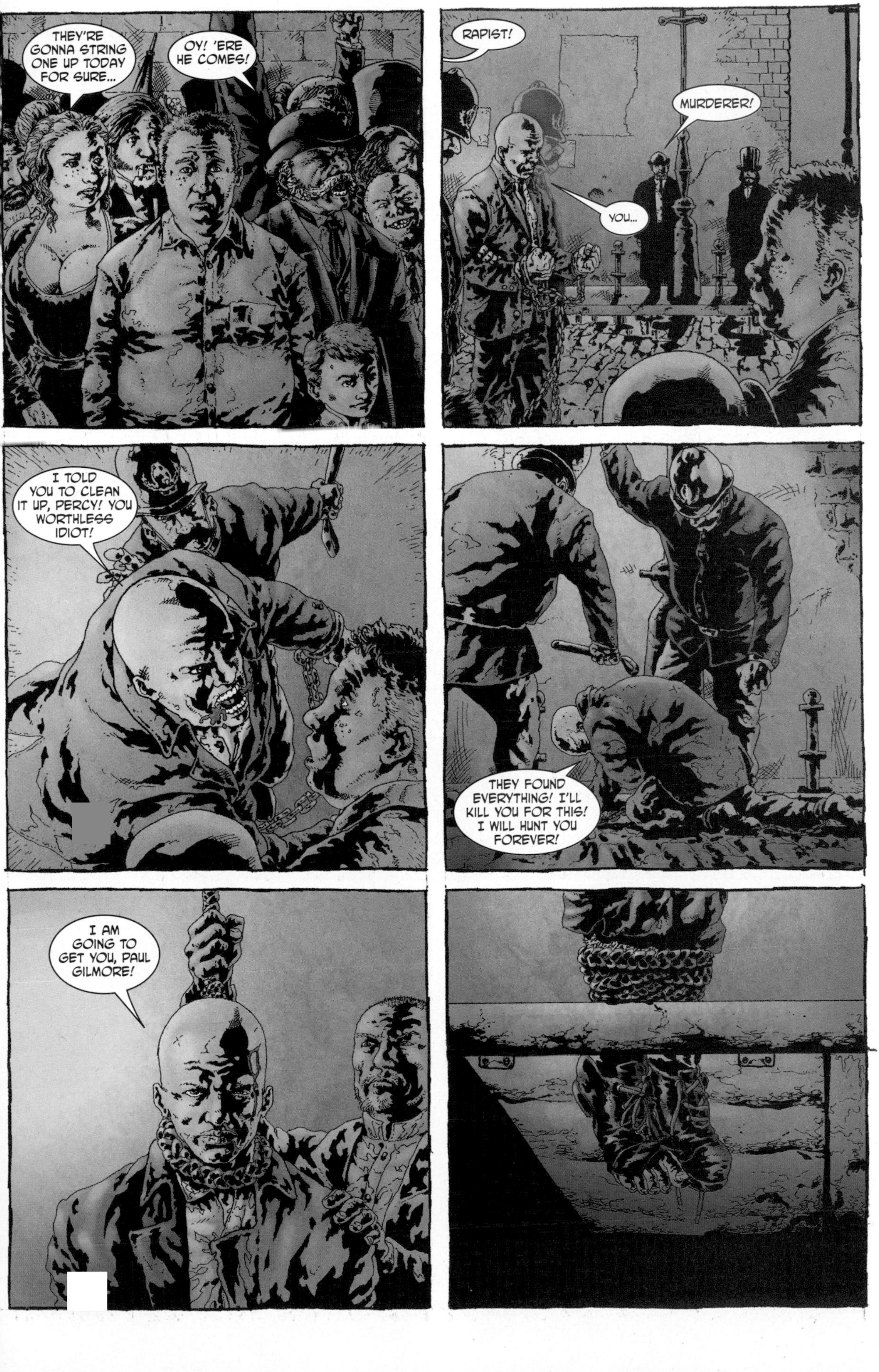
THEY'RE GONNA STRING ONE UP TODAY FOR SURE...
OY! 'ERE HE COMES!
RAPIST!
MURDERER!
YOU...
I TOLD YOU TO CLEAN IT UP, PERCY! YOU WORTHLESS IDIOT!
THEY FOUND EVERYTHING! I'LL KILL YOU FOR THIS! I WILL HUNT YOU FOREVER!
I AM GOING TO GET YOU, PAUL GILMORE!

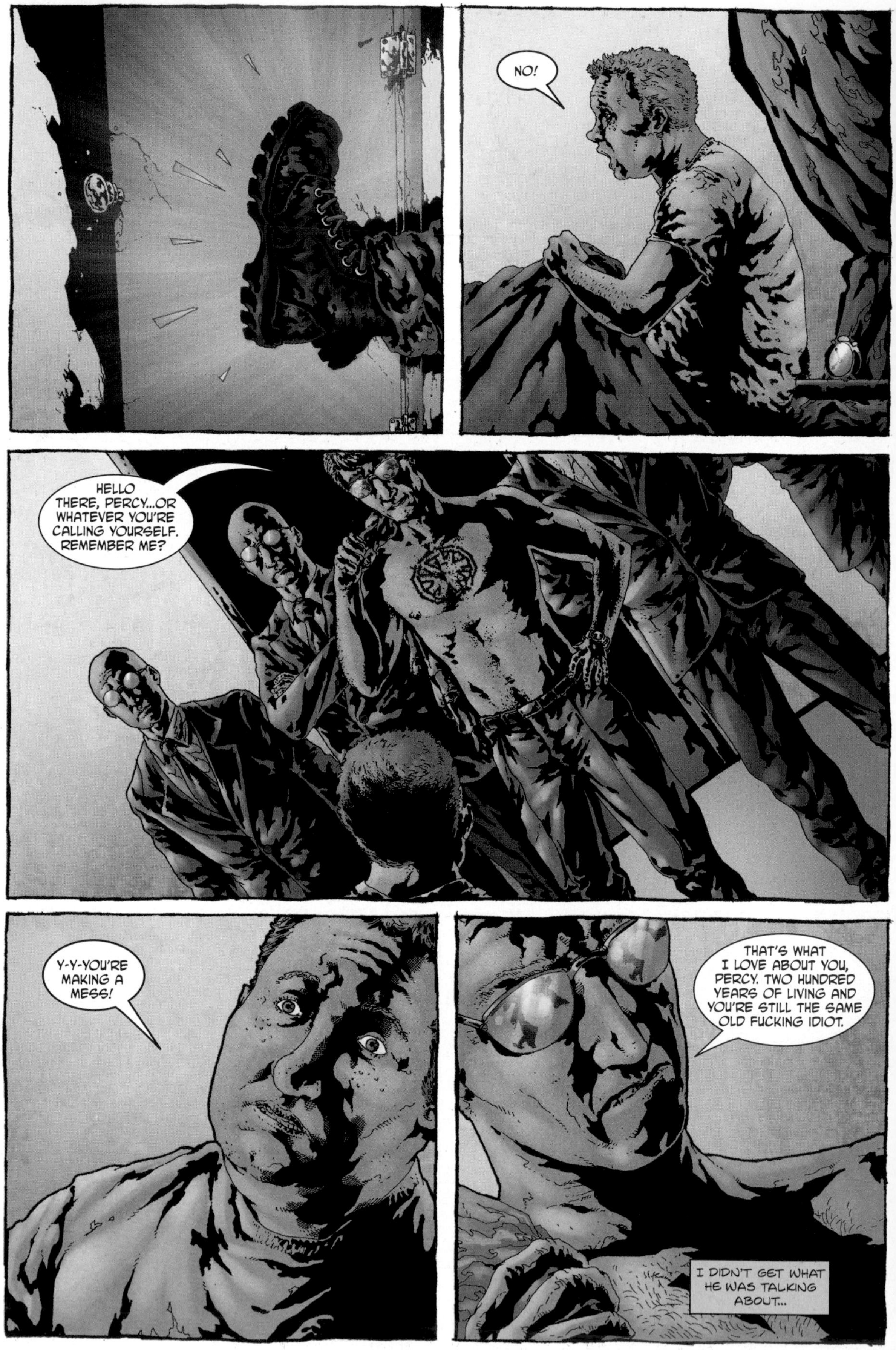

NO!
HELLO THERE, PERCY...OR WHATEVER YOU'RE CALLING YOURSELF. REMEMBER ME?
Y-Y-YOU'RE MAKING A MESS!
THAT'S WHAT I LOVE ABOUT YOU, PERCY. TWO HUNDRED YEARS OF LIVING AND YOU'RE STILL THE SAME OLD FUCKING IDIOT.
I DIDN'T GET WHAT HE WAS TALKING ABOUT...

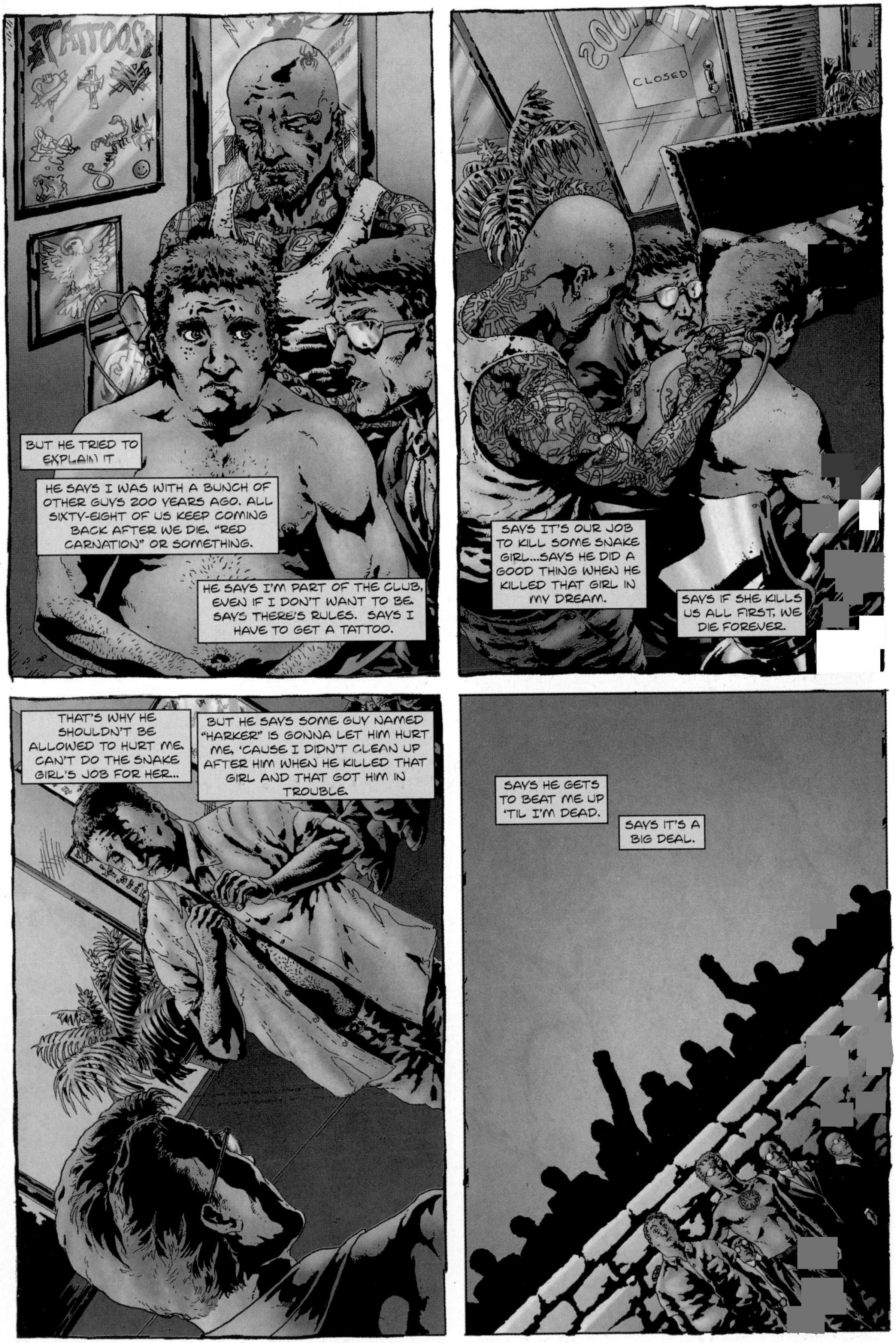
TATTOOS
BUT HE TRIED TO EXPLAIN IT.
HE SAYS I WAS WITH A BUNCH OF OTHER GUYS 200 YEARS AGO. ALL SIXTY-EIGHT OF US KEEP COMING BACK AFTER WE DIE. "RED CARNATION" OR SOMETHING.
HE SAYS I'M PART OF THE CLUB, EVEN IF I DON'T WANT TO BE. SAYS THERE'S RULES. SAYS I HAVE TO GET A TATTOO.
CLOSED
SAYS IT'S OUR JOB TO KILL SOME SNAKE GIRL...SAYS HE DID A GOOD THING WHEN HE KILLED THAT GIRL IN MY DREAM.
SAYS IF SHE KILLS US ALL FIRST, WE DIE FOREVER.
THAT'S WHY HE SHOULDN'T BE ALLOWED TO HURT ME. CAN'T DO THE SNAKE GIRL'S JOB FOR HER...
BUT HE SAYS SOME GUY NAMED "HARKER" IS GONNA LET HIM HURT ME, 'CAUSE I DIDN'T CLEAN UP AFTER HIM WHEN HE KILLED THAT GIRL AND THAT GOT HIM IN TROUBLE.
SAYS HE GETS TO BEAT ME UP 'TIL I'M DEAD.
SAYS IT'S A BIG DEAL.

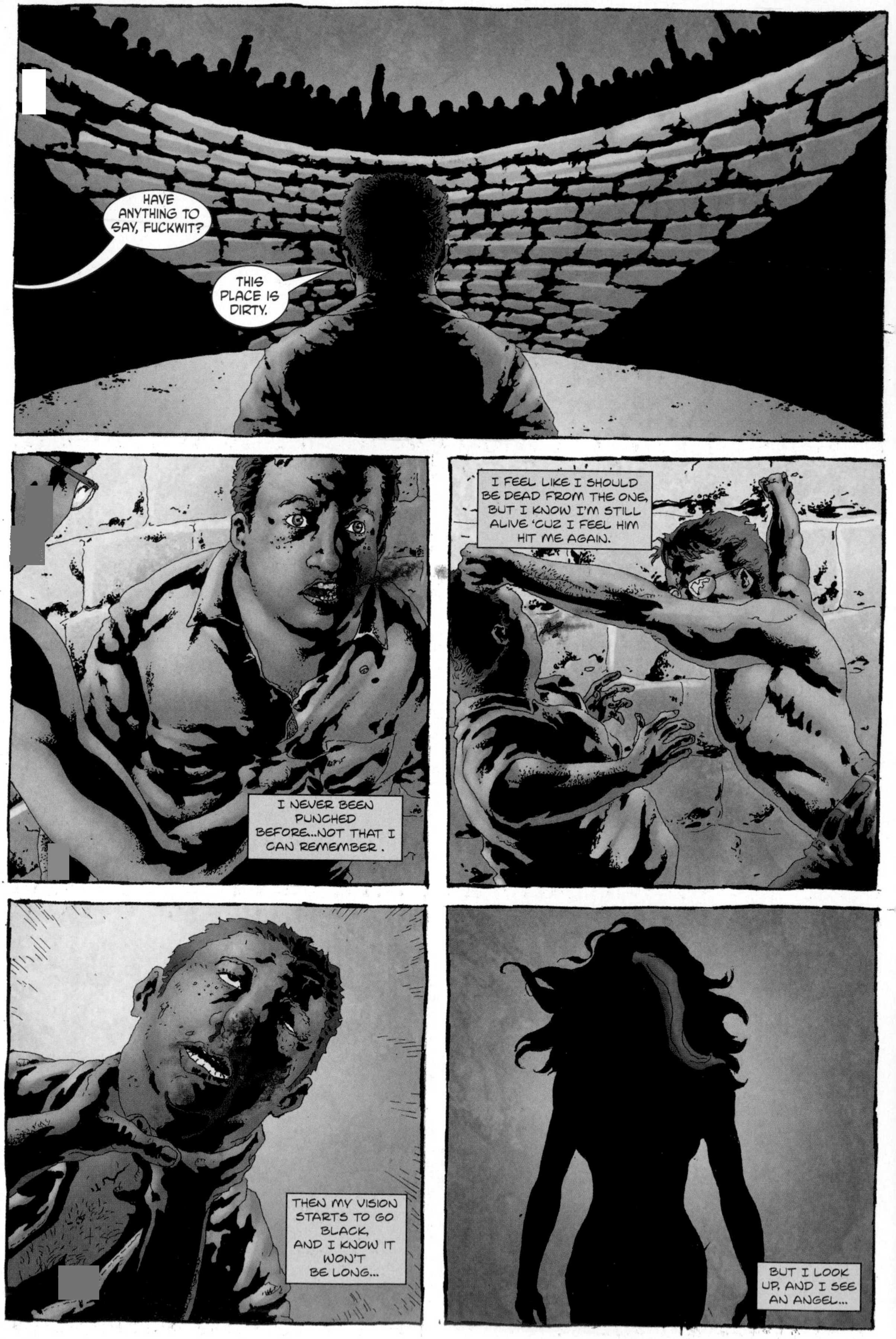
HAVE ANYTHING TO SAY, FUCKWIT?
THIS PLACE IS DIRTY.
I NEVER BEEN PUNCHED BEFORE...NOT THAT I CAN REMEMBER.
I FEEL LIKE I SHOULD BE DEAD FROM THE ONE, BUT I KNOW I'M STILL ALIVE 'CUZ I FEEL HIM HIT ME AGAIN.
THEN MY VISION STARTS TO GO BLACK, AND I KNOW IT WON'T BE LONG...
BUT I LOOK UP, AND I SEE AN ANGEL...

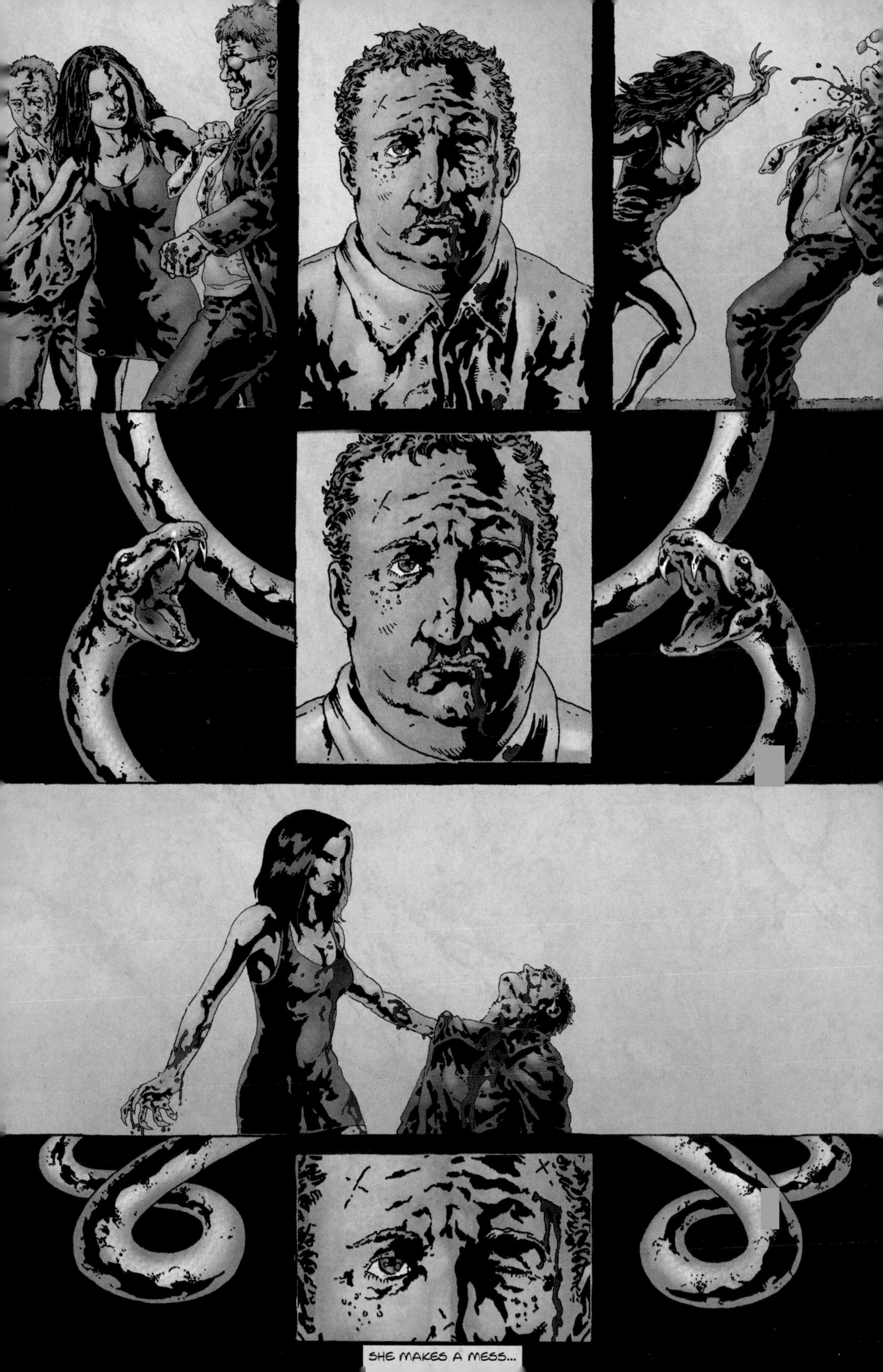
SHE MAKES A MESS...

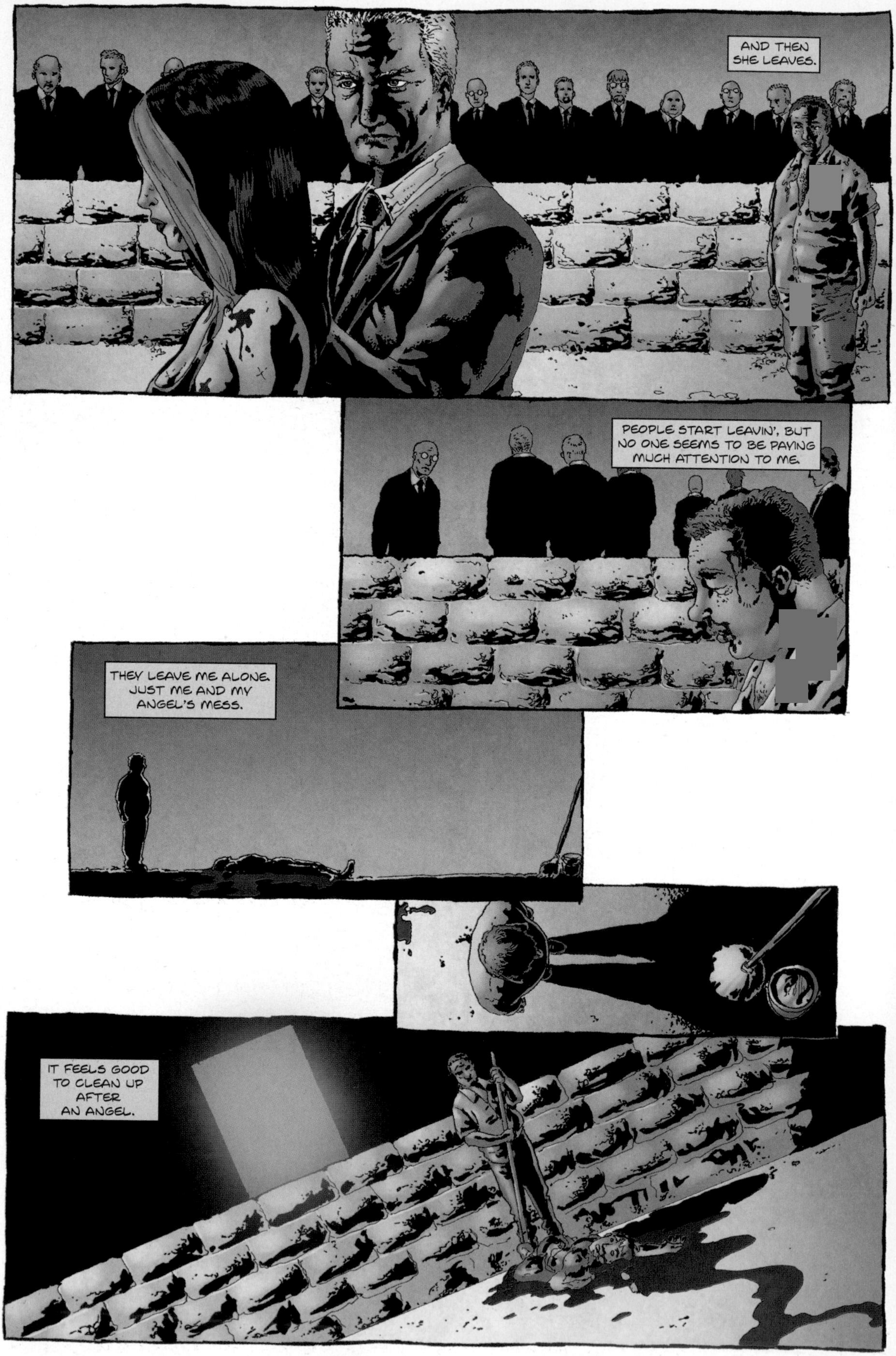
AND THEN SHE LEAVES.
PEOPLE START LEAVIN', BUT NO ONE SEEMS TO BE PAYING MUCH ATTENTION TO ME.
THEY LEAVE ME ALONE. JUST ME AND MY ANGEL'S MESS.
IT FEELS GOOD TO CLEAN UP AFTER AN ANGEL.

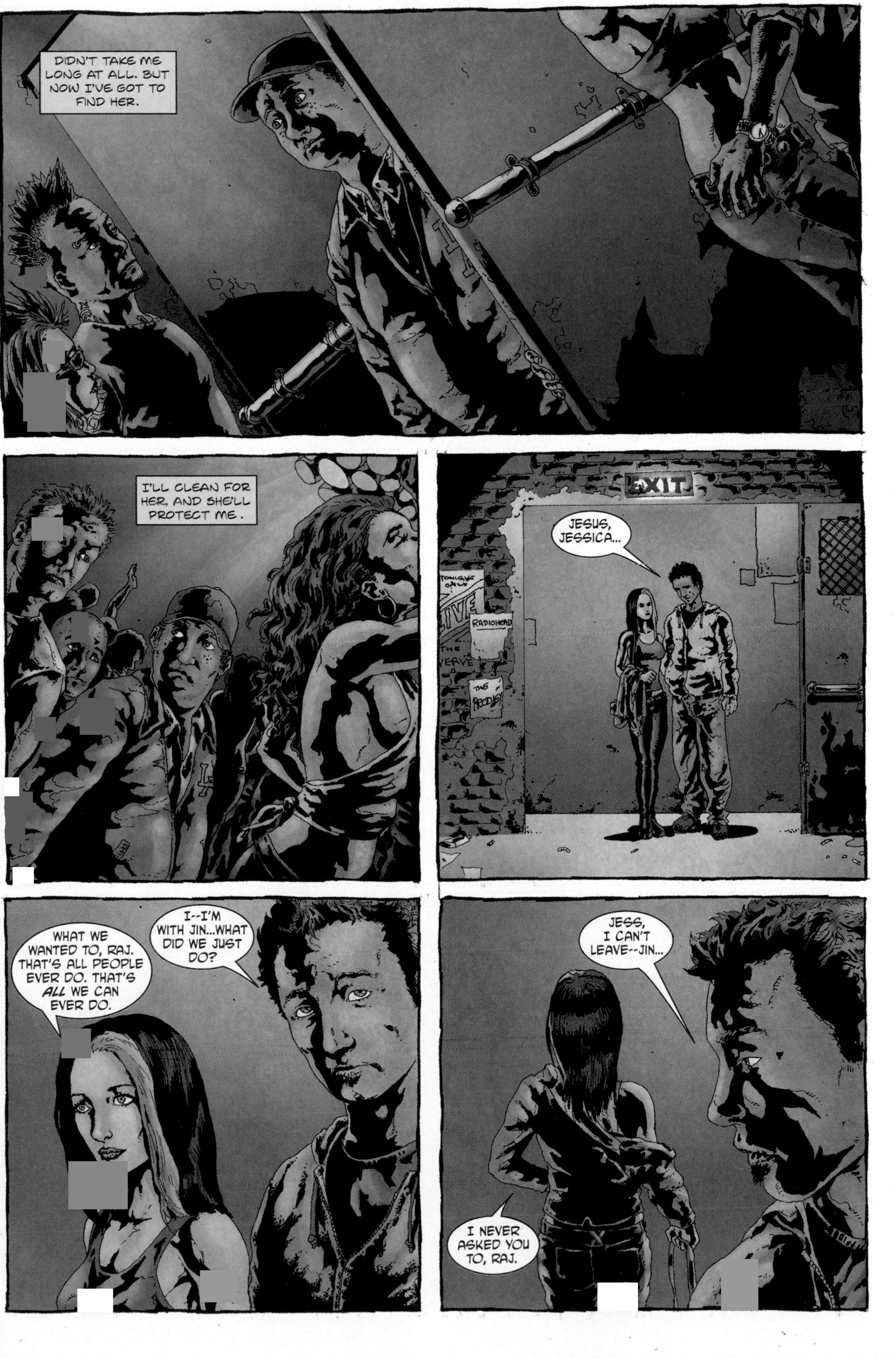
DIDN'T TAKE ME LONG AT ALL. BUT NOW I'VE GOT TO FIND HER.
I'LL CLEAN FOR HER, AND SHE'LL PROTECT ME.
EXIT
RADIOHEAD
JESUS, JESSICA...
I--I'M WITH JIN...WHAT DID WE JUST DO?
WHAT WE WANTED TO, RAJ. THAT'S ALL PEOPLE EVER DO. THAT'S *ALL* WE CAN EVER DO.
JESS, I CAN'T LEAVE--JIN...
I NEVER ASKED YOU TO, RAJ.

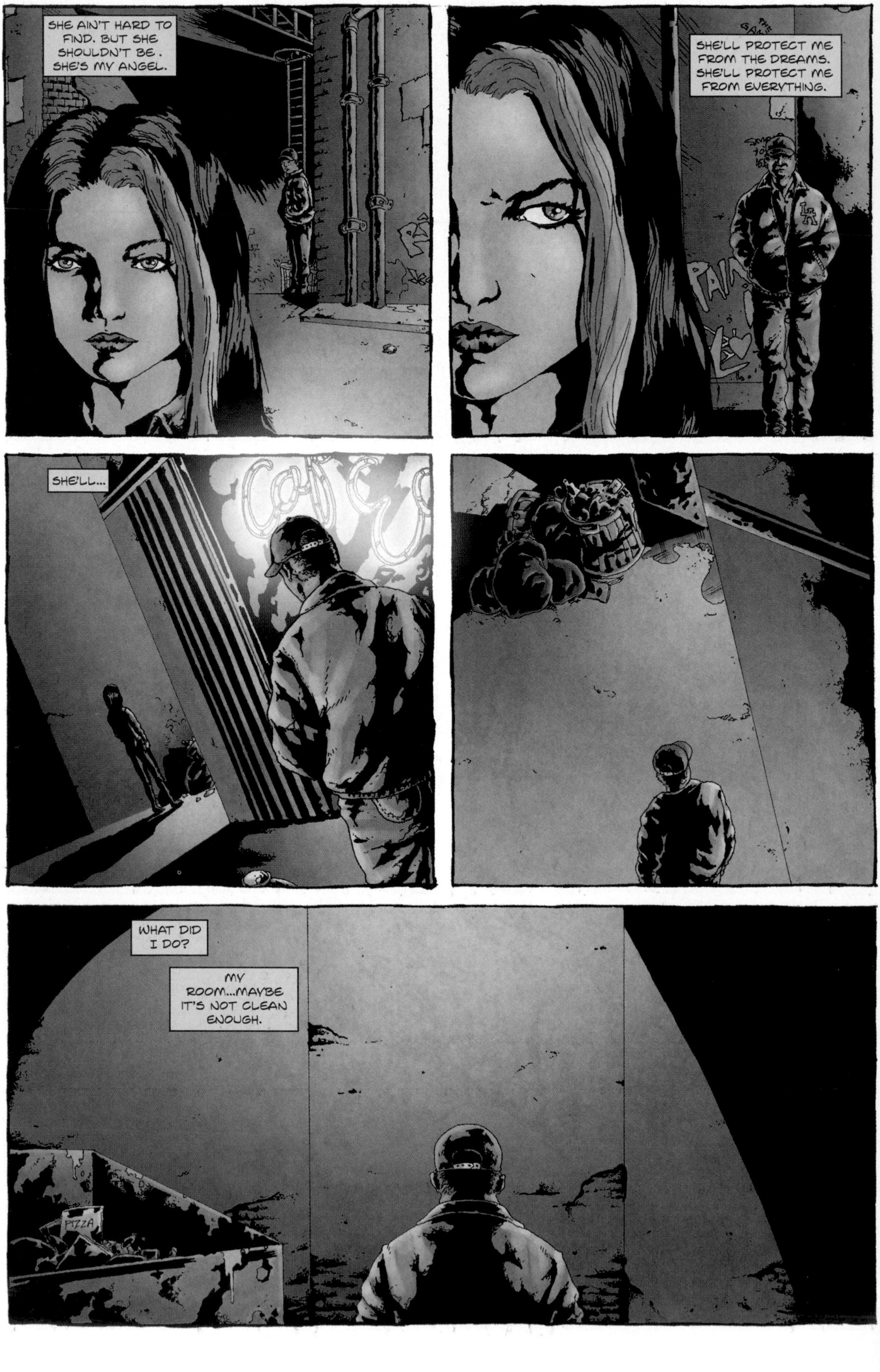
SHE AIN'T HARD TO FIND. BUT SHE SHOULDN'T BE. SHE'S MY ANGEL.
SHE'LL PROTECT ME FROM THE DREAMS. SHE'LL PROTECT ME FROM EVERYTHING.
SHE'LL...
WHAT DID I DO?
MY ROOM...MAYBE IT'S NOT CLEAN ENOUGH.
PIZZA

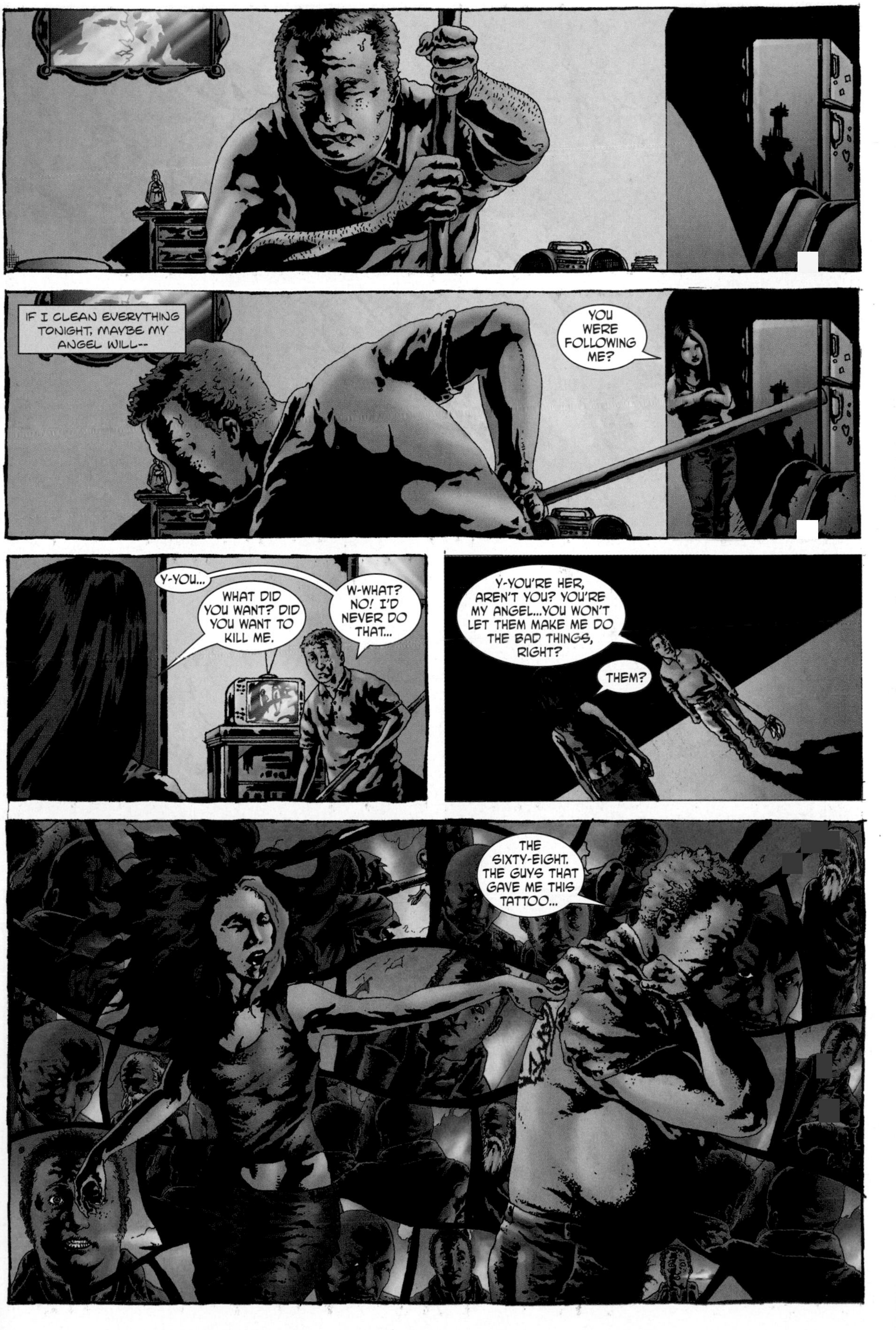
IF I CLEAN EVERYTHING TONIGHT, MAYBE MY ANGEL WILL--
YOU WERE FOLLOWING ME?
Y-YOU...
WHAT DID YOU WANT? DID YOU WANT TO KILL ME.
W-WHAT? NO! I'D NEVER DO THAT...
Y-YOU'RE HER, AREN'T YOU? YOU'RE MY ANGEL...YOU WON'T LET THEM MAKE ME DO THE BAD THINGS, RIGHT?
THEM?
THE SIXTY-EIGHT. THE GUYS THAT GAVE ME THIS TATTOO...

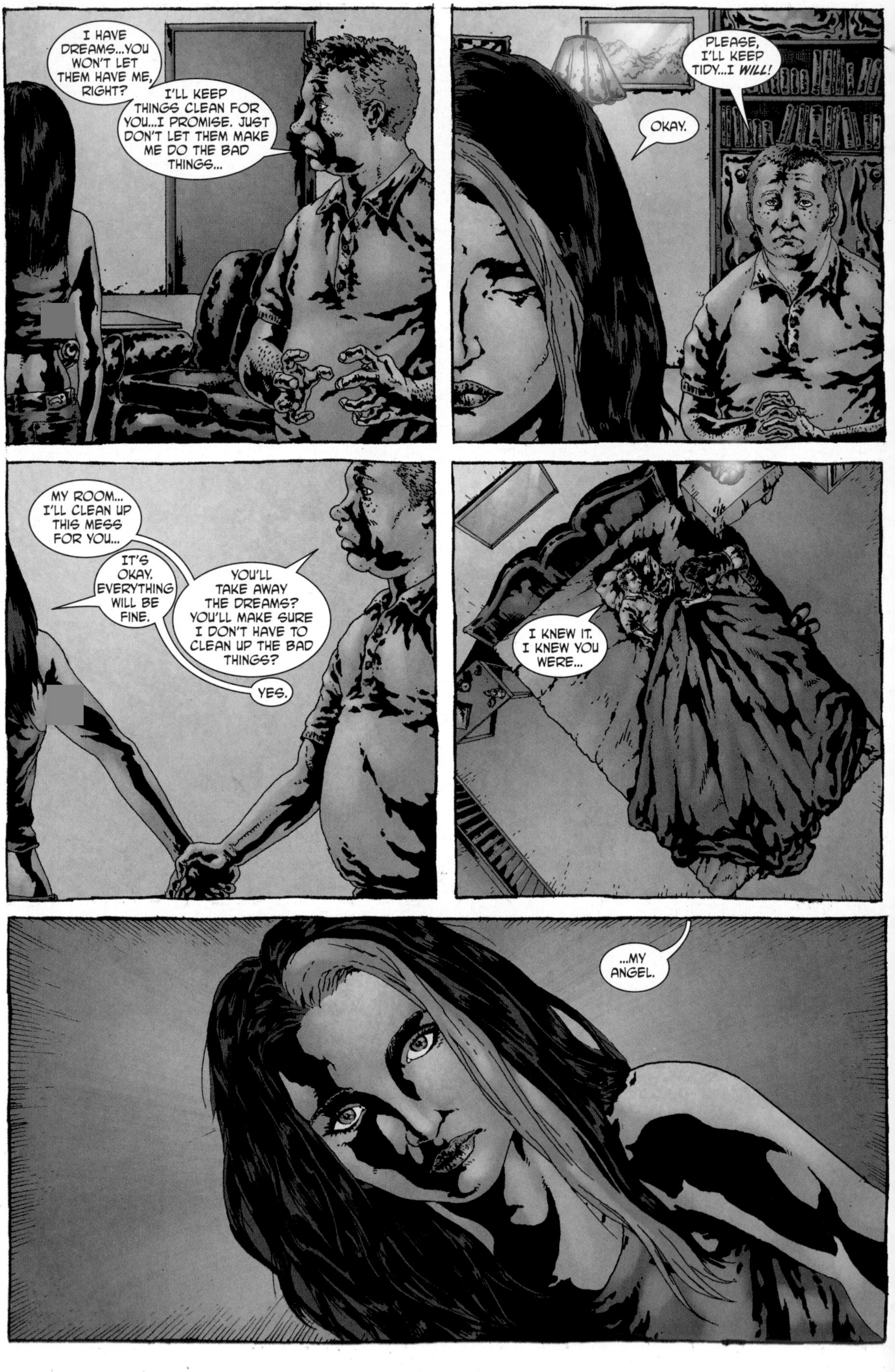
I HAVE DREAMS...YOU WON'T LET THEM HAVE ME, RIGHT?
I'LL KEEP THINGS CLEAN FOR YOU...I PROMISE. JUST DON'T LET THEM MAKE ME DO THE BAD THINGS...
PLEASE, I'LL KEEP TIDY...I *WILL!*
OKAY.
MY ROOM... I'LL CLEAN UP THIS MESS FOR YOU...
IT'S OKAY. EVERYTHING WILL BE FINE.
YOU'LL TAKE AWAY THE DREAMS? YOU'LL MAKE SURE I DON'T HAVE TO CLEAN UP THE BAD THINGS?
YES.
I KNEW IT. I KNEW YOU WERE...
...MY ANGEL.

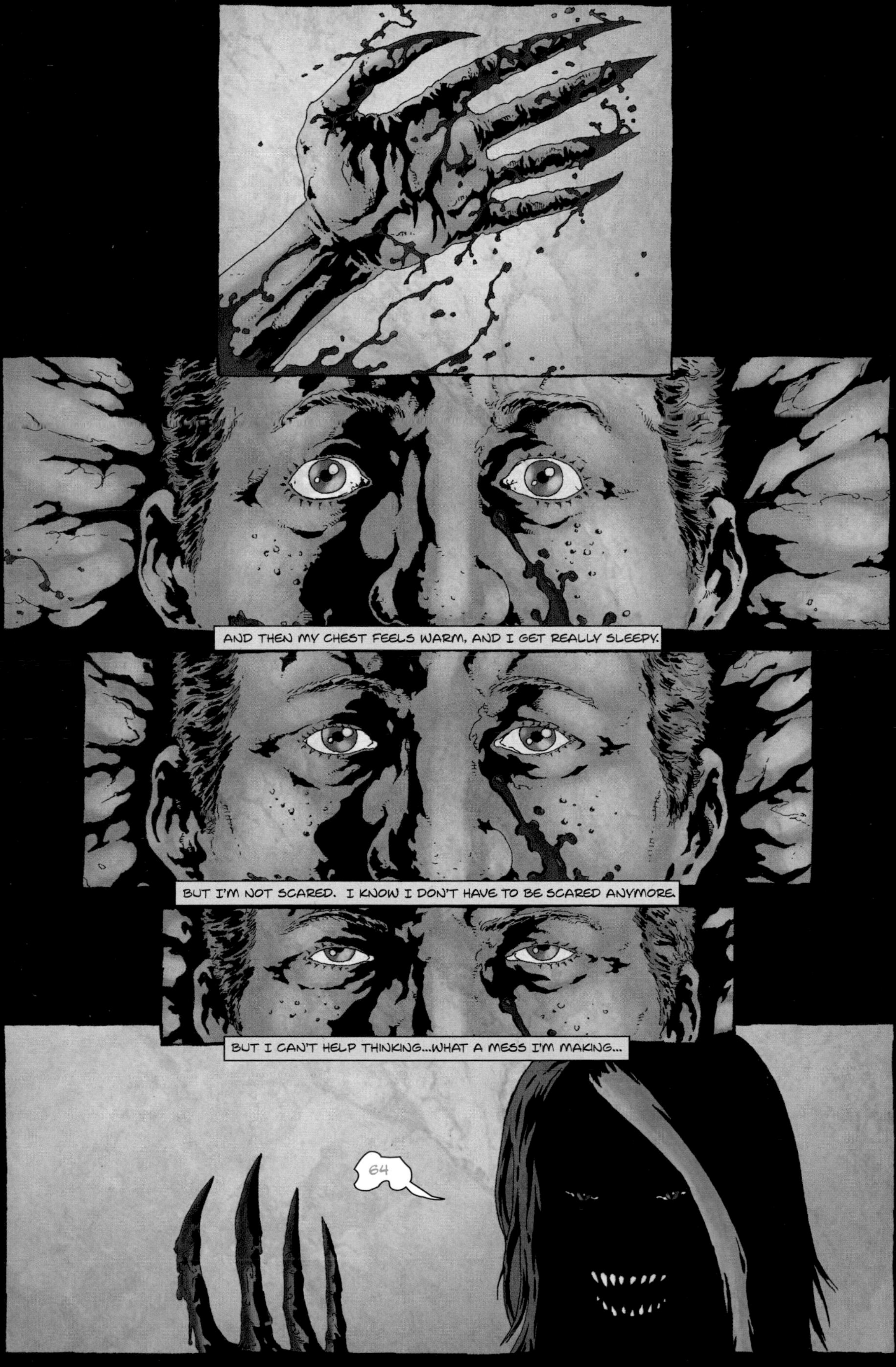
AND THEN MY CHEST FEELS WARM, AND I GET REALLY SLEEPY.
BUT I'M NOT SCARED. I KNOW I DON'T HAVE TO BE SCARED ANYMORE.
BUT I CAN'T HELP THINKING...WHAT A MESS I'M MAKING...
64

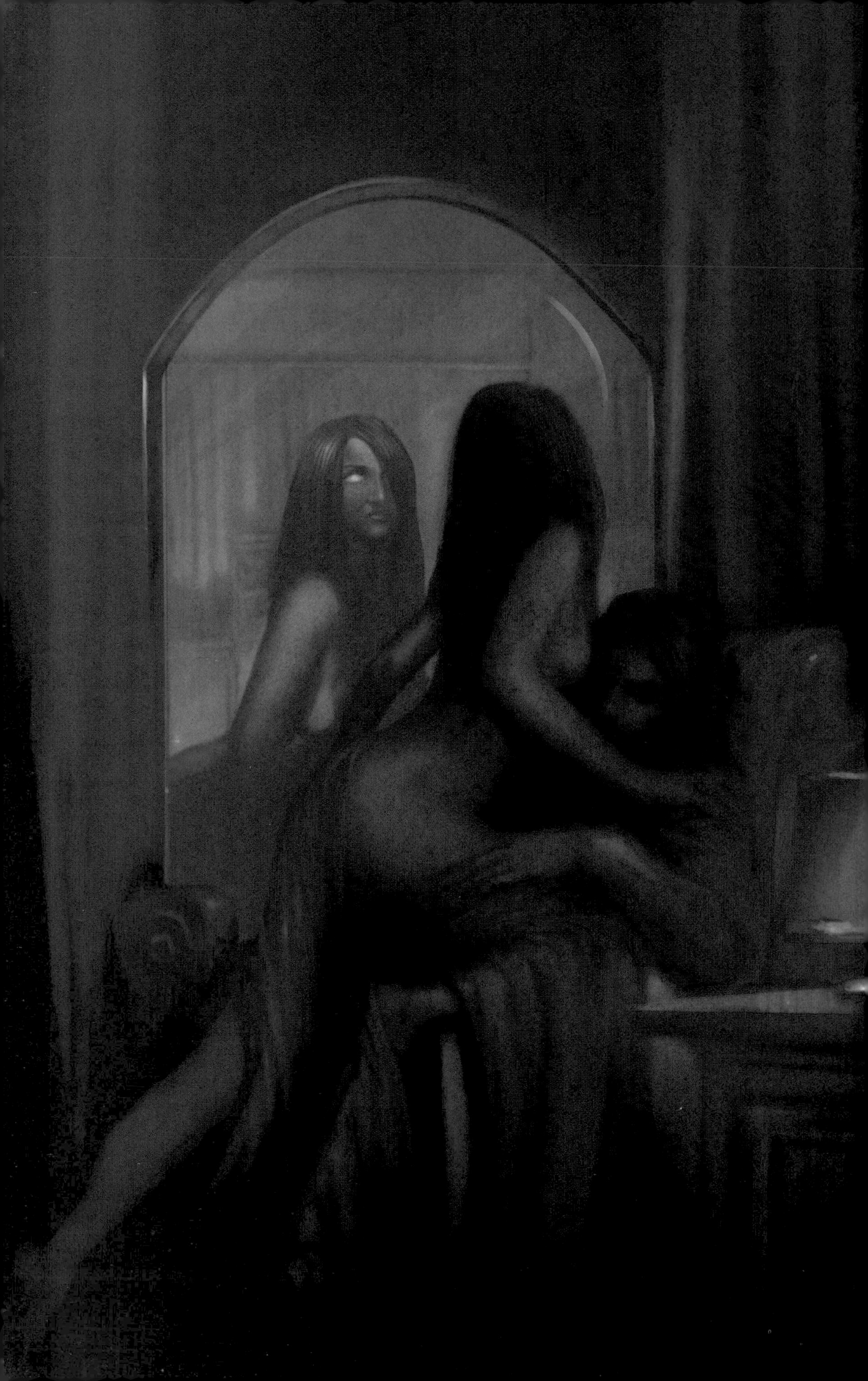

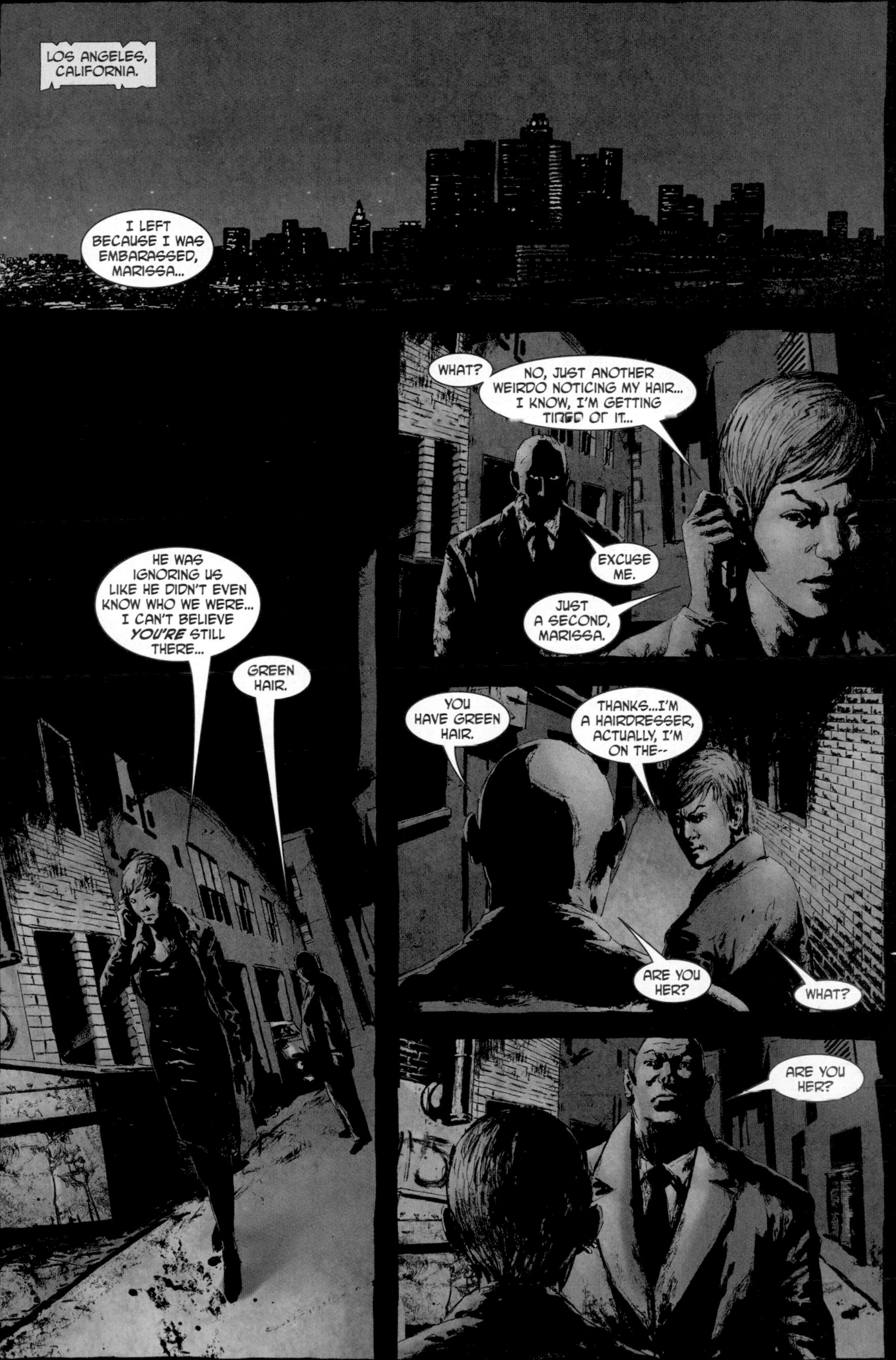
LOS ANGELES, CALIFORNIA.
I LEFT BECAUSE I WAS EMBARASSED, MARISSA...
WHAT?
NO, JUST ANOTHER WEIRDO NOTICING MY HAIR... I KNOW, I'M GETTING TIRED OF IT...
EXCUSE ME.
JUST A SECOND, MARISSA.
HE WAS IGNORING US LIKE HE DIDN'T EVEN KNOW WHO WE WERE... I CAN'T BELIEVE *YOU'RE* STILL THERE...
GREEN HAIR.
YOU HAVE GREEN HAIR.
THANKS...I'M A HAIRDRESSER, ACTUALLY, I'M ON THE--
ARE YOU HER?
WHAT?
ARE YOU HER?

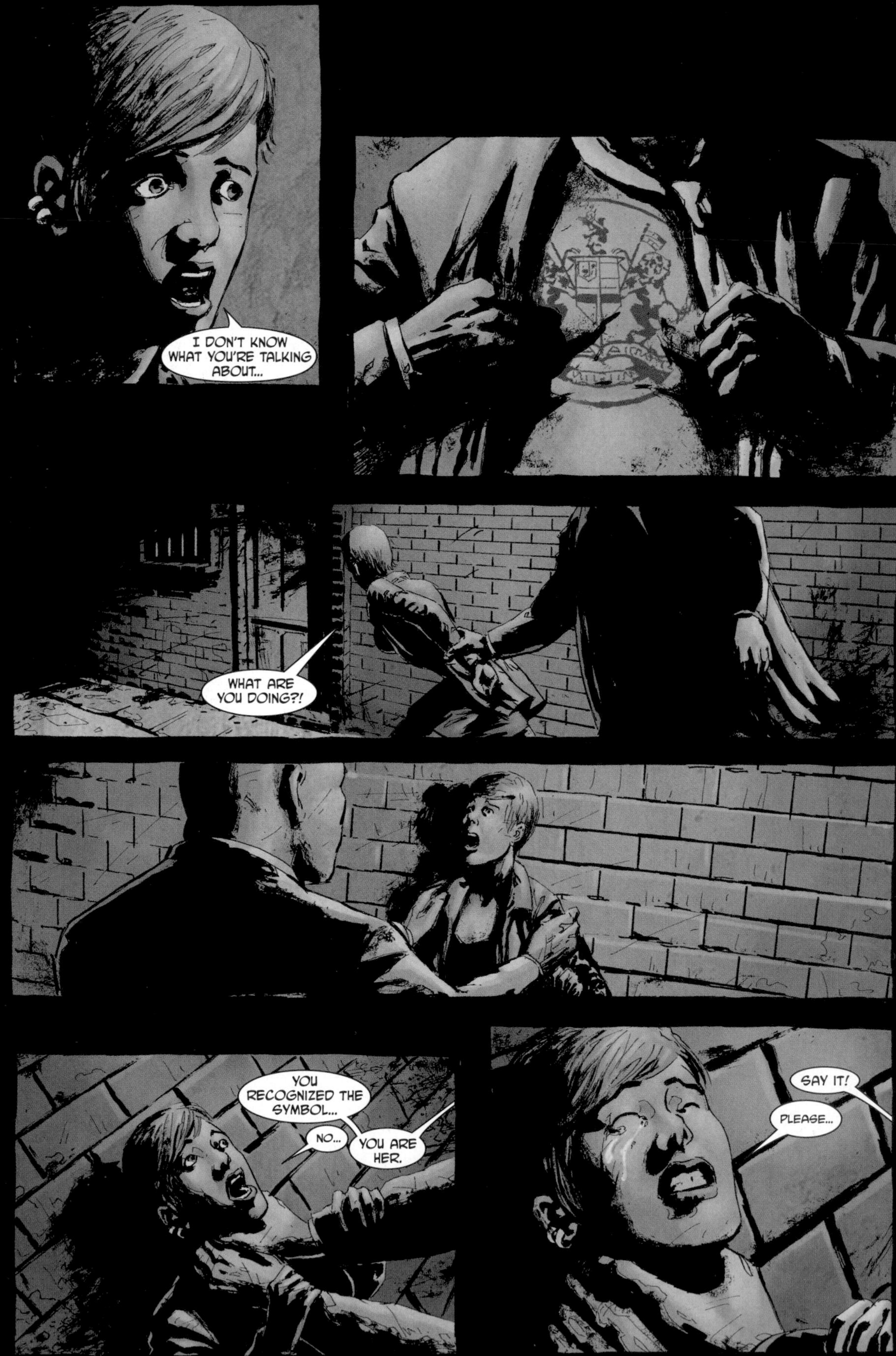
I DON'T KNOW WHAT YOU'RE TALKING ABOUT...
WHAT ARE YOU DOING?!
YOU RECOGNIZED THE SYMBOL...
NO...
YOU ARE HER.
SAY IT!
PLEASE...

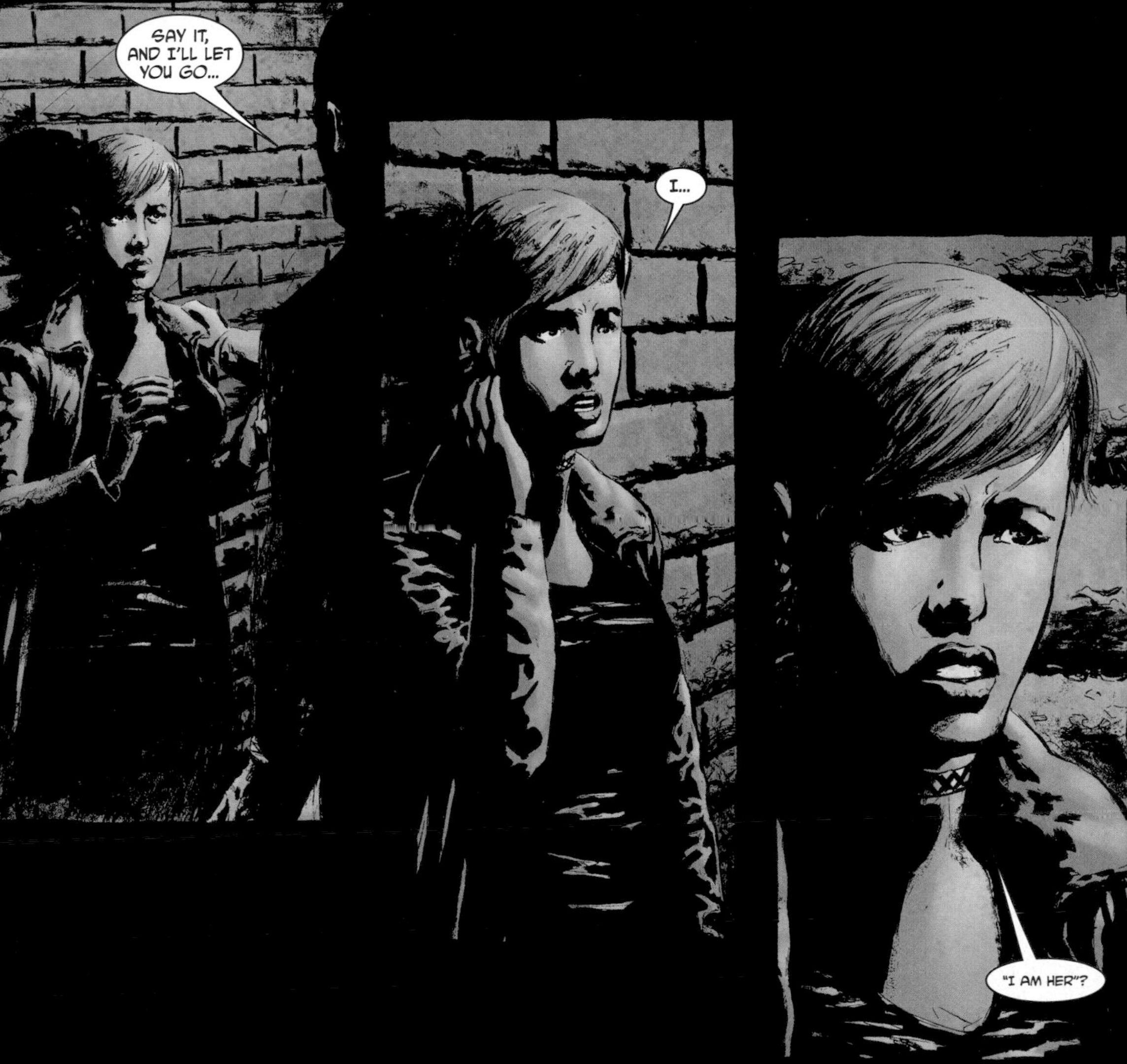
SAY IT, AND I'LL LET YOU GO...
I...
"I AM HER"?

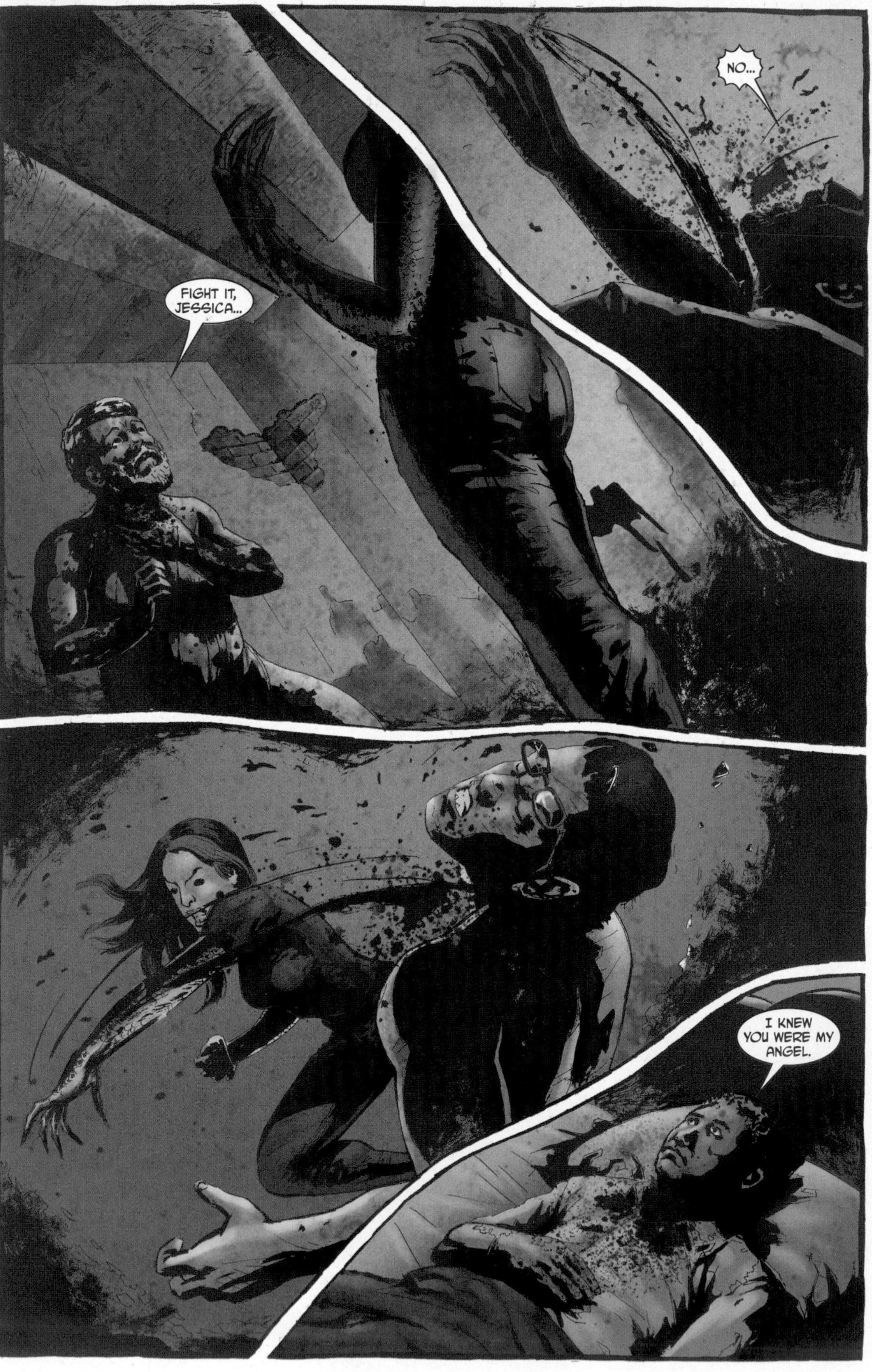
NO...
FIGHT IT, JESSICA...
I KNEW YOU WERE MY ANGEL.

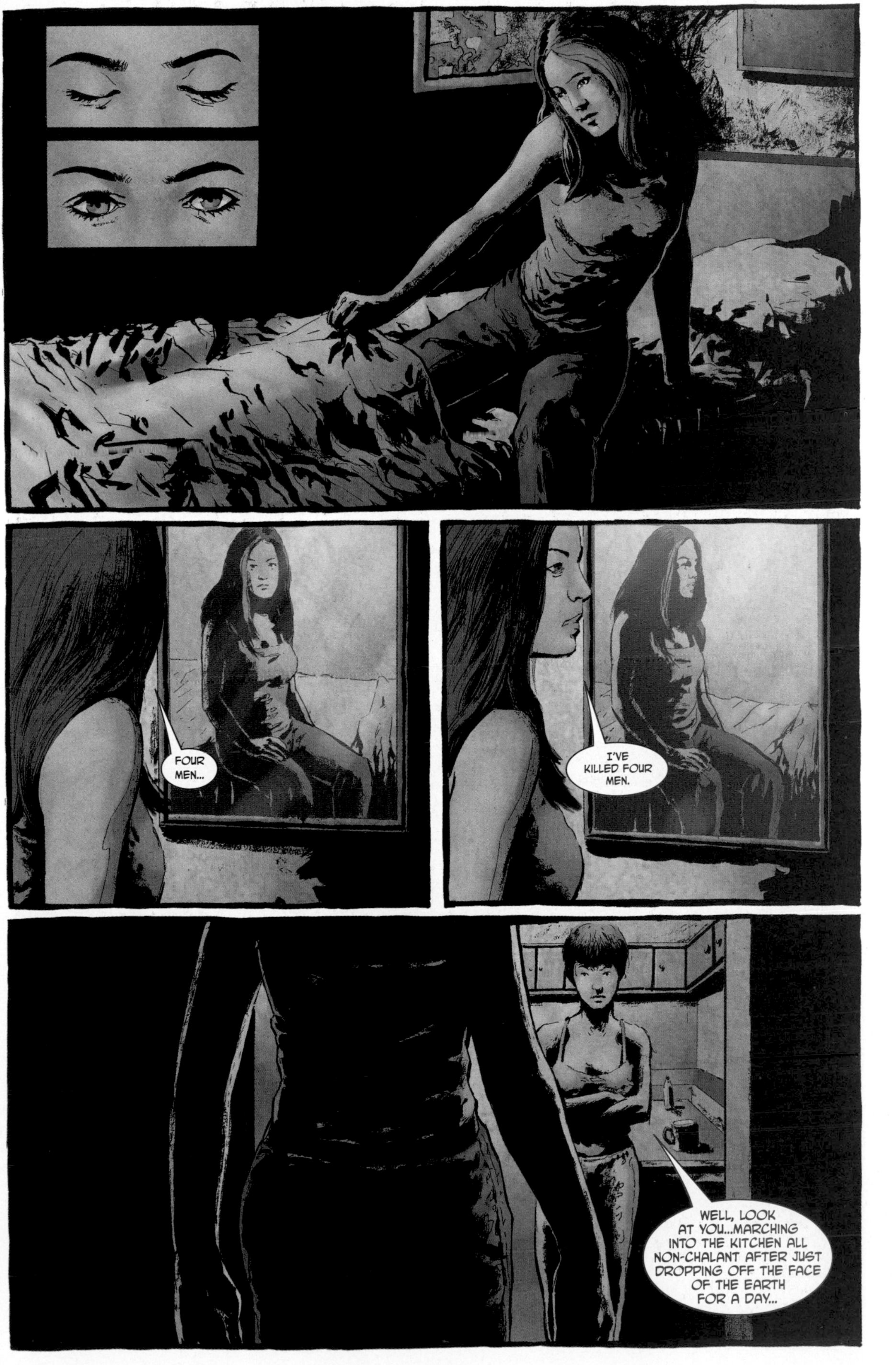
FOUR MEN...
I'VE KILLED FOUR MEN.
WELL, LOOK AT YOU...MARCHING INTO THE KITCHEN ALL NON-CHALANT AFTER JUST DROPPING OFF THE FACE OF THE EARTH FOR A DAY...

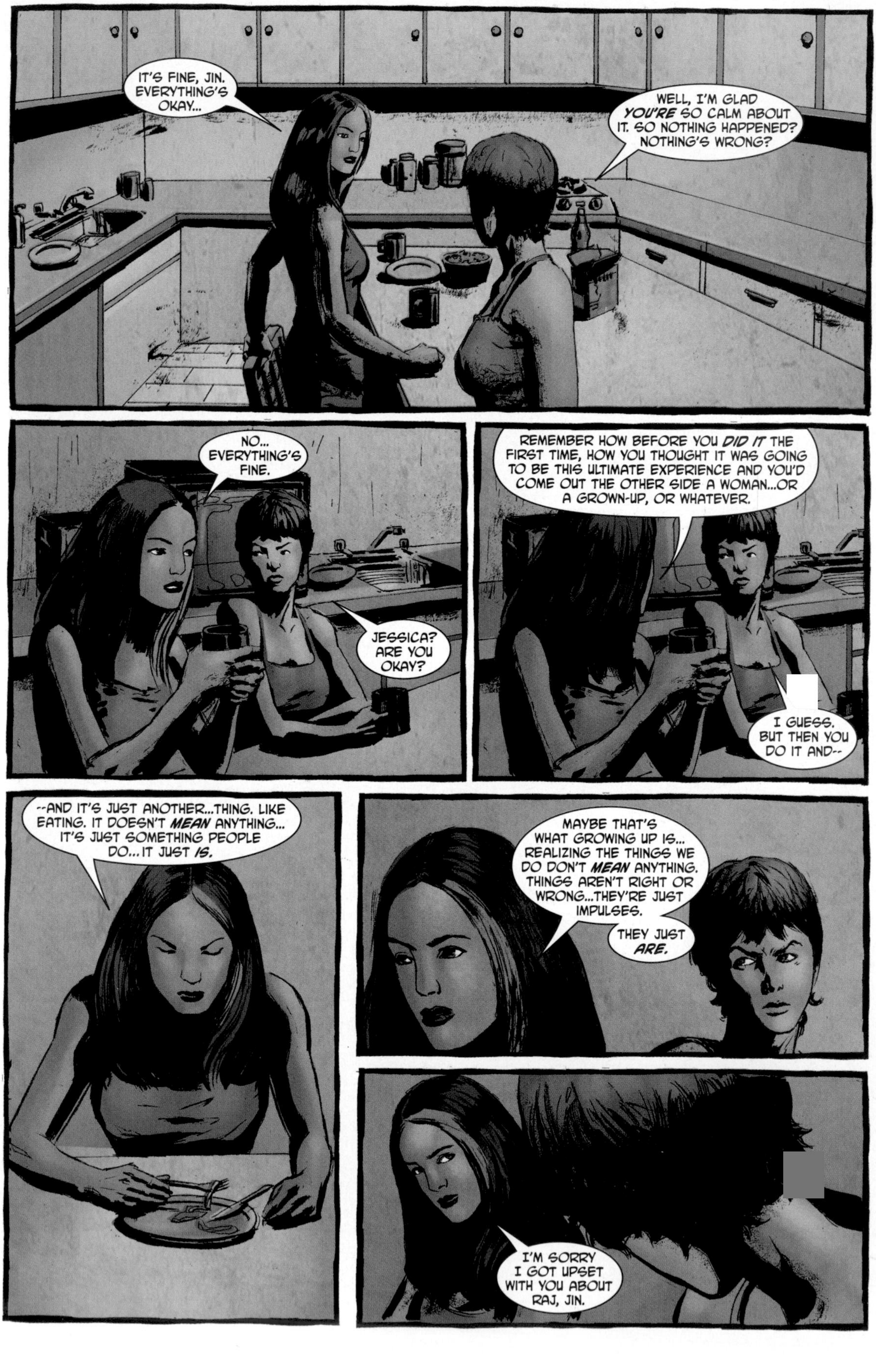
IT'S FINE, JIN. EVERYTHING'S OKAY...
WELL, I'M GLAD ***YOU'RE*** SO CALM ABOUT IT. SO NOTHING HAPPENED? NOTHING'S WRONG?
NO... EVERYTHING'S FINE.
JESSICA? ARE YOU OKAY?
REMEMBER HOW BEFORE YOU ***DID IT*** THE FIRST TIME, HOW YOU THOUGHT IT WAS GOING TO BE THIS ULTIMATE EXPERIENCE AND YOU'D COME OUT THE OTHER SIDE A WOMAN...OR A GROWN-UP, OR WHATEVER.
I GUESS. BUT THEN YOU DO IT AND--
--AND IT'S JUST ANOTHER...THING. LIKE EATING. IT DOESN'T ***MEAN*** ANYTHING... IT'S JUST SOMETHING PEOPLE DO...IT JUST ***IS.***
MAYBE THAT'S WHAT GROWING UP IS... REALIZING THE THINGS WE DO DON'T ***MEAN*** ANYTHING. THINGS AREN'T RIGHT OR WRONG...THEY'RE JUST IMPULSES.
THEY JUST ***ARE.***
I'M SORRY I GOT UPSET WITH YOU ABOUT RAJ, JIN.

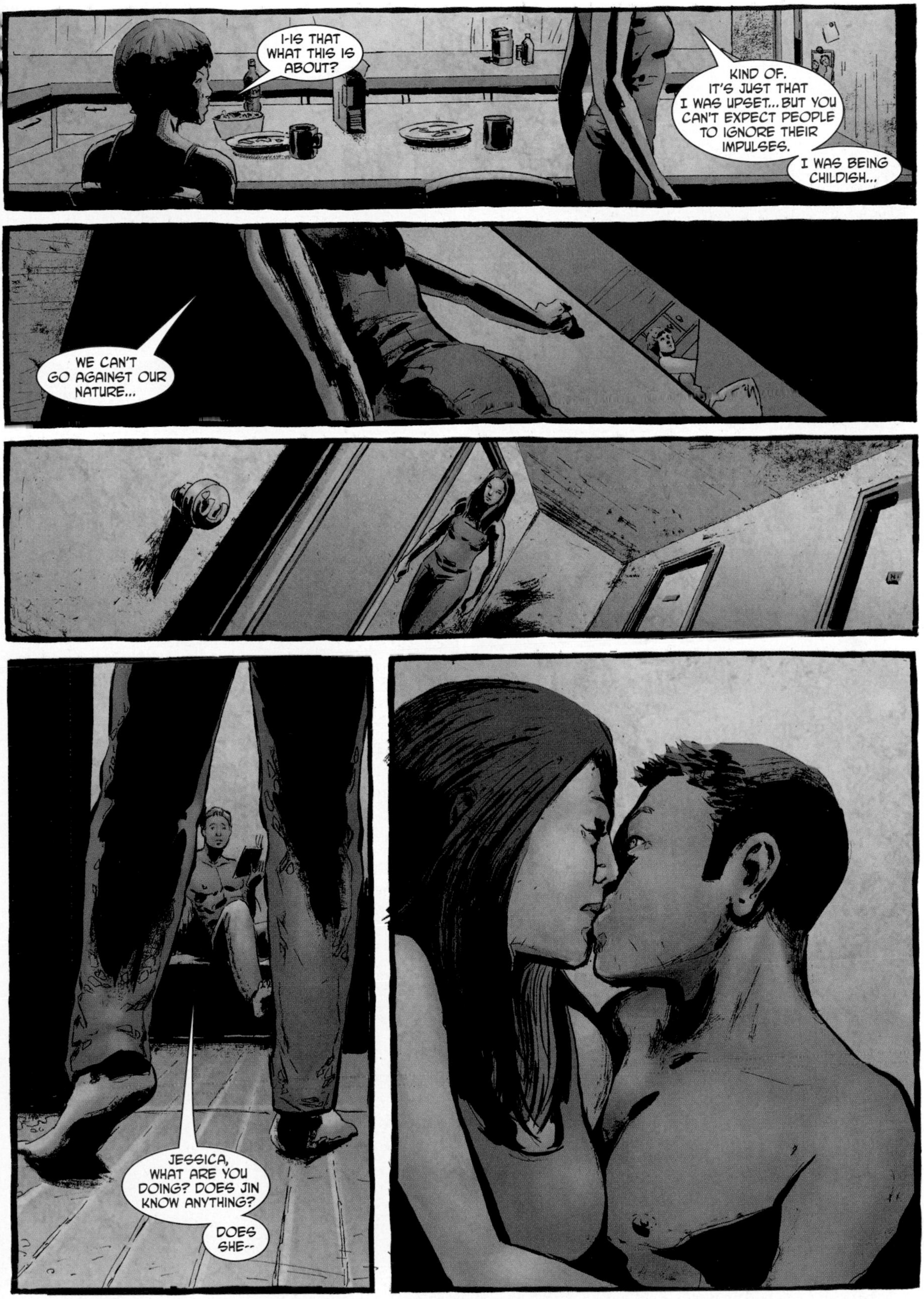

I-IS THAT WHAT THIS IS ABOUT?
KIND OF. IT'S JUST THAT I WAS UPSET... BUT YOU CAN'T EXPECT PEOPLE TO IGNORE THEIR IMPULSES.
I WAS BEING CHILDISH...
WE CAN'T GO AGAINST OUR NATURE...
JESSICA, WHAT ARE YOU DOING? DOES JIN KNOW ANYTHING?
DOES SHE--

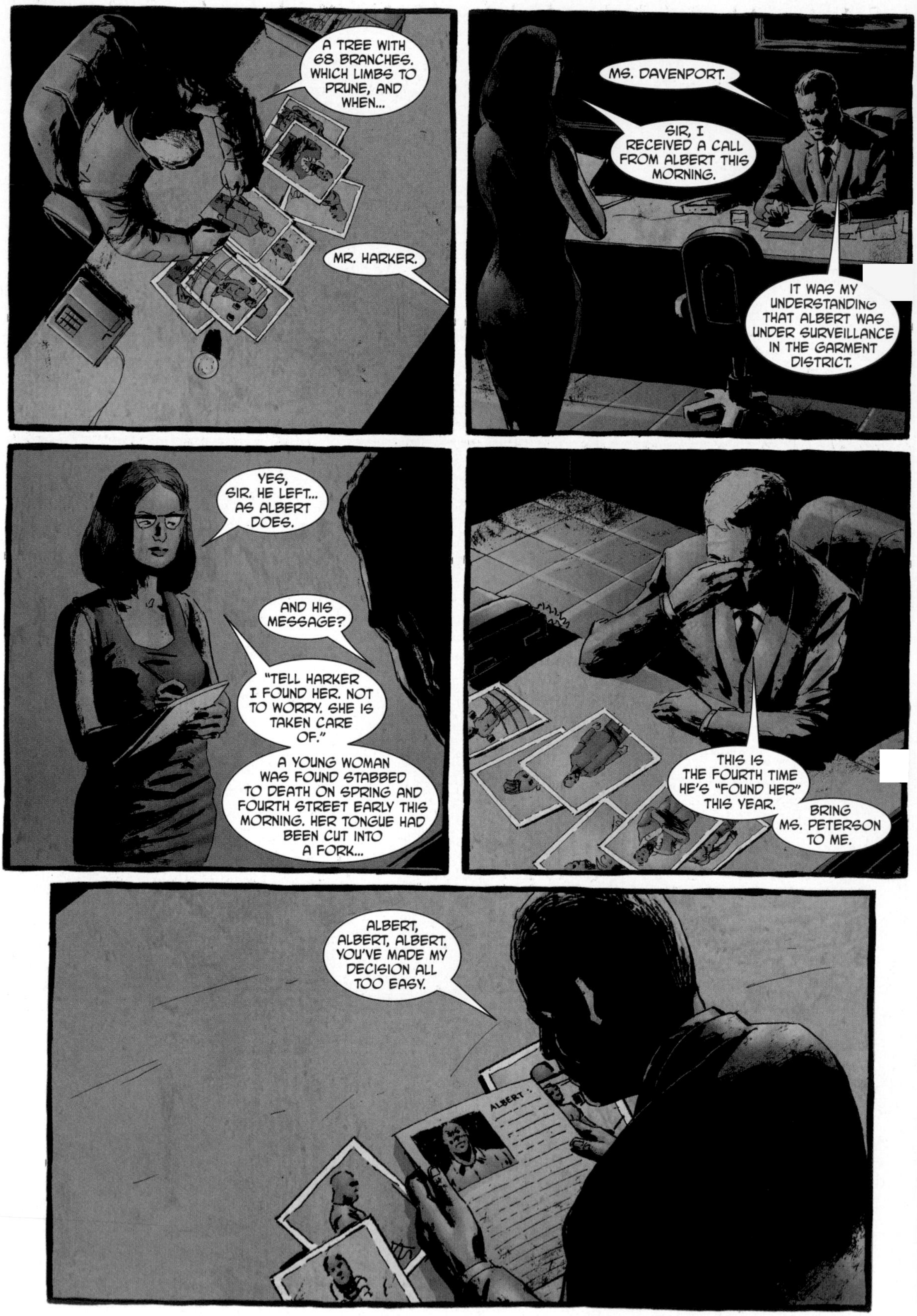
A TREE WITH 68 BRANCHES. WHICH LIMBS TO PRUNE, AND WHEN...
MR. HARKER.
MS. DAVENPORT.
SIR, I RECEIVED A CALL FROM ALBERT THIS MORNING.
IT WAS MY UNDERSTANDING THAT ALBERT WAS UNDER SURVEILLANCE IN THE GARMENT DISTRICT.
YES, SIR. HE LEFT... AS ALBERT DOES.
AND HIS MESSAGE?
"TELL HARKER I FOUND HER. NOT TO WORRY. SHE IS TAKEN CARE OF."
A YOUNG WOMAN WAS FOUND STABBED TO DEATH ON SPRING AND FOURTH STREET EARLY THIS MORNING. HER TONGUE HAD BEEN CUT INTO A FORK...
THIS IS THE FOURTH TIME HE'S "FOUND HER" THIS YEAR.
BRING MS. PETERSON TO ME.
ALBERT, ALBERT, ALBERT. YOU'VE MADE MY DECISION ALL TOO EASY.
ALBERT

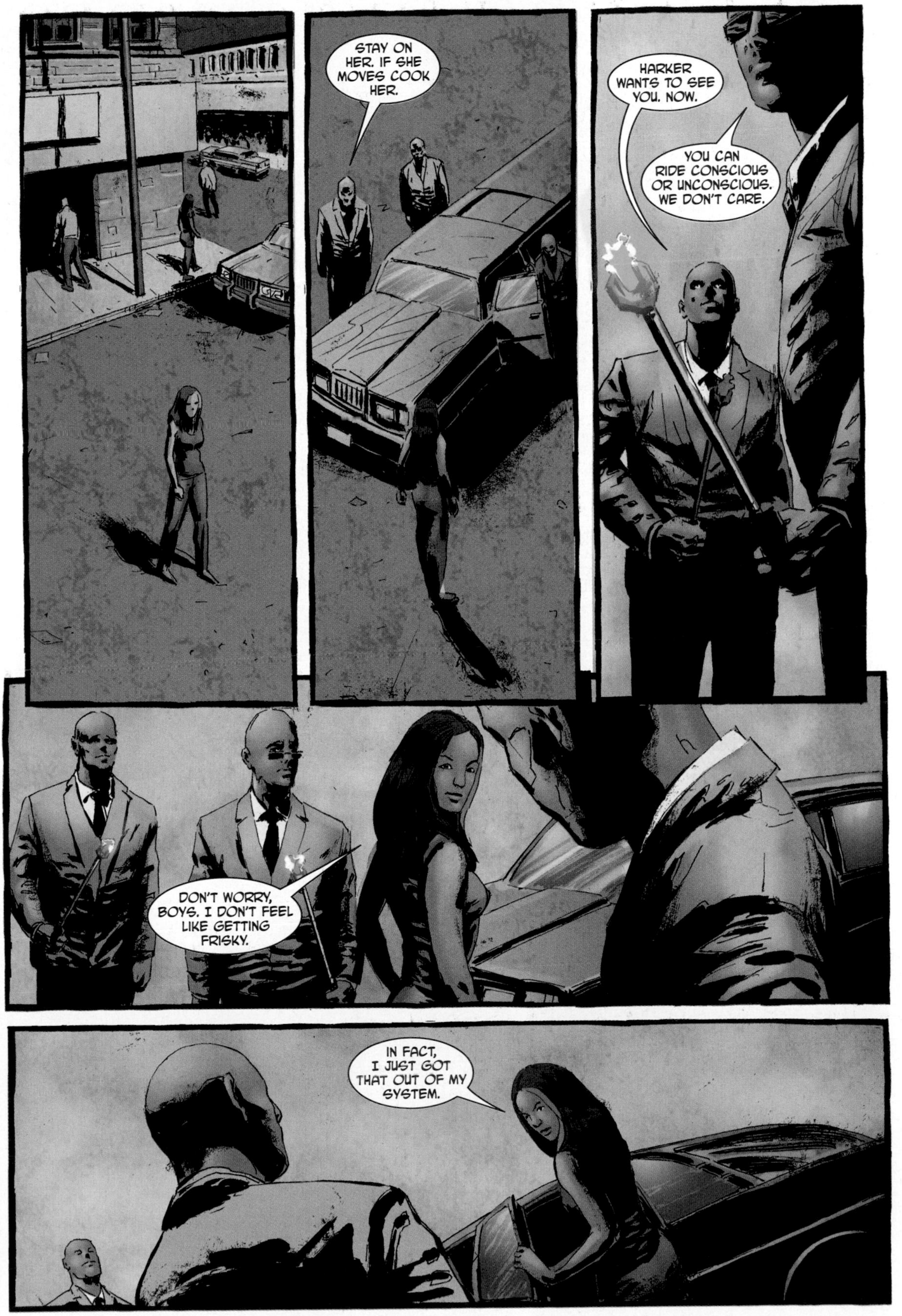
STAY ON HER. IF SHE MOVES COOK HER.
HARKER WANTS TO SEE YOU. NOW.
YOU CAN RIDE CONSCIOUS OR UNCONSCIOUS. WE DON'T CARE.
DON'T WORRY, BOYS. I DON'T FEEL LIKE GETTING FRISKY.
IN FACT, I JUST GOT THAT OUT OF MY SYSTEM.

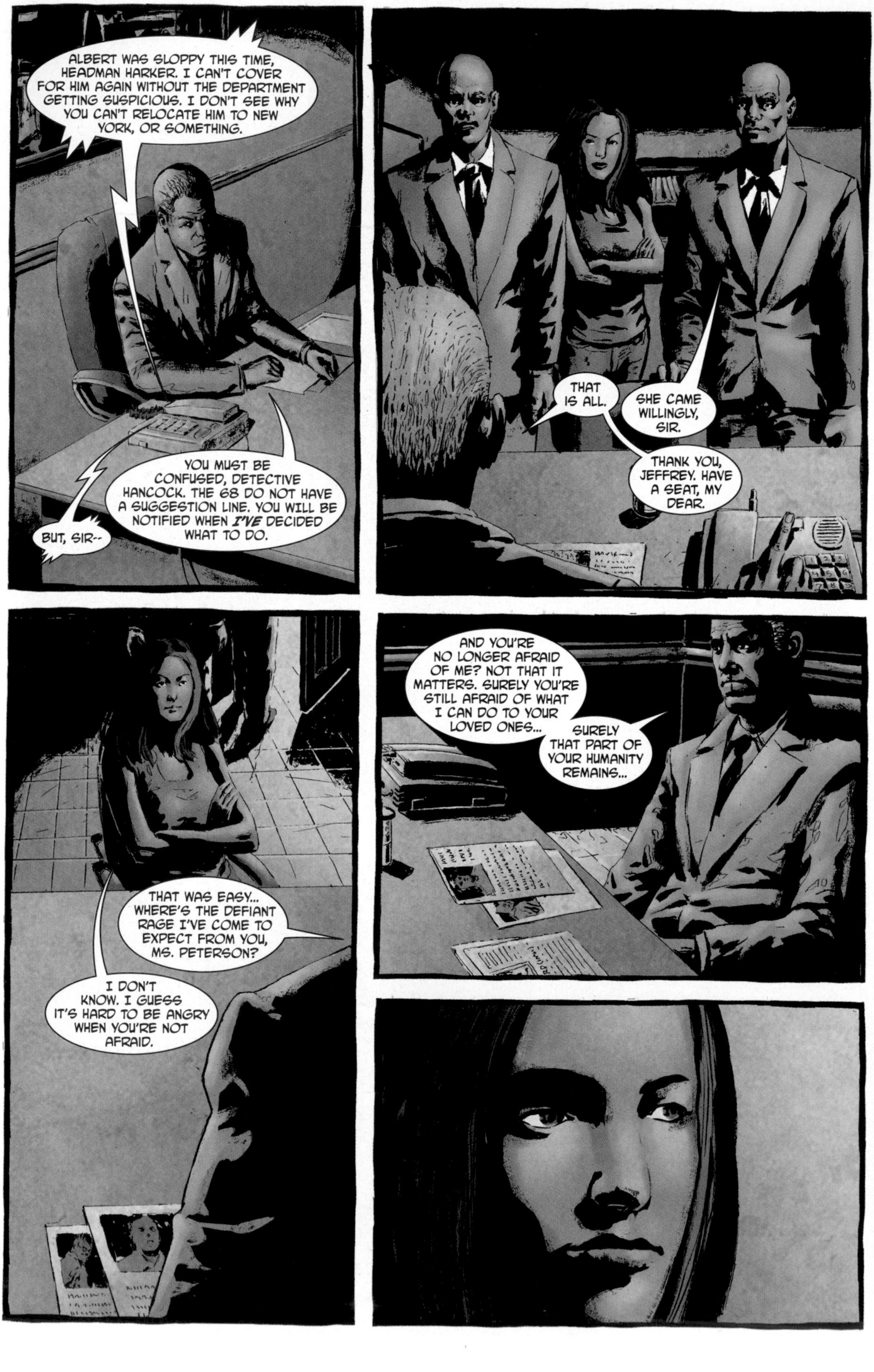
ALBERT WAS SLOPPY THIS TIME, HEADMAN HARKER. I CAN'T COVER FOR HIM AGAIN WITHOUT THE DEPARTMENT GETTING SUSPICIOUS. I DON'T SEE WHY YOU CAN'T RELOCATE HIM TO NEW YORK, OR SOMETHING.
YOU MUST BE CONFUSED, DETECTIVE HANCOCK. THE 68 DO NOT HAVE A SUGGESTION LINE. YOU WILL BE NOTIFIED WHEN *I'VE* DECIDED WHAT TO DO.
BUT, SIR--
SHE CAME WILLINGLY, SIR.
THAT IS ALL.
THANK YOU, JEFFREY. HAVE A SEAT, MY DEAR.
THAT WAS EASY... WHERE'S THE DEFIANT RAGE I'VE COME TO EXPECT FROM YOU, MS. PETERSON?
I DON'T KNOW. I GUESS IT'S HARD TO BE ANGRY WHEN YOU'RE NOT AFRAID.
AND YOU'RE NO LONGER AFRAID OF ME? NOT THAT IT MATTERS. SURELY YOU'RE STILL AFRAID OF WHAT I CAN DO TO YOUR LOVED ONES...
SURELY THAT PART OF YOUR HUMANITY REMAINS...

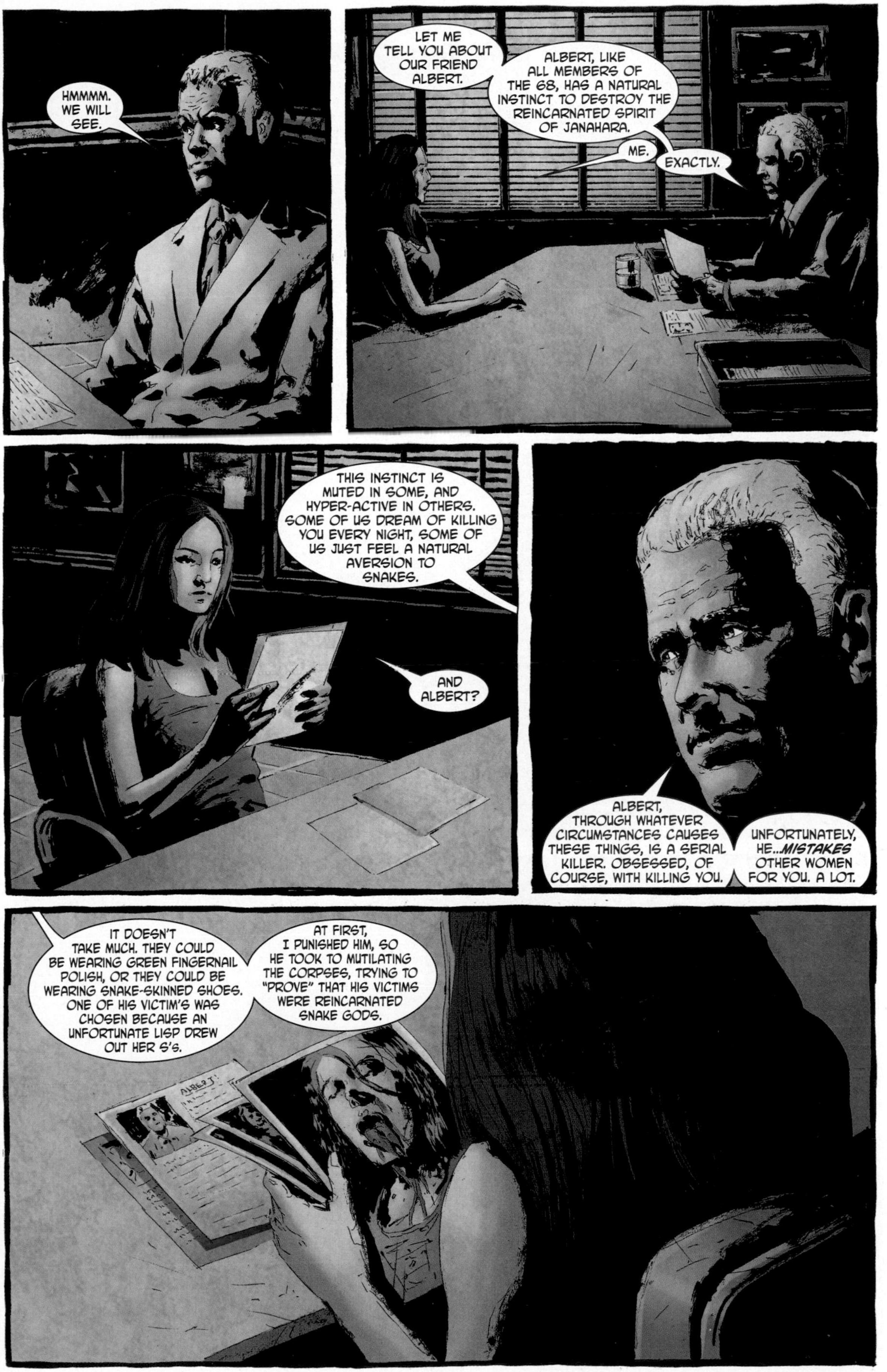
HMMMM. WE WILL SEE.
LET ME TELL YOU ABOUT OUR FRIEND ALBERT.
ALBERT, LIKE ALL MEMBERS OF THE 68, HAS A NATURAL INSTINCT TO DESTROY THE REINCARNATED SPIRIT OF JANAHARA.
ME.
EXACTLY.
THIS INSTINCT IS MUTED IN SOME, AND HYPER-ACTIVE IN OTHERS. SOME OF US DREAM OF KILLING YOU EVERY NIGHT, SOME OF US JUST FEEL A NATURAL AVERSION TO SNAKES.
AND ALBERT?
ALBERT, THROUGH WHATEVER CIRCUMSTANCES CAUSES THESE THINGS, IS A SERIAL KILLER. OBSESSED, OF COURSE, WITH KILLING YOU.
UNFORTUNATELY, HE...*MISTAKES* OTHER WOMEN FOR YOU. A LOT.
IT DOESN'T TAKE MUCH. THEY COULD BE WEARING GREEN FINGERNAIL POLISH, OR THEY COULD BE WEARING SNAKE-SKINNED SHOES. ONE OF HIS VICTIM'S WAS CHOSEN BECAUSE AN UNFORTUNATE LISP DREW OUT HER S'S.
AT FIRST, I PUNISHED HIM, SO HE TOOK TO MUTILATING THE CORPSES, TRYING TO "PROVE" THAT HIS VICTIMS WERE REINCARNATED SNAKE GODS.
ALBERT

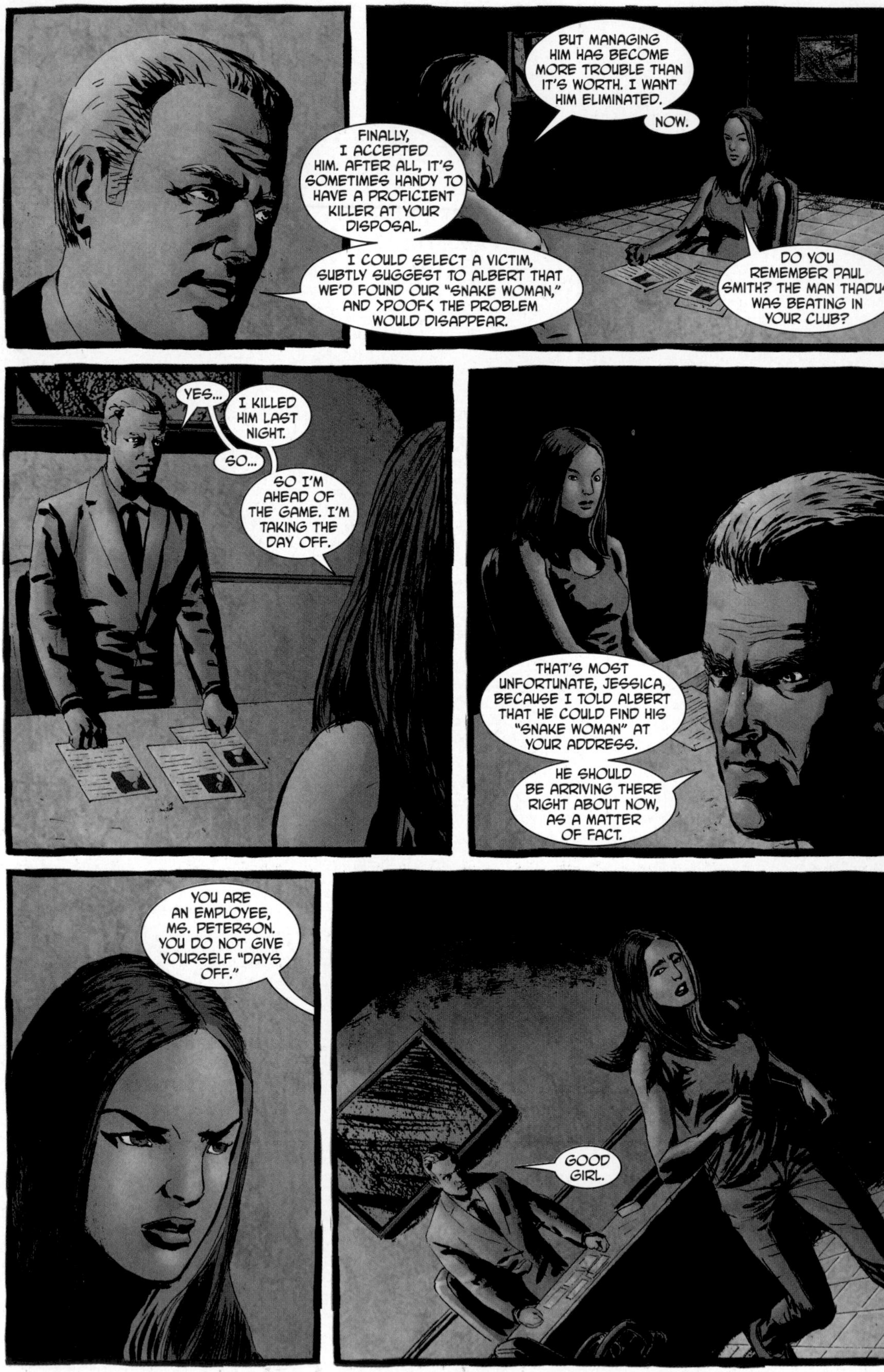
FINALLY, I ACCEPTED HIM. AFTER ALL, IT'S SOMETIMES HANDY TO HAVE A PROFICIENT KILLER AT YOUR DISPOSAL.
I COULD SELECT A VICTIM, SUBTLY SUGGEST TO ALBERT THAT WE'D FOUND OUR "SNAKE WOMAN," AND >POOF< THE PROBLEM WOULD DISAPPEAR.
BUT MANAGING HIM HAS BECOME MORE TROUBLE THAN IT'S WORTH. I WANT HIM ELIMINATED.
NOW.
DO YOU REMEMBER PAUL SMITH? THE MAN THADUS WAS BEATING IN YOUR CLUB?
YES...
I KILLED HIM LAST NIGHT.
SO...
SO I'M AHEAD OF THE GAME. I'M TAKING THE DAY OFF.
THAT'S MOST UNFORTUNATE, JESSICA, BECAUSE I TOLD ALBERT THAT HE COULD FIND HIS "SNAKE WOMAN" AT YOUR ADDRESS.
HE SHOULD BE ARRIVING THERE RIGHT ABOUT NOW, AS A MATTER OF FACT.
YOU ARE AN EMPLOYEE, MS. PETERSON. YOU DO NOT GIVE YOURSELF "DAYS OFF."
GOOD GIRL.

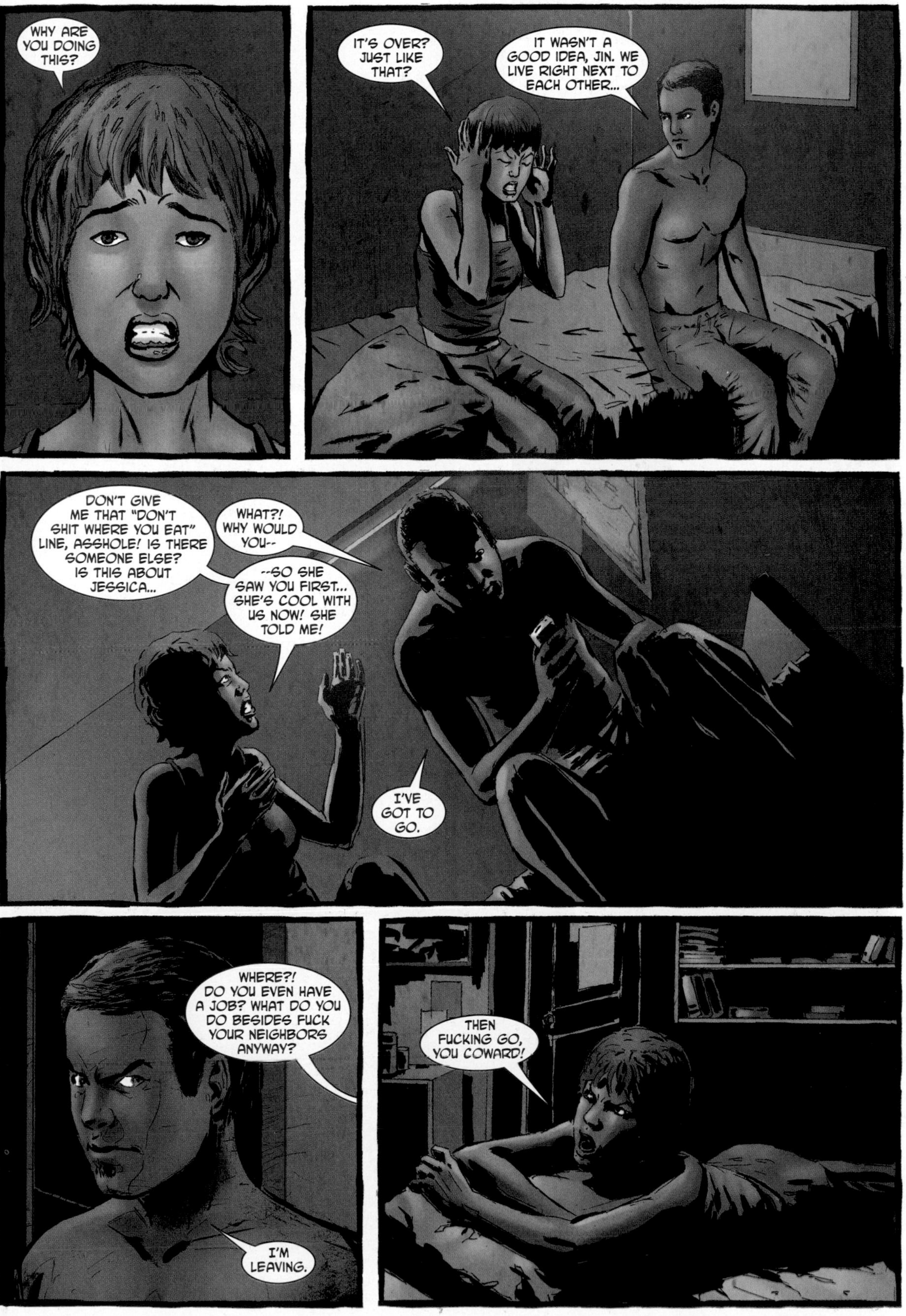
WHY ARE YOU DOING THIS?
IT'S OVER? JUST LIKE THAT?
IT WASN'T A GOOD IDEA, JIN. WE LIVE RIGHT NEXT TO EACH OTHER...
DON'T GIVE ME THAT "DON'T SHIT WHERE YOU EAT" LINE, ASSHOLE! IS THERE SOMEONE ELSE? IS THIS ABOUT JESSICA...
WHAT?! WHY WOULD YOU--
--SO SHE SAW YOU FIRST... SHE'S COOL WITH US NOW! SHE TOLD ME!
I'VE GOT TO GO.
WHERE?! DO YOU EVEN HAVE A JOB? WHAT DO YOU DO BESIDES FUCK YOUR NEIGHBORS ANYWAY?
I'M LEAVING.
THEN FUCKING GO, YOU COWARD!

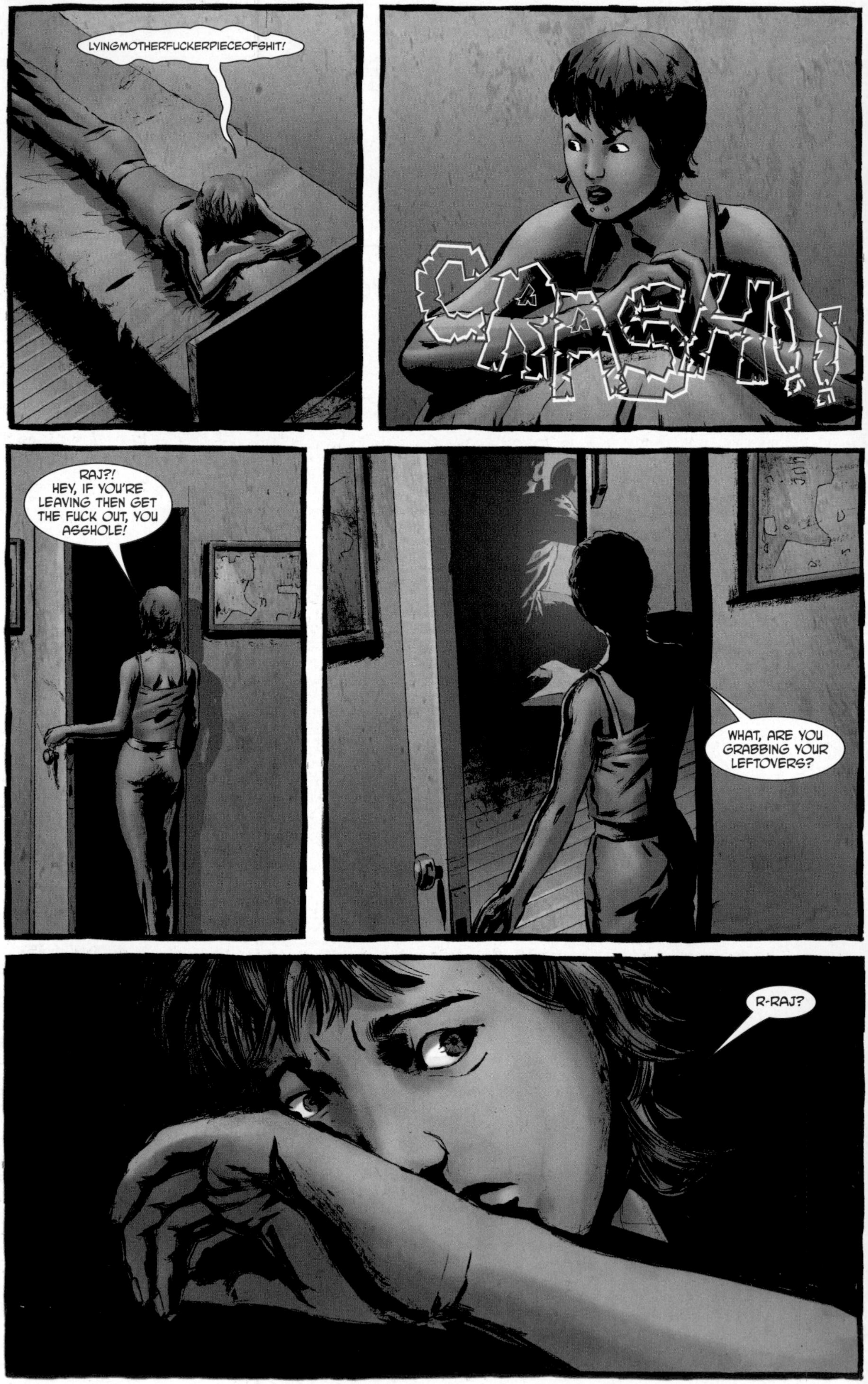
LYINGMOTHERFUCKERPIECEOFSHIT!
CRASH!!
RAJ?! HEY, IF YOU'RE LEAVING THEN GET THE FUCK OUT, YOU ASSHOLE!
WHAT, ARE YOU GRABBING YOUR LEFTOVERS?
R-RAJ?

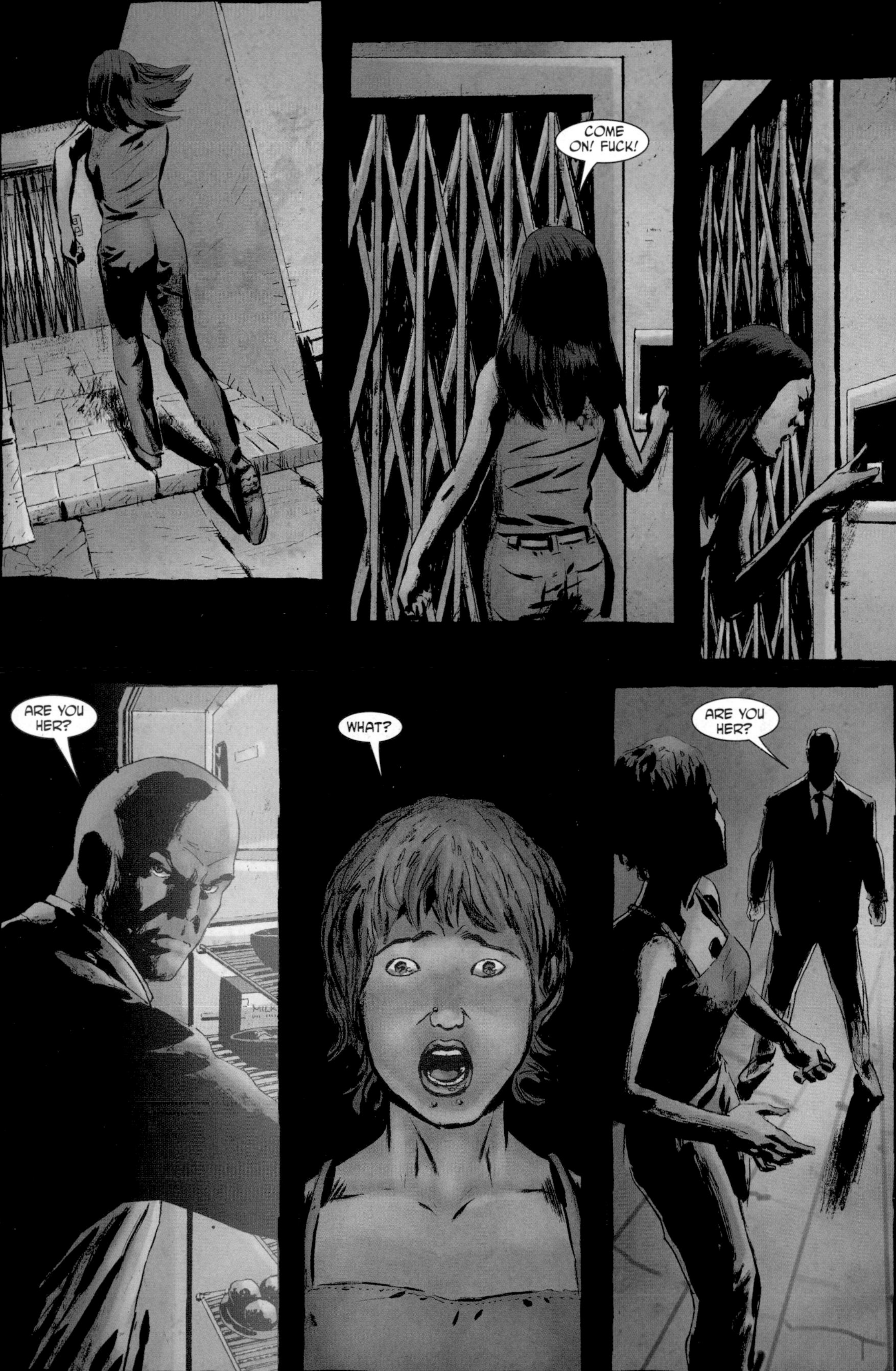
COME ON! FUCK!
ARE YOU HER?
WHAT?
MILK
ARE YOU HER?

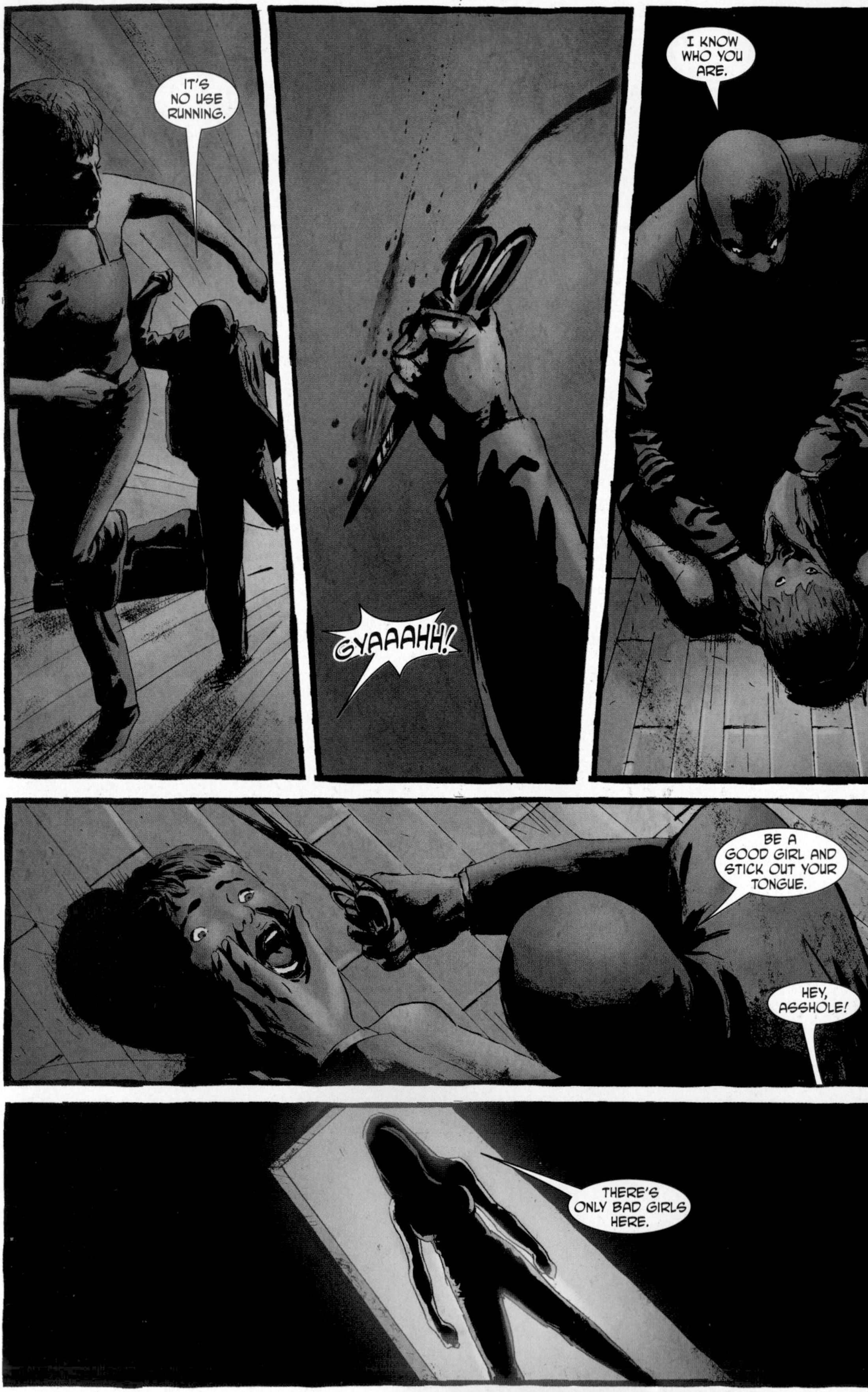
IT'S NO USE RUNNING.
GYAAAHH!
I KNOW WHO YOU ARE.
BE A GOOD GIRL AND STICK OUT YOUR TONGUE.
HEY, ASSHOLE!
THERE'S ONLY BAD GIRLS HERE.

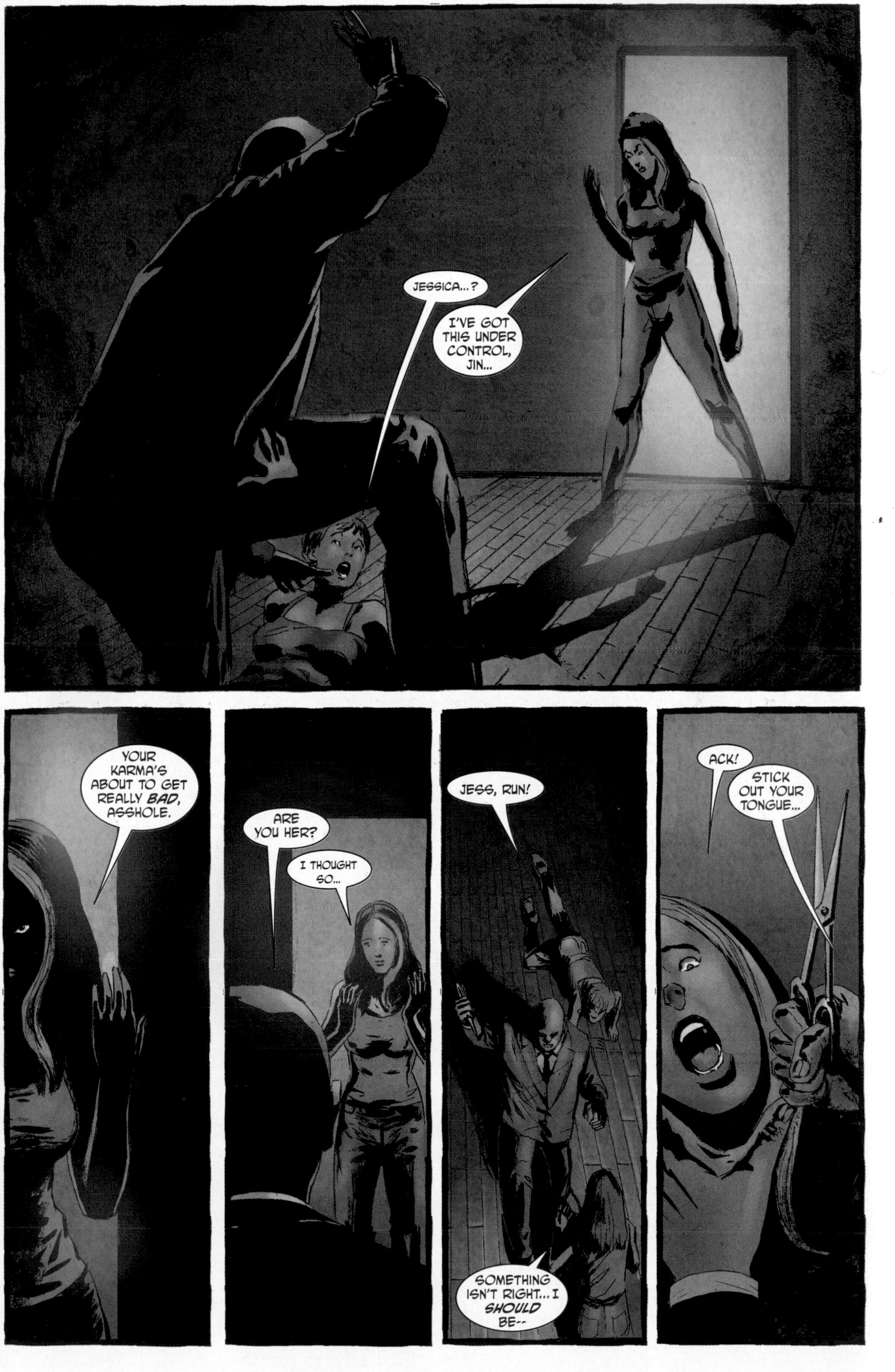
JESSICA...?
I'VE GOT THIS UNDER CONTROL, JIN...
YOUR KARMA'S ABOUT TO GET REALLY *BAD*, ASSHOLE.
ARE YOU HER?
I THOUGHT SO...
JESS, RUN!
SOMETHING ISN'T RIGHT... I *SHOULD* BE--
ACK!
STICK OUT YOUR TONGUE...

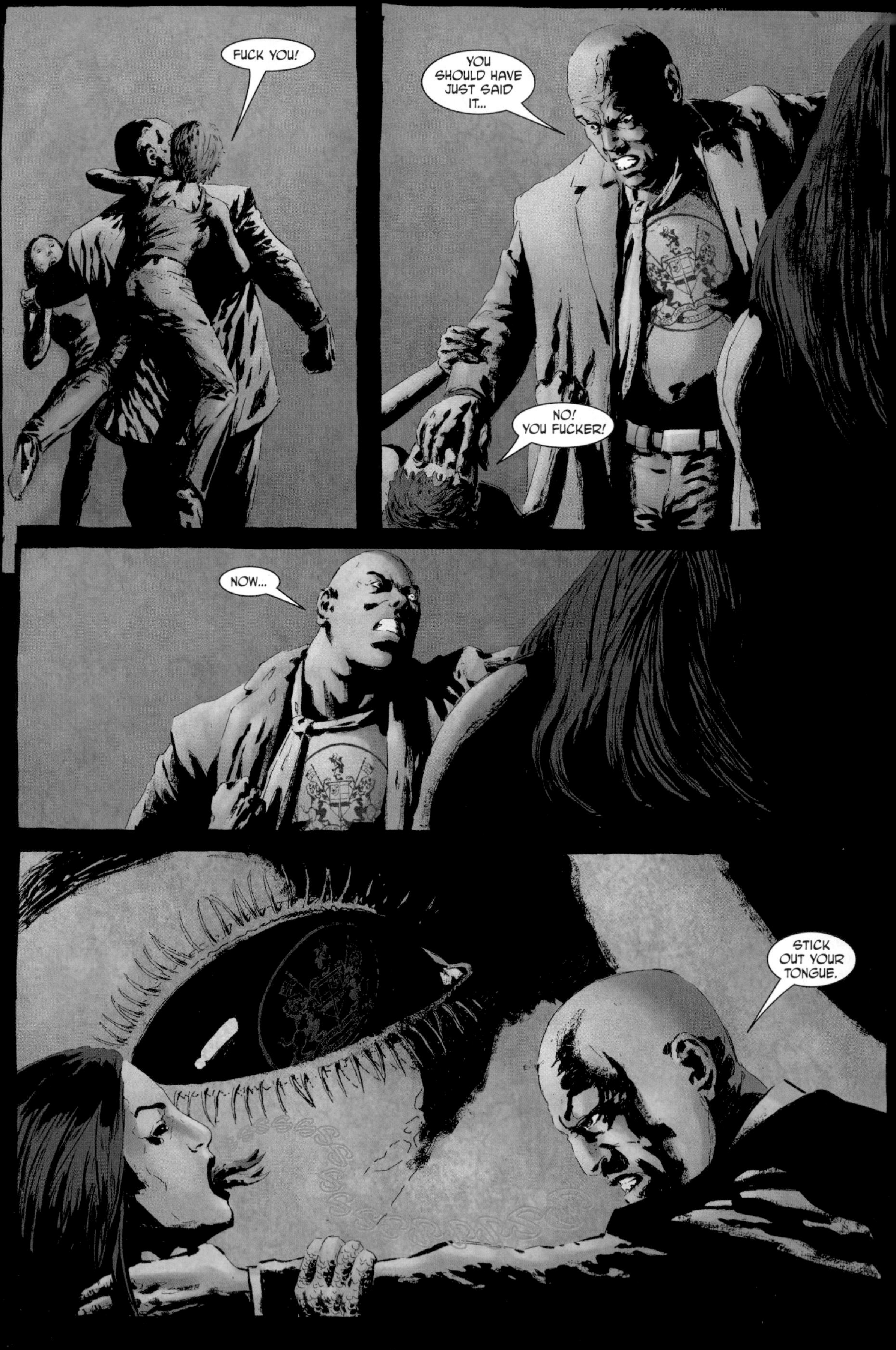
FUCK YOU!
YOU SHOULD HAVE JUST SAID IT...
NO! YOU FUCKER!
NOW...
STICK OUT YOUR TONGUE.

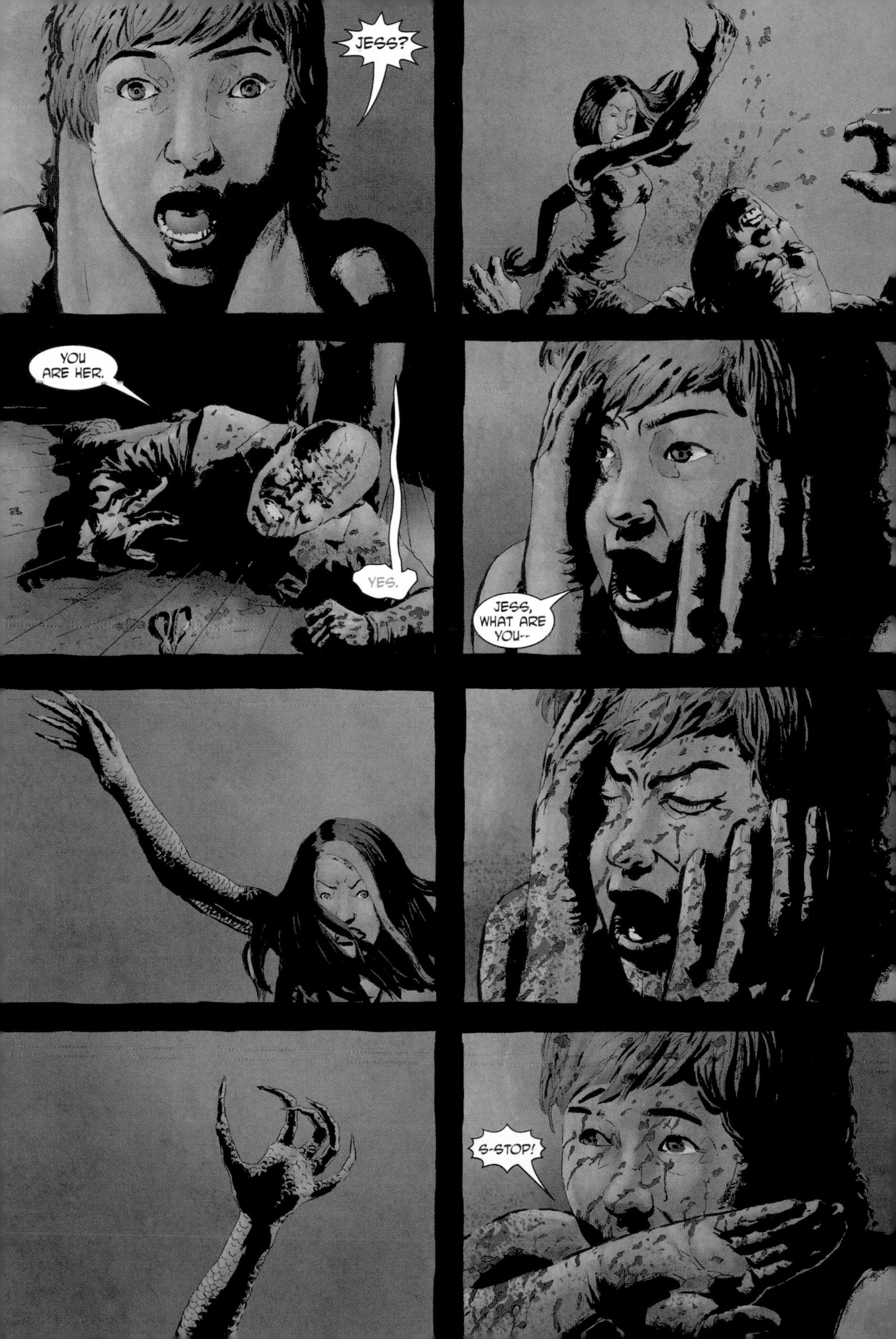
JESS?
YOU ARE HER.
YES.
JESS, WHAT ARE YOU--
S-STOP!

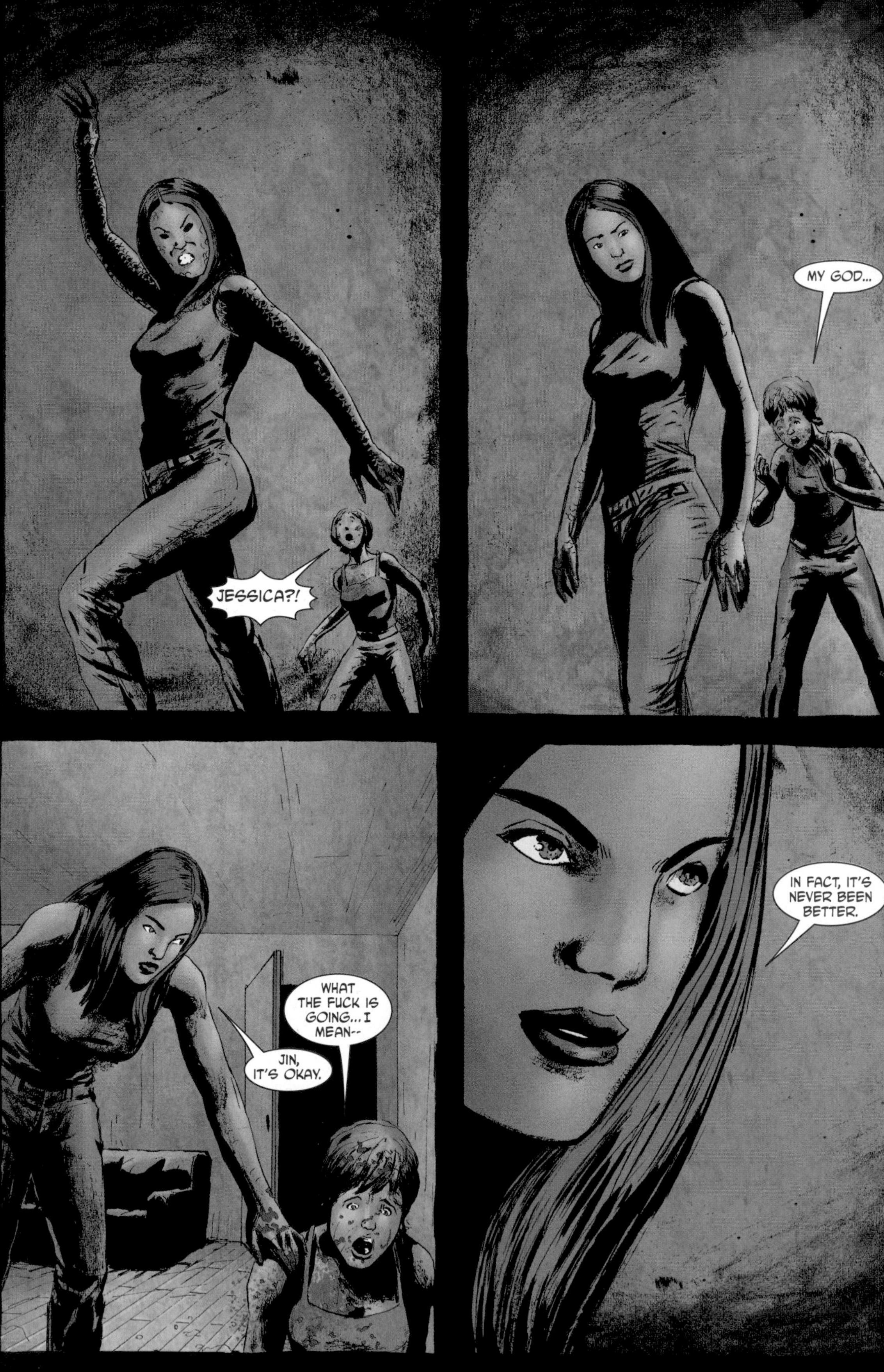
JESSICA?!
MY GOD...
WHAT THE FUCK IS GOING... I MEAN--
JIN, IT'S OKAY.
IN FACT, IT'S NEVER BEEN BETTER.

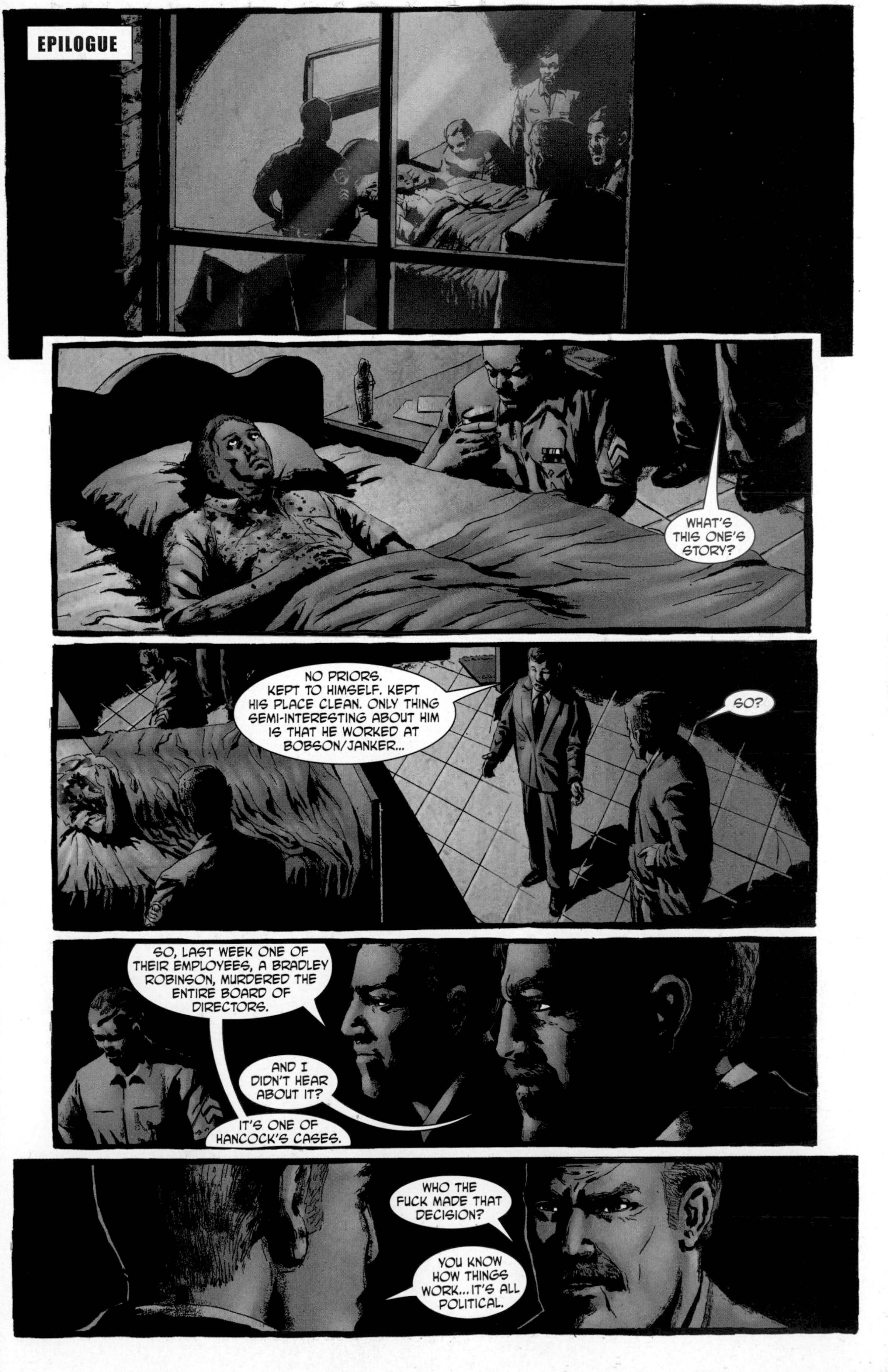
EPILOGUE
WHAT'S THIS ONE'S STORY?
NO PRIORS. KEPT TO HIMSELF. KEPT HIS PLACE CLEAN. ONLY THING SEMI-INTERESTING ABOUT HIM IS THAT HE WORKED AT BOBSON/JANKER...
SO?
SO, LAST WEEK ONE OF THEIR EMPLOYEES, A BRADLEY ROBINSON, MURDERED THE ENTIRE BOARD OF DIRECTORS.
AND I DIDN'T HEAR ABOUT IT?
IT'S ONE OF HANCOCK'S CASES.
WHO THE FUCK MADE THAT DECISION?
YOU KNOW HOW THINGS WORK... IT'S ALL POLITICAL.

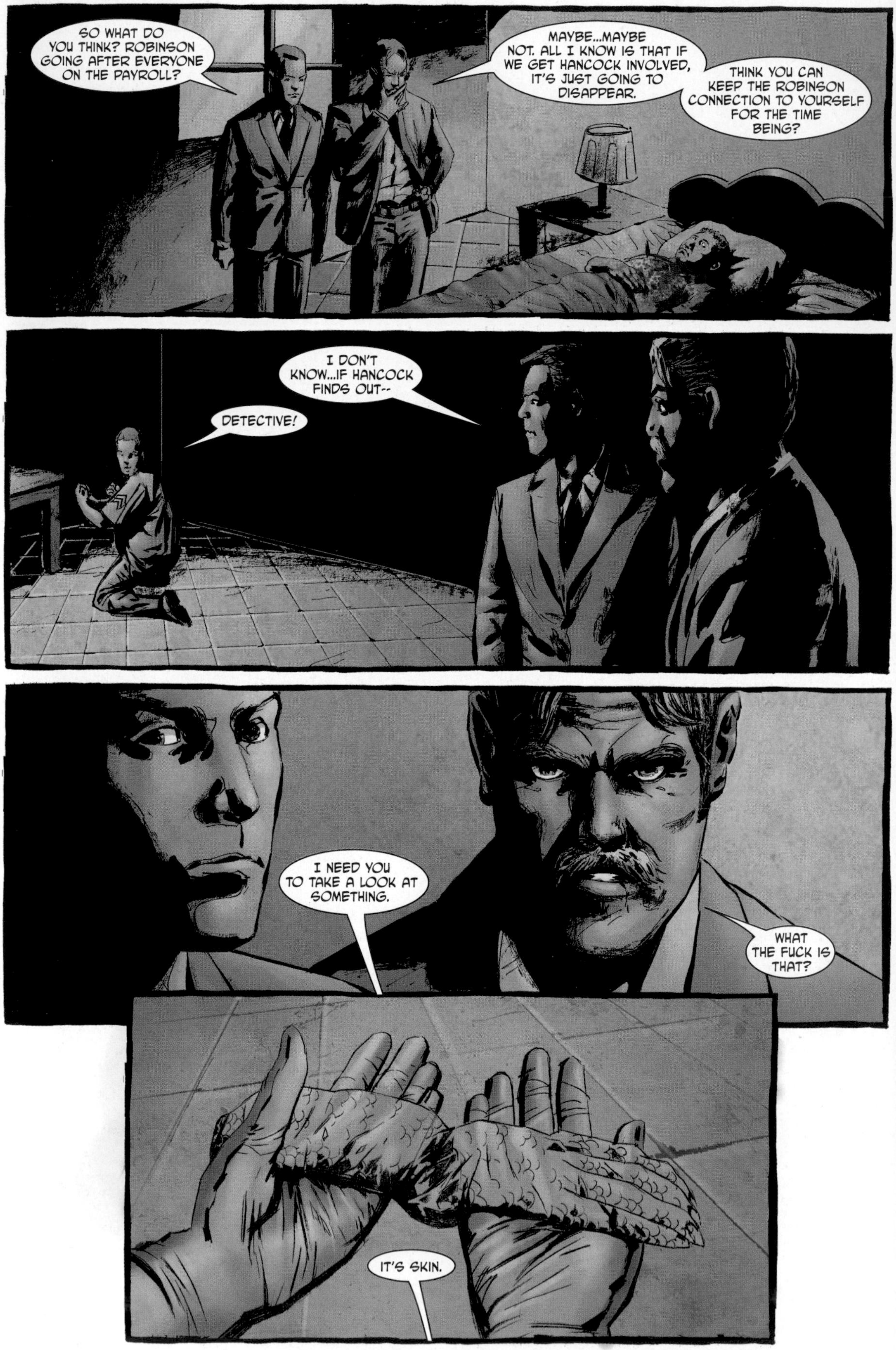
SO WHAT DO YOU THINK? ROBINSON GOING AFTER EVERYONE ON THE PAYROLL?
MAYBE...MAYBE NOT. ALL I KNOW IS THAT IF WE GET HANCOCK INVOLVED, IT'S JUST GOING TO DISAPPEAR.
THINK YOU CAN KEEP THE ROBINSON CONNECTION TO YOURSELF FOR THE TIME BEING?
I DON'T KNOW...IF HANCOCK FINDS OUT--
DETECTIVE!
I NEED YOU TO TAKE A LOOK AT SOMETHING.
WHAT THE FUCK IS THAT?
IT'S SKIN.

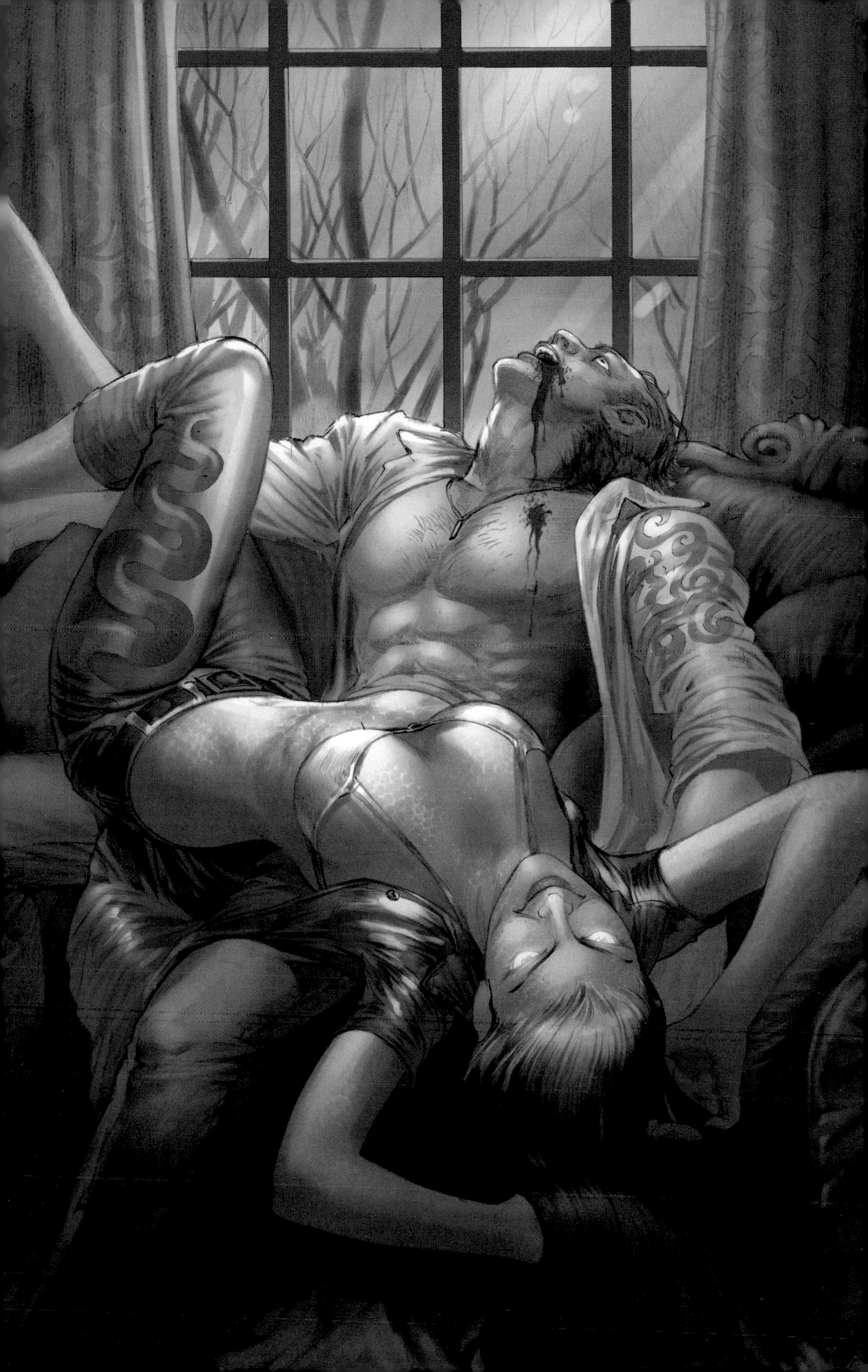

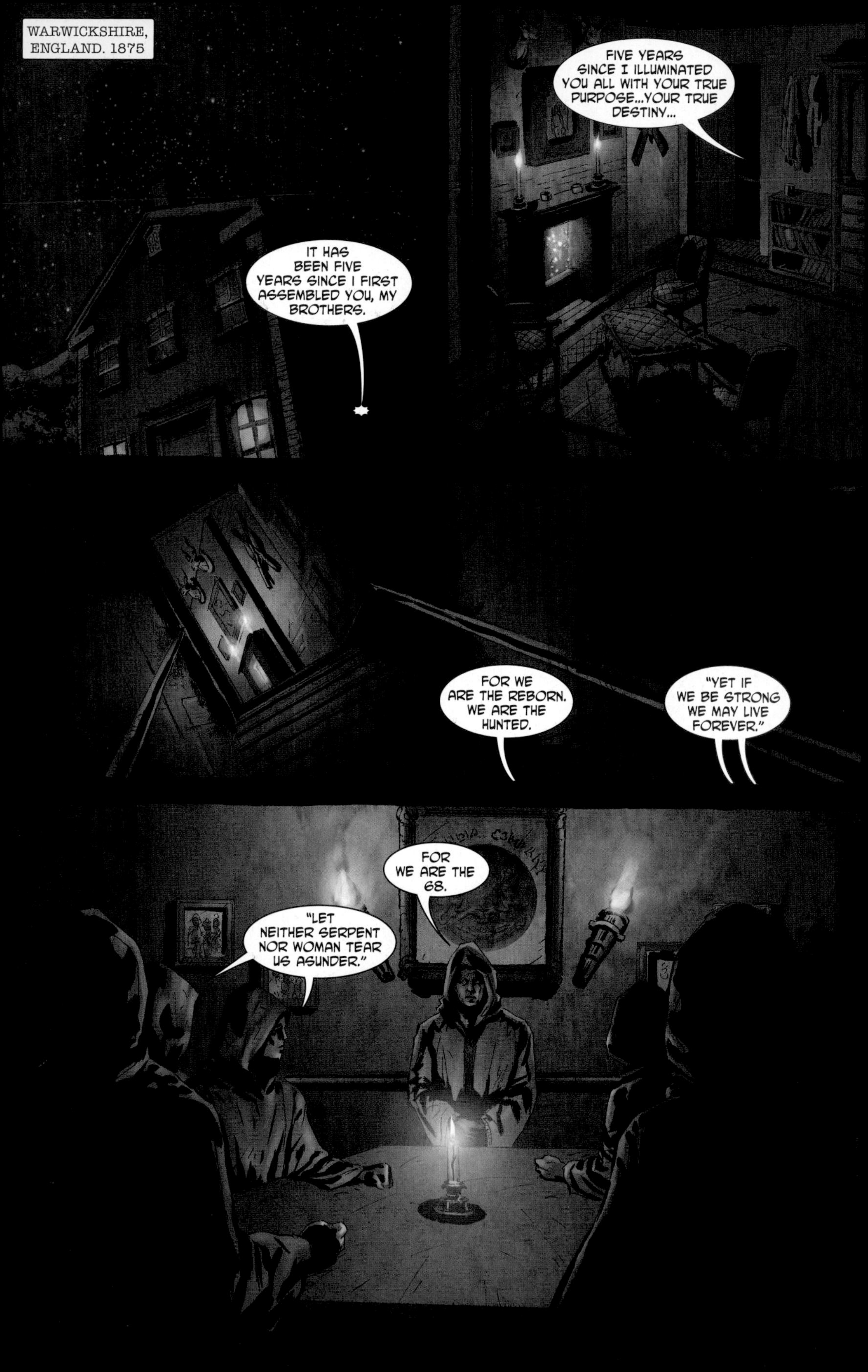
WARWICKSHIRE, ENGLAND. 1875
IT HAS BEEN FIVE YEARS SINCE I FIRST ASSEMBLED YOU, MY BROTHERS.
FIVE YEARS SINCE I ILLUMINATED YOU ALL WITH YOUR TRUE PURPOSE...YOUR TRUE DESTINY...
FOR WE ARE THE REBORN. WE ARE THE HUNTED.
"YET IF WE BE STRONG WE MAY LIVE FOREVER."
FOR WE ARE THE 68.
"LET NEITHER SERPENT NOR WOMAN TEAR US ASUNDER."

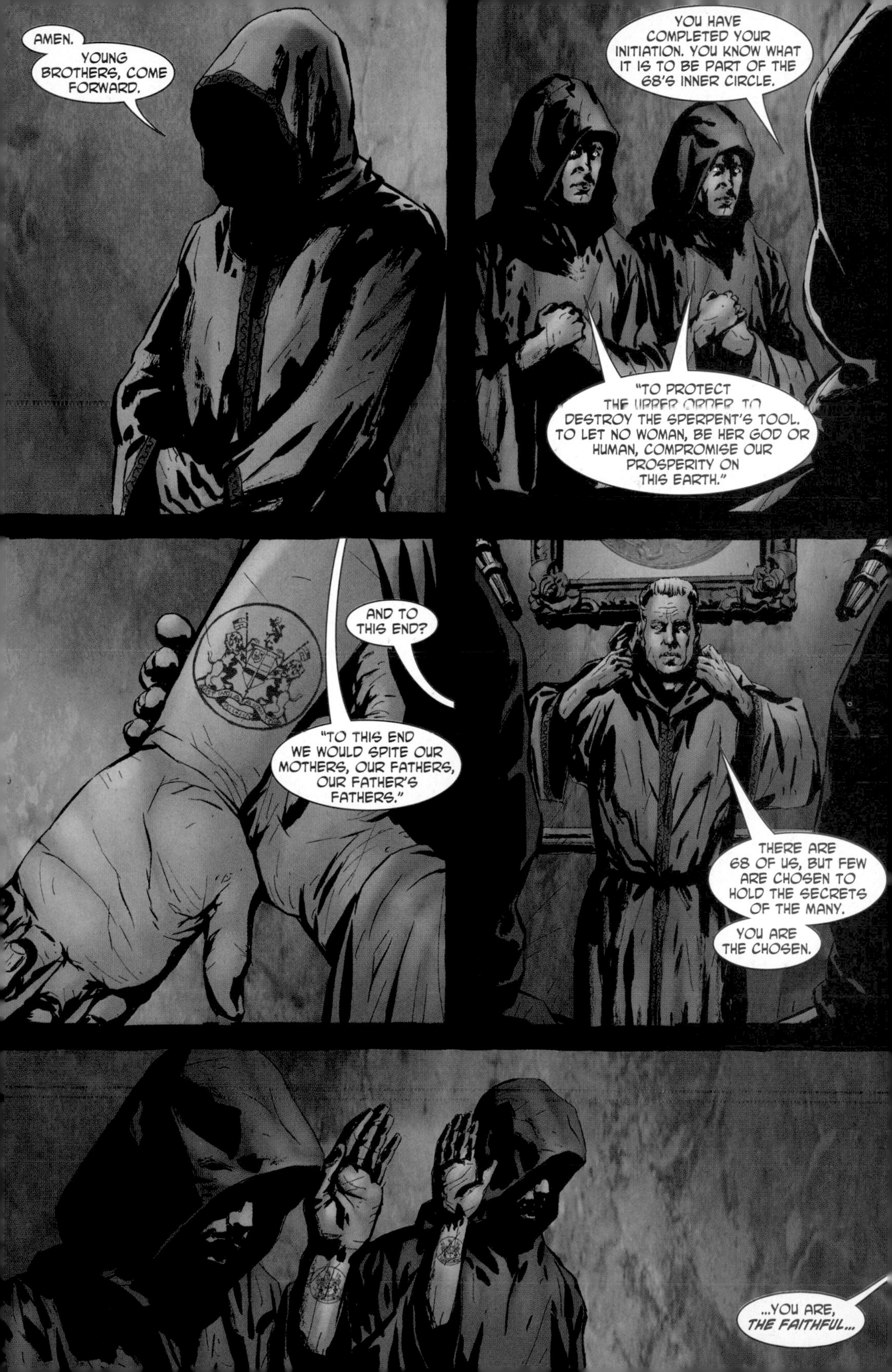
AMEN.
YOUNG BROTHERS, COME FORWARD.
YOU HAVE COMPLETED YOUR INITIATION. YOU KNOW WHAT IT IS TO BE PART OF THE 68'S INNER CIRCLE.
"TO PROTECT THE UPPER ORDER. TO DESTROY THE SPERPENT'S TOOL. TO LET NO WOMAN, BE HER GOD OR HUMAN, COMPROMISE OUR PROSPERITY ON THIS EARTH."
AND TO THIS END?
"TO THIS END WE WOULD SPITE OUR MOTHERS, OUR FATHERS, OUR FATHER'S FATHERS."
THERE ARE 68 OF US, BUT FEW ARE CHOSEN TO HOLD THE SECRETS OF THE MANY.
YOU ARE THE CHOSEN.
...YOU ARE, *THE FAITHFUL...*

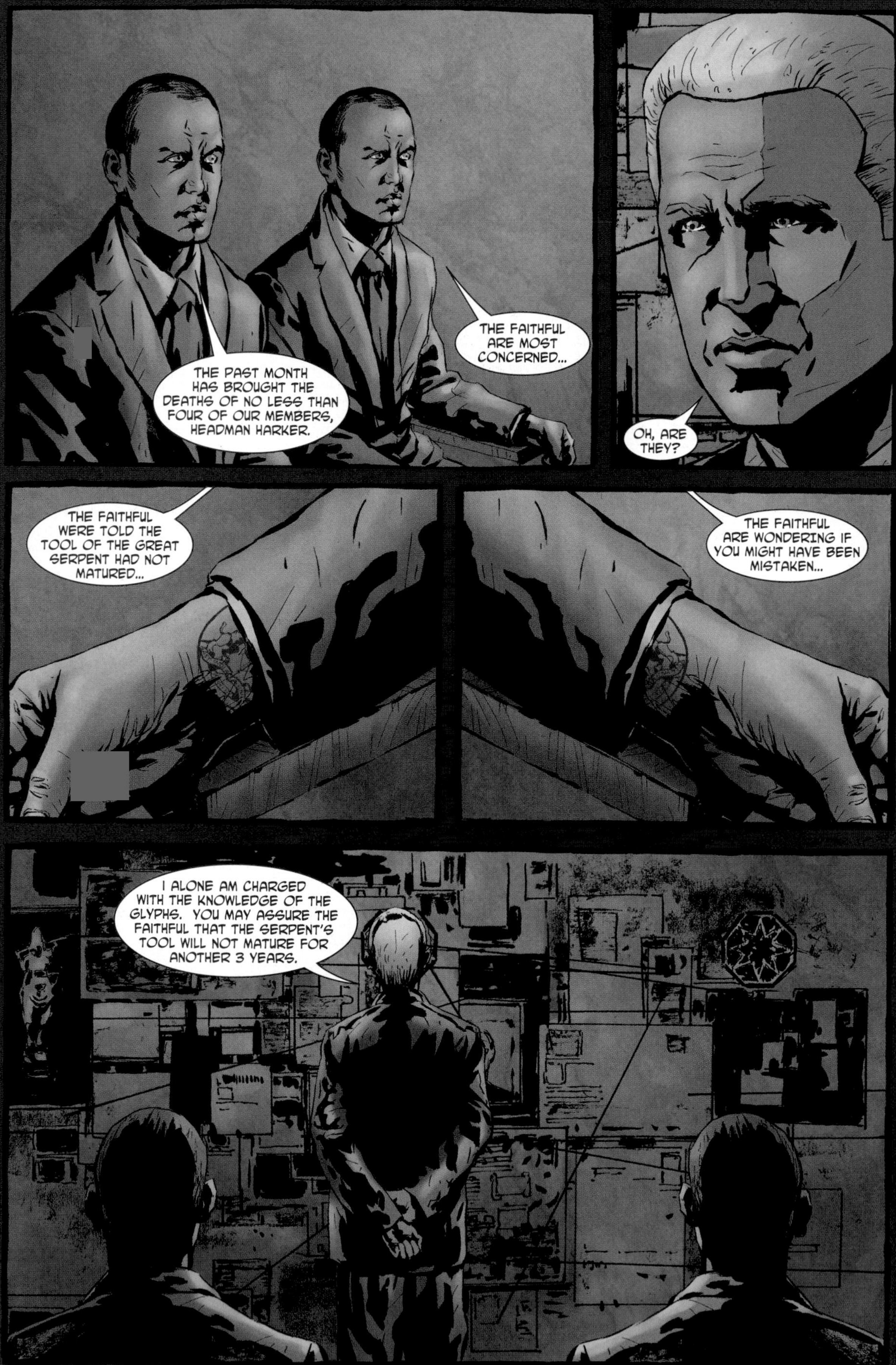
THE PAST MONTH HAS BROUGHT THE DEATHS OF NO LESS THAN FOUR OF OUR MEMBERS, HEADMAN HARKER.
THE FAITHFUL ARE MOST CONCERNED...
OH, ARE THEY?
THE FAITHFUL WERE TOLD THE TOOL OF THE GREAT SERPENT HAD NOT MATURED...
THE FAITHFUL ARE WONDERING IF YOU MIGHT HAVE BEEN MISTAKEN...
I ALONE AM CHARGED WITH THE KNOWLEDGE OF THE GLYPHS. YOU MAY ASSURE THE FAITHFUL THAT THE SERPENT'S TOOL WILL NOT MATURE FOR ANOTHER 3 YEARS.

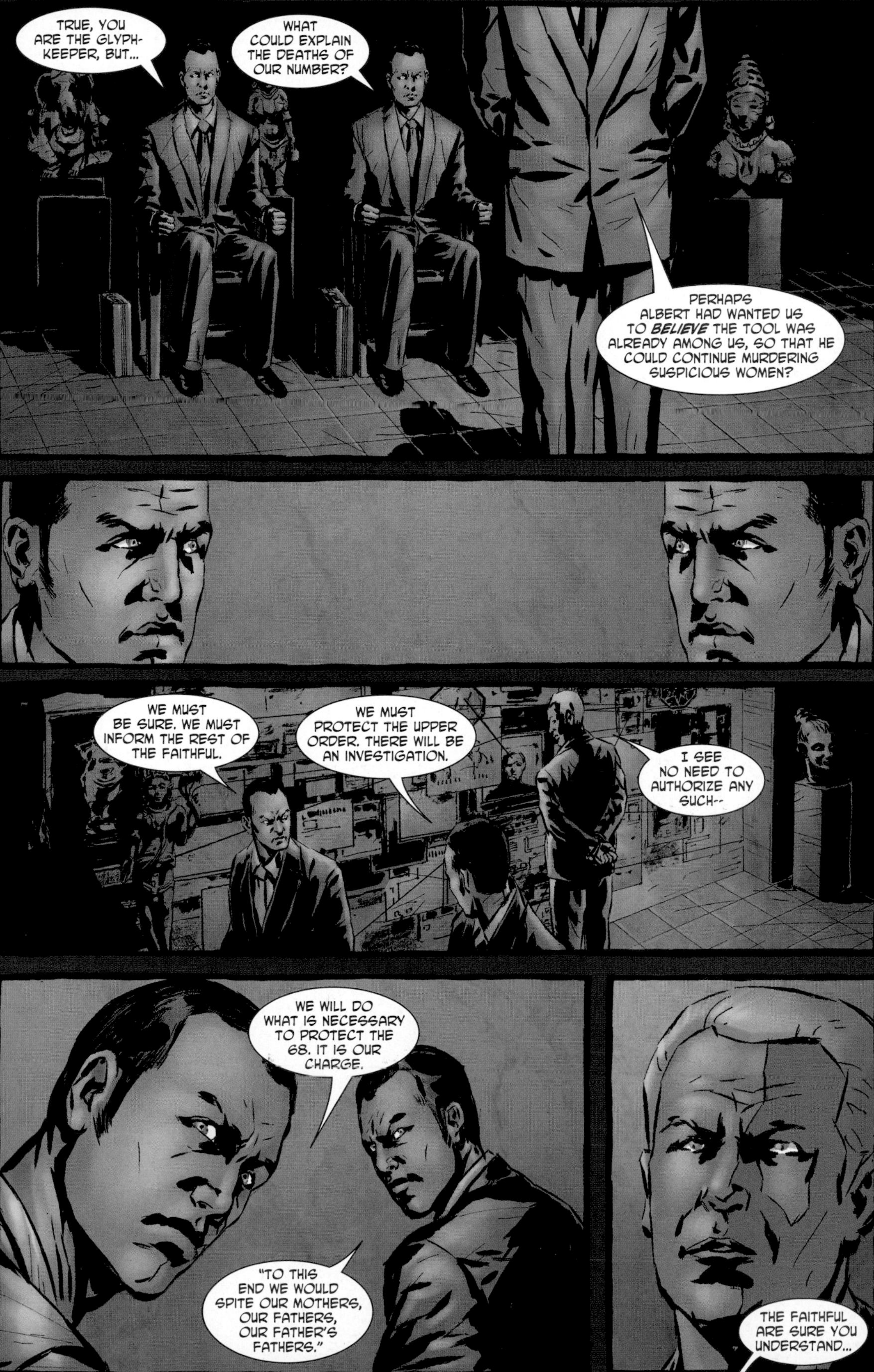
TRUE, YOU ARE THE GLYPH-KEEPER, BUT...
WHAT COULD EXPLAIN THE DEATHS OF OUR NUMBER?
PERHAPS ALBERT HAD WANTED US TO *BELIEVE* THE TOOL WAS ALREADY AMONG US, SO THAT HE COULD CONTINUE MURDERING SUSPICIOUS WOMEN?
WE MUST BE SURE. WE MUST INFORM THE REST OF THE FAITHFUL.
WE MUST PROTECT THE UPPER ORDER. THERE WILL BE AN INVESTIGATION.
I SEE NO NEED TO AUTHORIZE ANY SUCH--
WE WILL DO WHAT IS NECESSARY TO PROTECT THE 68. IT IS OUR CHARGE.
"TO THIS END WE WOULD SPITE OUR MOTHERS, OUR FATHERS, OUR FATHER'S FATHERS."
THE FAITHFUL ARE SURE YOU UNDERSTAND...

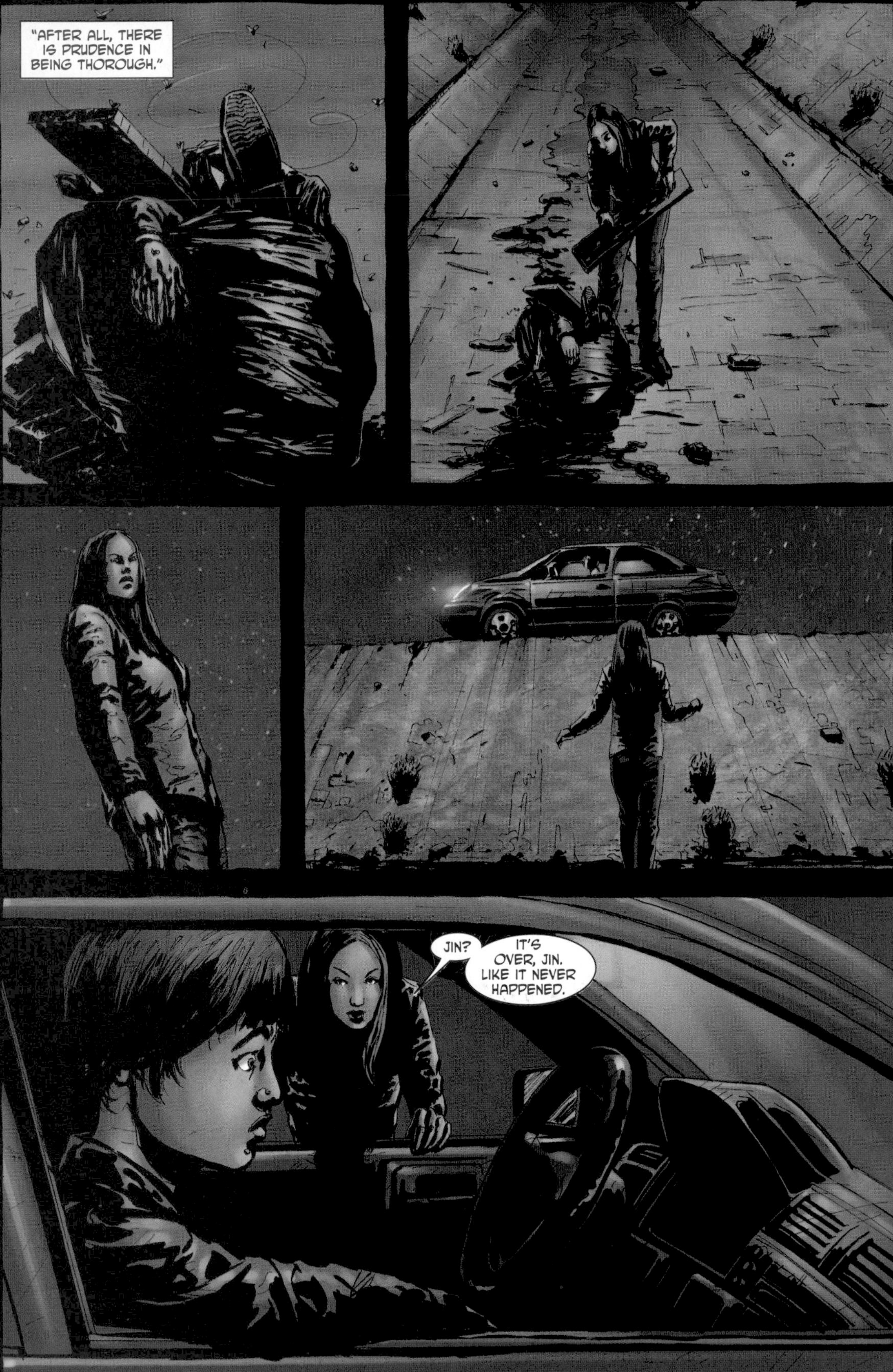
"AFTER ALL, THERE IS PRUDENCE IN BEING THOROUGH."
JIN?
IT'S OVER, JIN. LIKE IT NEVER HAPPENED.

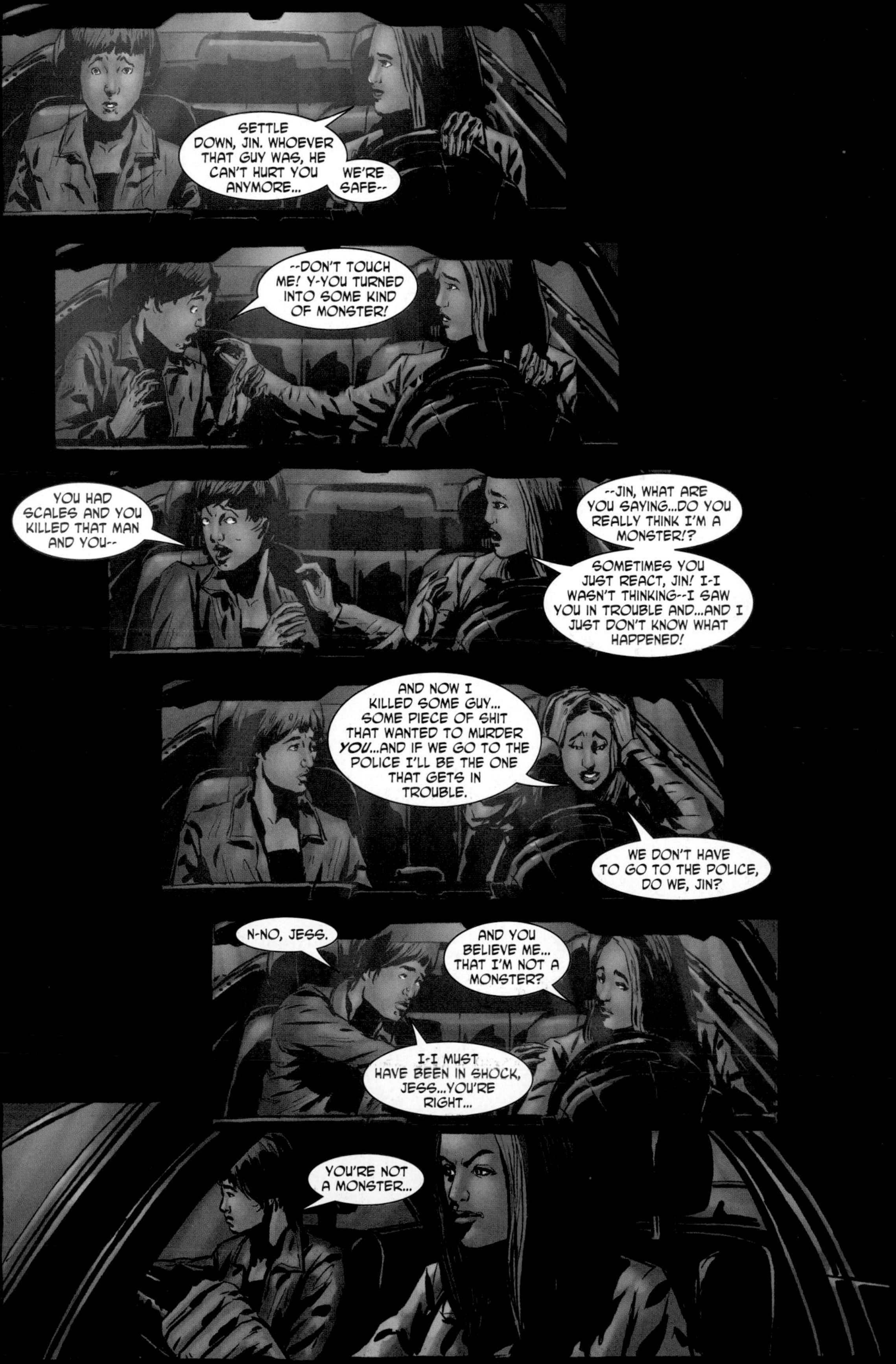
SETTLE DOWN, JIN. WHOEVER THAT GUY WAS, HE CAN'T HURT YOU ANYMORE...
WE'RE SAFE--
--DON'T TOUCH ME! Y-YOU TURNED INTO SOME KIND OF MONSTER!
YOU HAD SCALES AND YOU KILLED THAT MAN AND YOU--
--JIN, WHAT ARE YOU SAYING...DO YOU REALLY THINK I'M A MONSTER!?
SOMETIMES YOU JUST REACT, JIN! I-I WASN'T THINKING--I SAW YOU IN TROUBLE AND...AND I JUST DON'T KNOW WHAT HAPPENED!
AND NOW I KILLED SOME GUY... SOME PIECE OF SHIT THAT WANTED TO MURDER *YOU*...AND IF WE GO TO THE POLICE I'LL BE THE ONE THAT GETS IN TROUBLE.
WE DON'T HAVE TO GO TO THE POLICE, DO WE, JIN?
N-NO, JESS.
AND YOU BELIEVE ME... THAT I'M NOT A MONSTER?
I-I MUST HAVE BEEN IN SHOCK, JESS...YOU'RE RIGHT...
YOU'RE NOT A MONSTER...

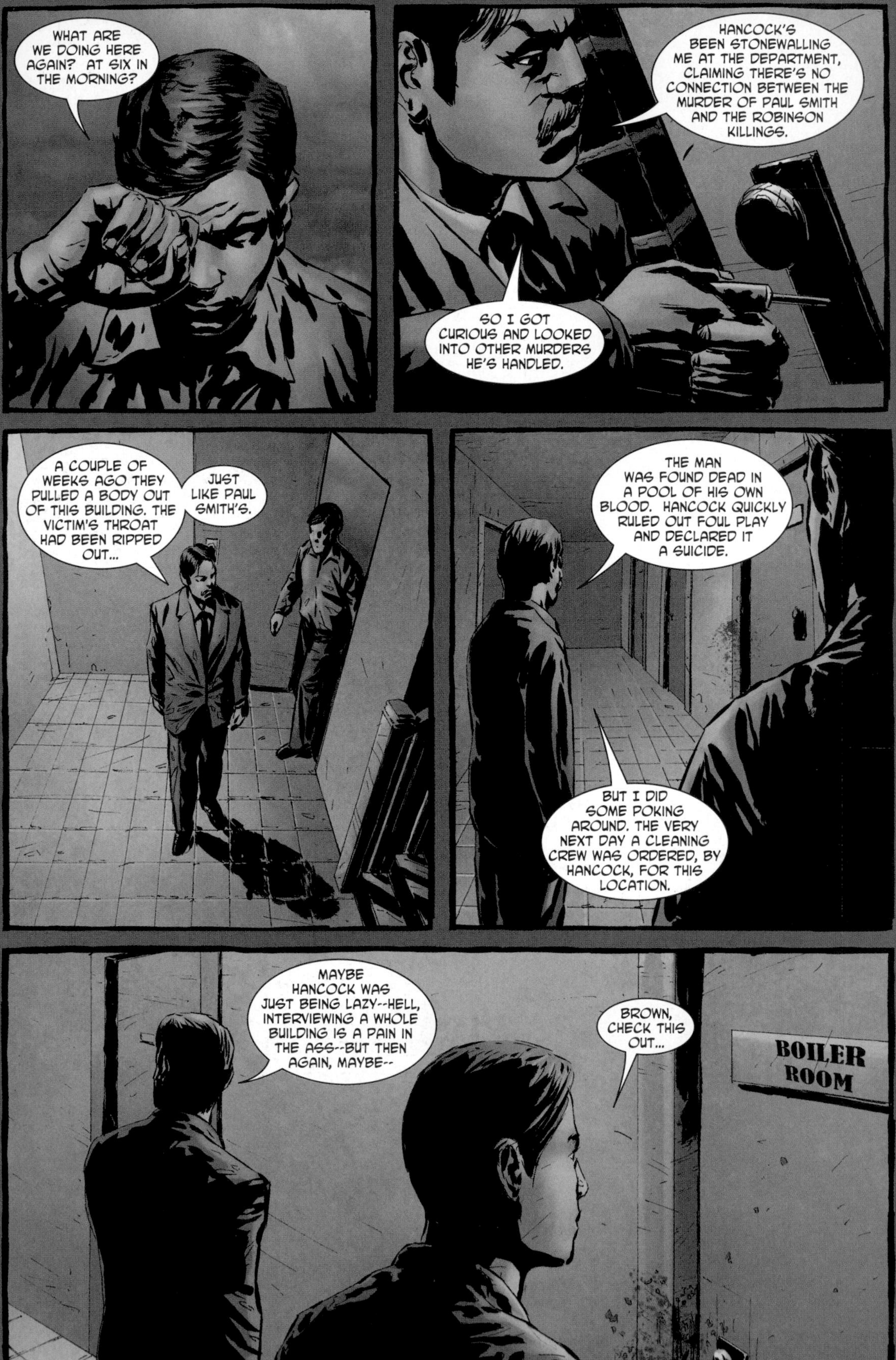
WHAT ARE WE DOING HERE AGAIN? AT SIX IN THE MORNING?
HANCOCK'S BEEN STONEWALLING ME AT THE DEPARTMENT, CLAIMING THERE'S NO CONNECTION BETWEEN THE MURDER OF PAUL SMITH AND THE ROBINSON KILLINGS.
SO I GOT CURIOUS AND LOOKED INTO OTHER MURDERS HE'S HANDLED.
A COUPLE OF WEEKS AGO THEY PULLED A BODY OUT OF THIS BUILDING. THE VICTIM'S THROAT HAD BEEN RIPPED OUT...
JUST LIKE PAUL SMITH'S.
THE MAN WAS FOUND DEAD IN A POOL OF HIS OWN BLOOD. HANCOCK QUICKLY RULED OUT FOUL PLAY AND DECLARED IT A SUICIDE.
BUT I DID SOME POKING AROUND. THE VERY NEXT DAY A CLEANING CREW WAS ORDERED, BY HANCOCK, FOR THIS LOCATION.
MAYBE HANCOCK WAS JUST BEING LAZY--HELL, INTERVIEWING A WHOLE BUILDING IS A PAIN IN THE ASS--BUT THEN AGAIN, MAYBE--
BROWN, CHECK THIS OUT...
BOILER ROOM

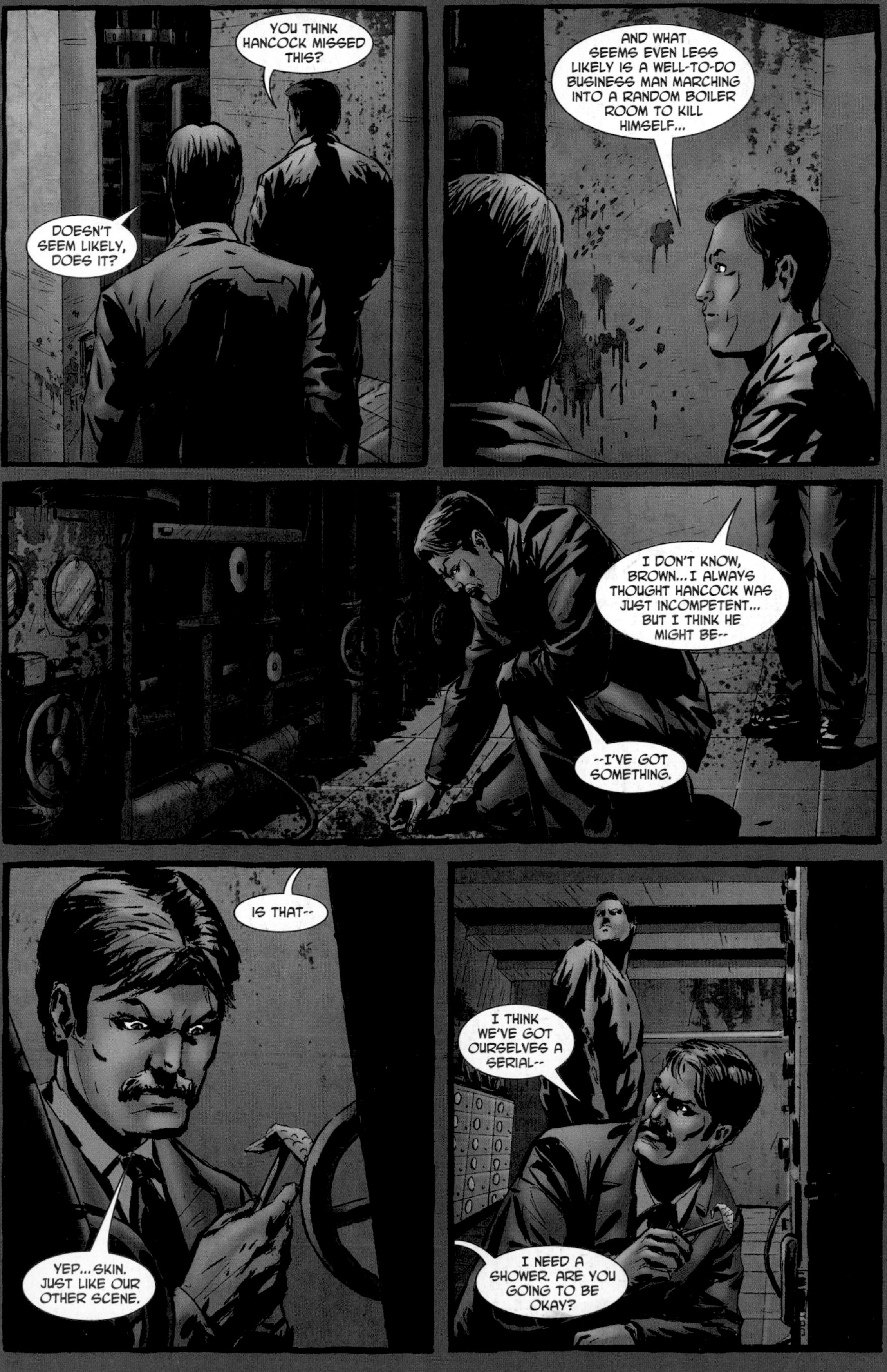

YOU THINK HANCOCK MISSED THIS?
DOESN'T SEEM LIKELY, DOES IT?
AND WHAT SEEMS EVEN LESS LIKELY IS A WELL-TO-DO BUSINESS MAN MARCHING INTO A RANDOM BOILER ROOM TO KILL HIMSELF...
I DON'T KNOW, BROWN... I ALWAYS THOUGHT HANCOCK WAS JUST INCOMPETENT... BUT I THINK HE MIGHT BE--
--I'VE GOT SOMETHING.
IS THAT--
YEP... SKIN. JUST LIKE OUR OTHER SCENE.
I THINK WE'VE GOT OURSELVES A SERIAL--
I NEED A SHOWER. ARE YOU GOING TO BE OKAY?

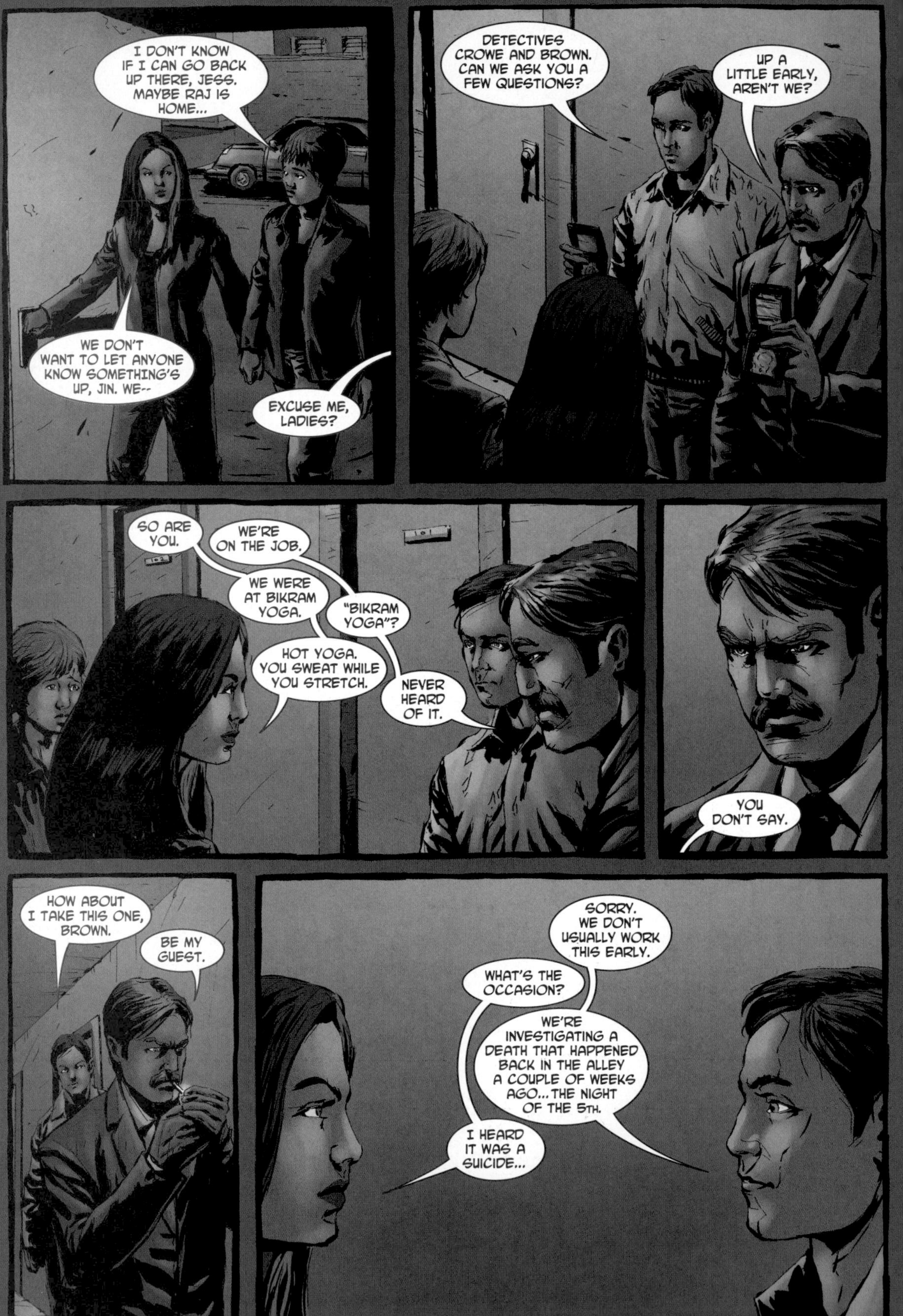
I DON'T KNOW IF I CAN GO BACK UP THERE, JESS. MAYBE RAJ IS HOME...
WE DON'T WANT TO LET ANYONE KNOW SOMETHING'S UP, JIN. WE--
EXCUSE ME, LADIES?
DETECTIVES CROWE AND BROWN. CAN WE ASK YOU A FEW QUESTIONS?
UP A LITTLE EARLY, AREN'T WE?
SO ARE YOU.
WE'RE ON THE JOB.
WE WERE AT BIKRAM YOGA.
"BIKRAM YOGA"?
HOT YOGA. YOU SWEAT WHILE YOU STRETCH.
NEVER HEARD OF IT.
YOU DON'T SAY.
HOW ABOUT I TAKE THIS ONE, BROWN.
BE MY GUEST.
SORRY. WE DON'T USUALLY WORK THIS EARLY.
WHAT'S THE OCCASION?
WE'RE INVESTIGATING A DEATH THAT HAPPENED BACK IN THE ALLEY A COUPLE OF WEEKS AGO...THE NIGHT OF THE 5TH.
I HEARD IT WAS A SUICIDE...

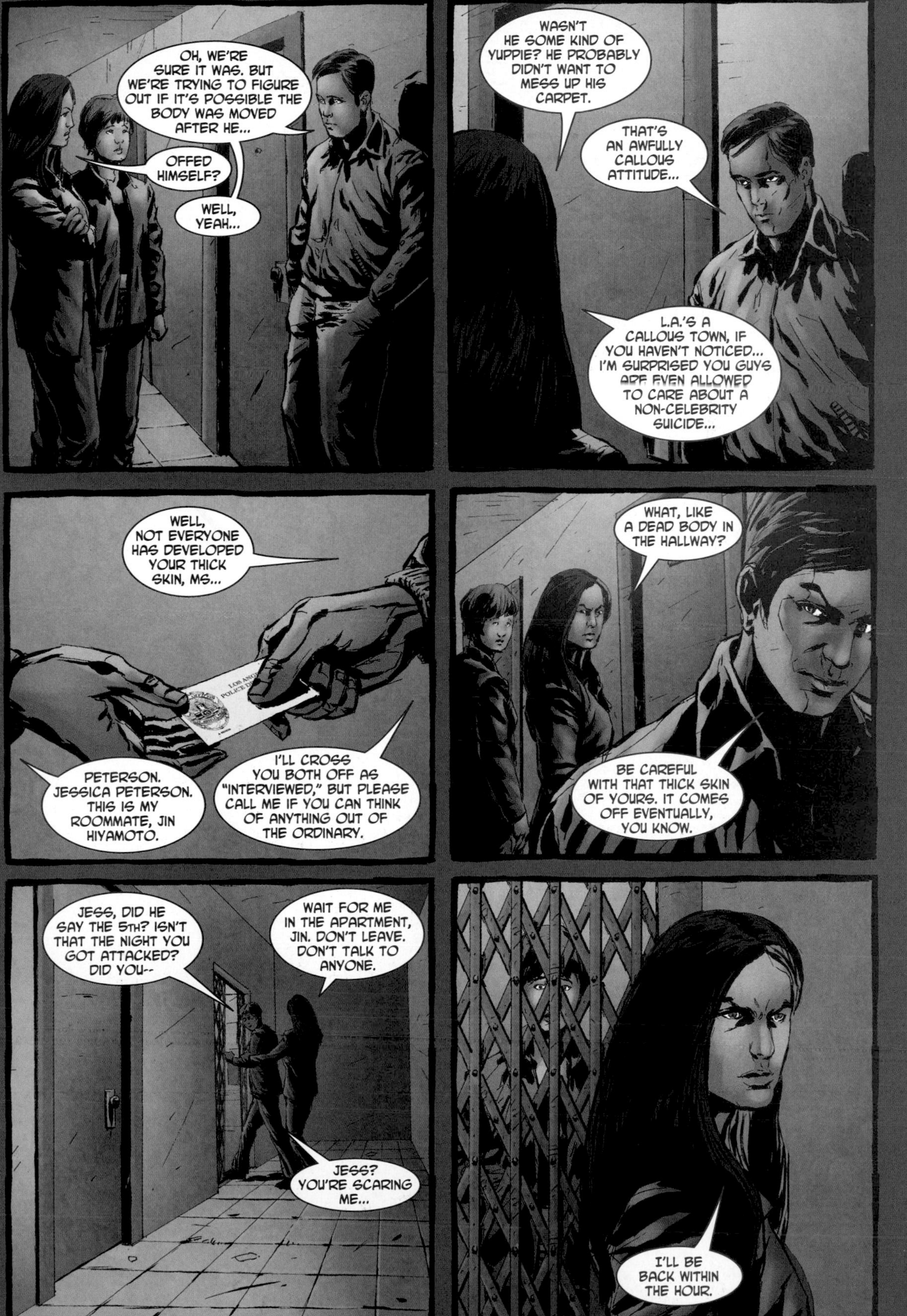
OH, WE'RE SURE IT WAS. BUT WE'RE TRYING TO FIGURE OUT IF IT'S POSSIBLE THE BODY WAS MOVED AFTER HE...
OFFED HIMSELF?
WELL, YEAH...
WASN'T HE SOME KIND OF YUPPIE? HE PROBABLY DIDN'T WANT TO MESS UP HIS CARPET.
THAT'S AN AWFULLY CALLOUS ATTITUDE...
L.A.'S A CALLOUS TOWN, IF YOU HAVEN'T NOTICED... I'M SURPRISED YOU GUYS ARE EVEN ALLOWED TO CARE ABOUT A NON-CELEBRITY SUICIDE...
WELL, NOT EVERYONE HAS DEVELOPED YOUR THICK SKIN, MS...
PETERSON. JESSICA PETERSON. THIS IS MY ROOMMATE, JIN HIYAMOTO.
I'LL CROSS YOU BOTH OFF AS "INTERVIEWED," BUT PLEASE CALL ME IF YOU CAN THINK OF ANYTHING OUT OF THE ORDINARY.
WHAT, LIKE A DEAD BODY IN THE HALLWAY?
BE CAREFUL WITH THAT THICK SKIN OF YOURS. IT COMES OFF EVENTUALLY, YOU KNOW.
JESS, DID HE SAY THE 5TH? ISN'T THAT THE NIGHT YOU GOT ATTACKED? DID YOU--
WAIT FOR ME IN THE APARTMENT, JIN. DON'T LEAVE. DON'T TALK TO ANYONE.
JESS? YOU'RE SCARING ME...
I'LL BE BACK WITHIN THE HOUR.

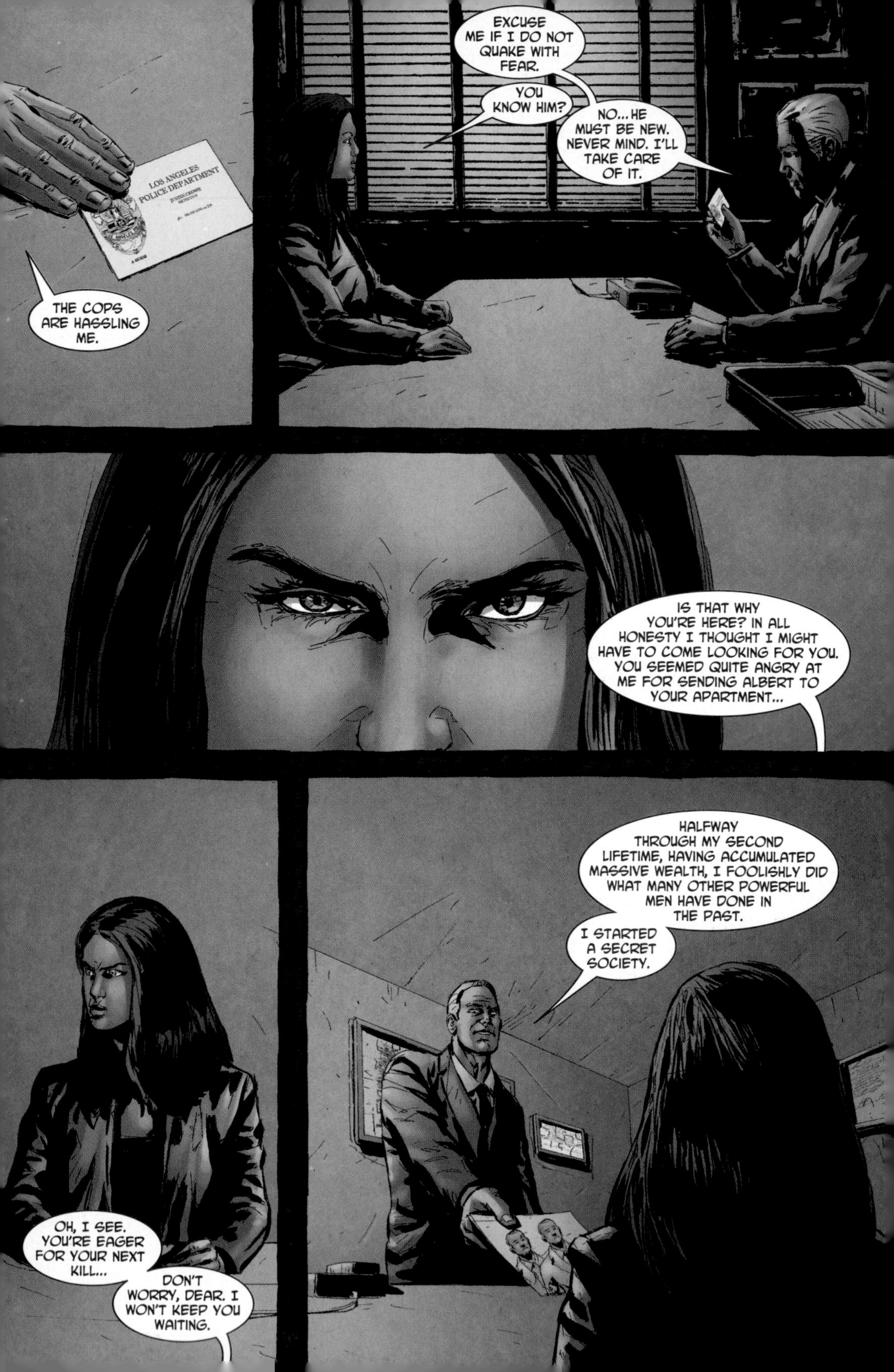
LOS ANGELES POLICE DEPARTMENT
THE COPS ARE HASSLING ME.
EXCUSE ME IF I DO NOT QUAKE WITH FEAR.
YOU KNOW HIM?
NO... HE MUST BE NEW. NEVER MIND. I'LL TAKE CARE OF IT.
IS THAT WHY YOU'RE HERE? IN ALL HONESTY I THOUGHT I MIGHT HAVE TO COME LOOKING FOR YOU. YOU SEEMED QUITE ANGRY AT ME FOR SENDING ALBERT TO YOUR APARTMENT...
OH, I SEE. YOU'RE EAGER FOR YOUR NEXT KILL...
DON'T WORRY, DEAR. I WON'T KEEP YOU WAITING.
HALFWAY THROUGH MY SECOND LIFETIME, HAVING ACCUMULATED MASSIVE WEALTH, I FOOLISHLY DID WHAT MANY OTHER POWERFUL MEN HAVE DONE IN THE PAST.
I STARTED A SECRET SOCIETY.

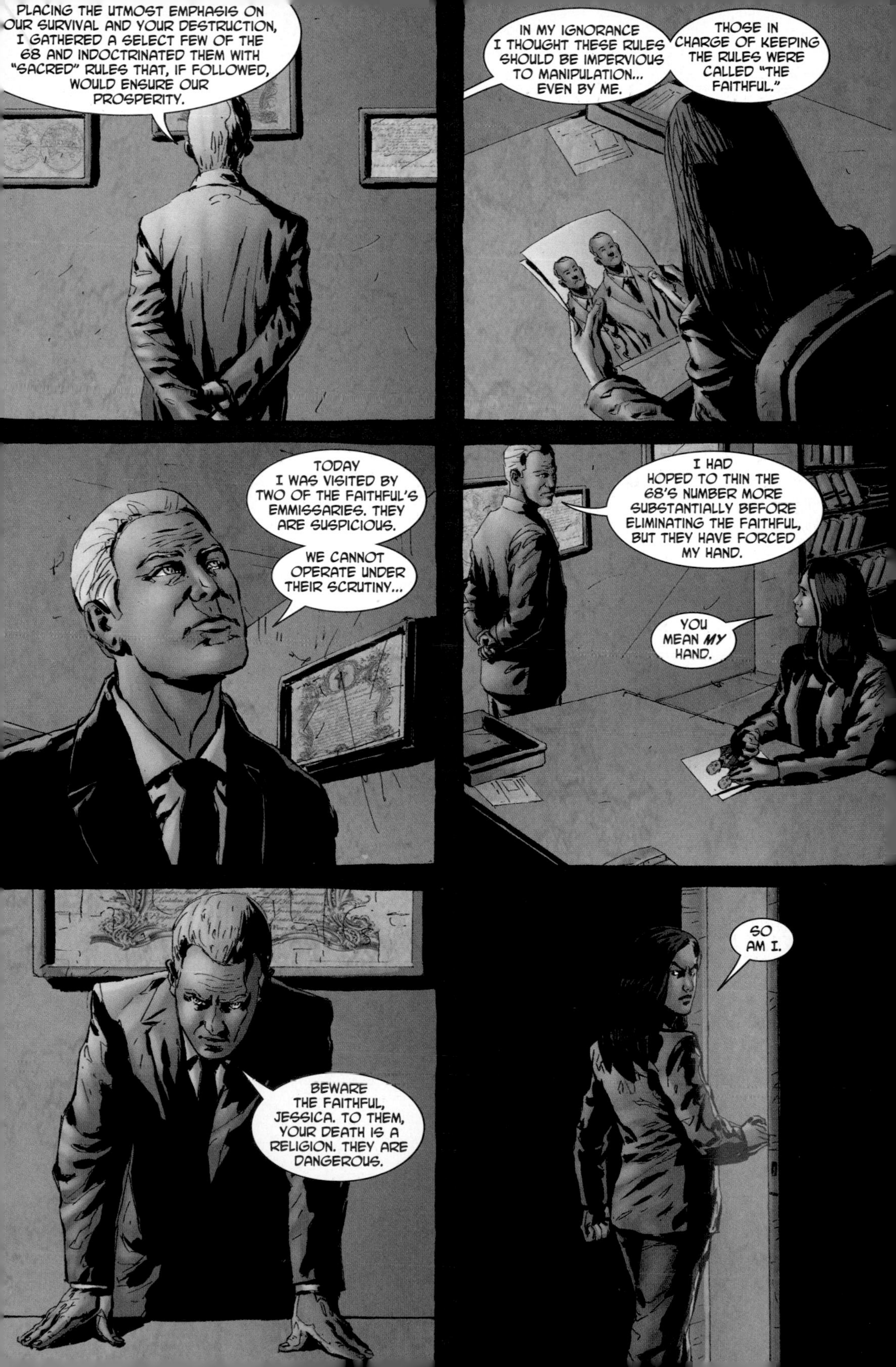
PLACING THE UTMOST EMPHASIS ON OUR SURVIVAL AND YOUR DESTRUCTION, I GATHERED A SELECT FEW OF THE 68 AND INDOCTRINATED THEM WITH "SACRED" RULES THAT, IF FOLLOWED, WOULD ENSURE OUR PROSPERITY.
IN MY IGNORANCE I THOUGHT THESE RULES SHOULD BE IMPERVIOUS TO MANIPULATION... EVEN BY ME.
THOSE IN CHARGE OF KEEPING THE RULES WERE CALLED "THE FAITHFUL."
TODAY I WAS VISITED BY TWO OF THE FAITHFUL'S EMMISSARIES. THEY ARE SUSPICIOUS.
WE CANNOT OPERATE UNDER THEIR SCRUTINY...
I HAD HOPED TO THIN THE 68'S NUMBER MORE SUBSTANTIALLY BEFORE ELIMINATING THE FAITHFUL, BUT THEY HAVE FORCED MY HAND.
YOU MEAN *MY* HAND.
BEWARE THE FAITHFUL, JESSICA. TO THEM, YOUR DEATH IS A RELIGION. THEY ARE DANGEROUS.
SO AM I.

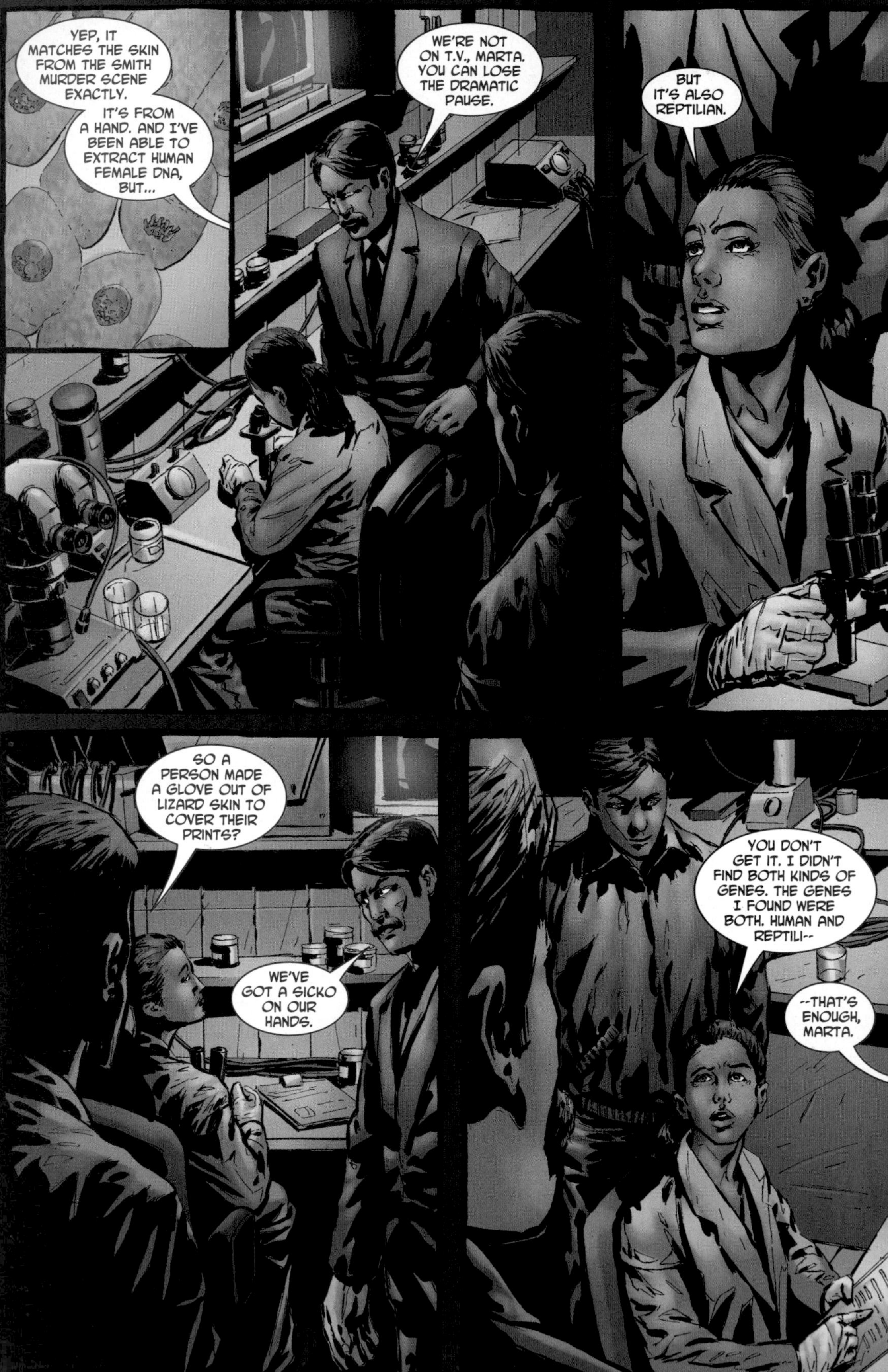
YEP, IT MATCHES THE SKIN FROM THE SMITH MURDER SCENE EXACTLY.
IT'S FROM A HAND. AND I'VE BEEN ABLE TO EXTRACT HUMAN FEMALE DNA, BUT...
WE'RE NOT ON T.V., MARTA. YOU CAN LOSE THE DRAMATIC PAUSE.
BUT IT'S ALSO REPTILIAN.
SO A PERSON MADE A GLOVE OUT OF LIZARD SKIN TO COVER THEIR PRINTS?
WE'VE GOT A SICKO ON OUR HANDS.
YOU DON'T GET IT. I DIDN'T FIND BOTH KINDS OF GENES. THE GENES I FOUND WERE BOTH. HUMAN AND REPTILI--
--THAT'S ENOUGH, MARTA.

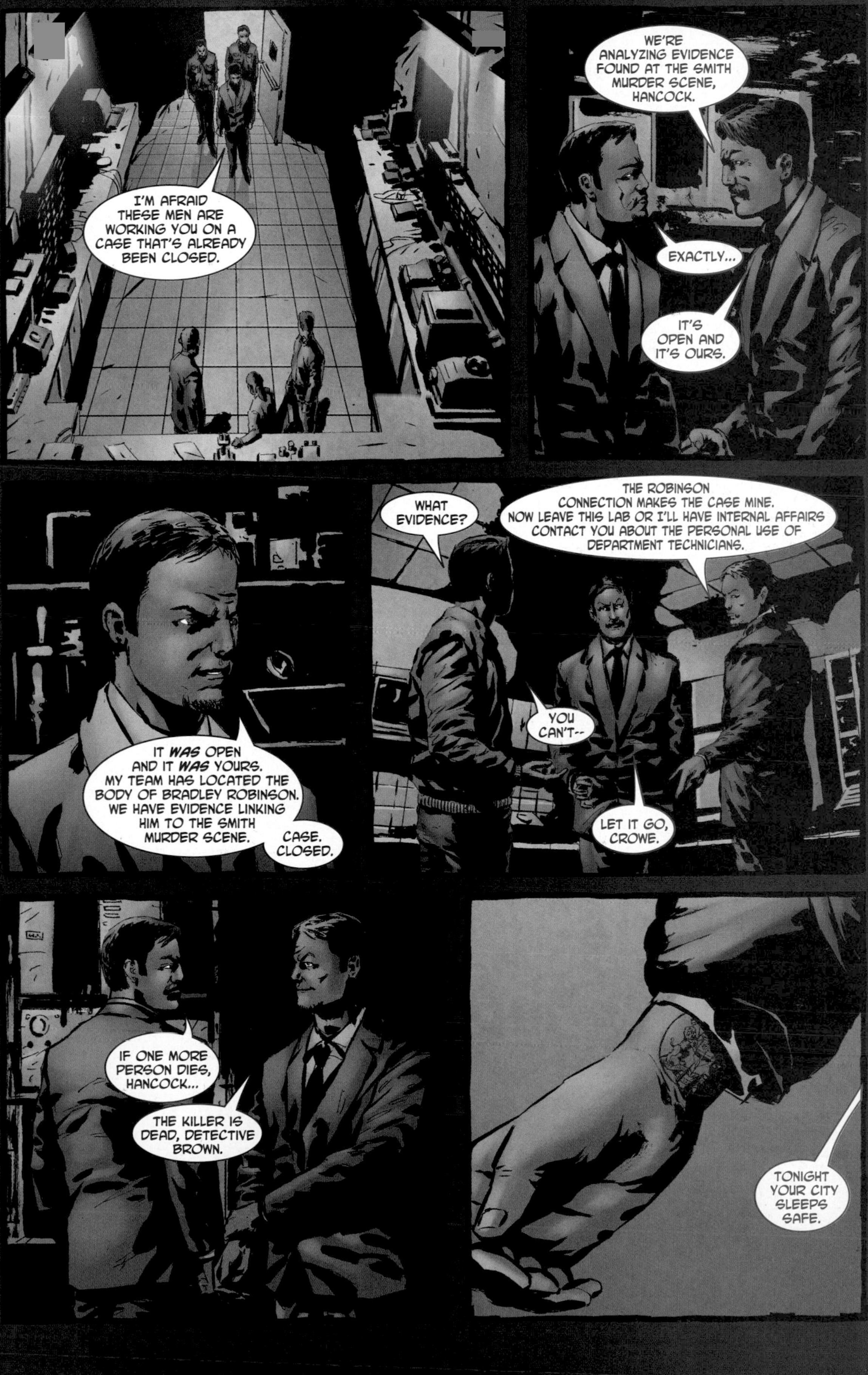
I'M AFRAID THESE MEN ARE WORKING YOU ON A CASE THAT'S ALREADY BEEN CLOSED.
WE'RE ANALYZING EVIDENCE FOUND AT THE SMITH MURDER SCENE, HANCOCK.
EXACTLY...
IT'S OPEN AND IT'S OURS.
IT *WAS* OPEN AND IT *WAS* YOURS. MY TEAM HAS LOCATED THE BODY OF BRADLEY ROBINSON. WE HAVE EVIDENCE LINKING HIM TO THE SMITH MURDER SCENE.
CASE. CLOSED.
WHAT EVIDENCE?
THE ROBINSON CONNECTION MAKES THE CASE MINE. NOW LEAVE THIS LAB OR I'LL HAVE INTERNAL AFFAIRS CONTACT YOU ABOUT THE PERSONAL USE OF DEPARTMENT TECHNICIANS.
YOU CAN'T--
LET IT GO, CROWE.
IF ONE MORE PERSON DIES, HANCOCK...
THE KILLER IS DEAD, DETECTIVE BROWN.
TONIGHT YOUR CITY SLEEPS SAFE.

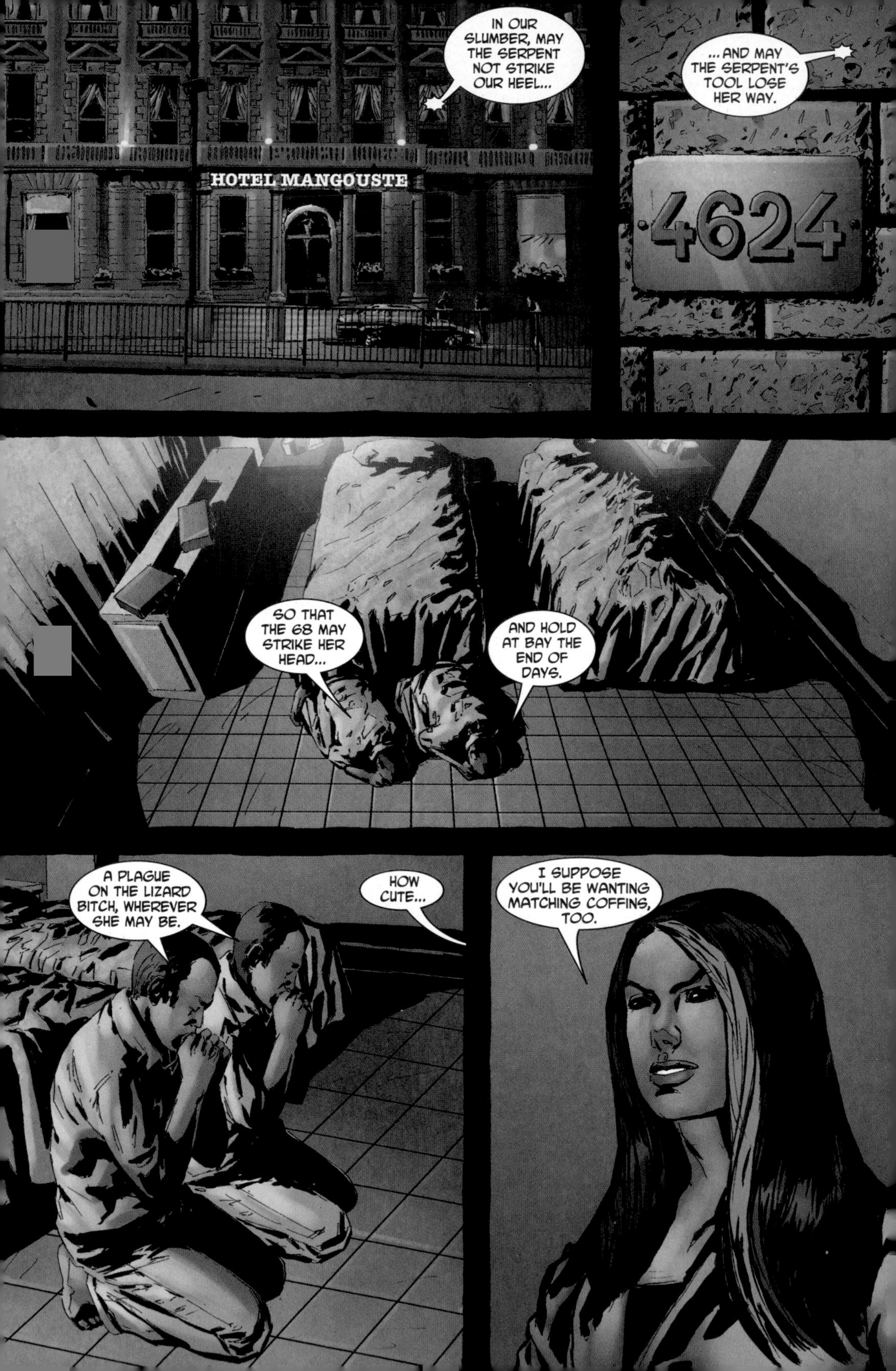
HOTEL MANGOUSTE
IN OUR SLUMBER, MAY THE SERPENT NOT STRIKE OUR HEEL...
...AND MAY THE SERPENT'S TOOL LOSE HER WAY.
4624
SO THAT THE 68 MAY STRIKE HER HEAD...
AND HOLD AT BAY THE END OF DAYS.
A PLAGUE ON THE LIZARD BITCH, WHEREVER SHE MAY BE.
HOW CUTE...
I SUPPOSE YOU'LL BE WANTING MATCHING COFFINS, TOO.

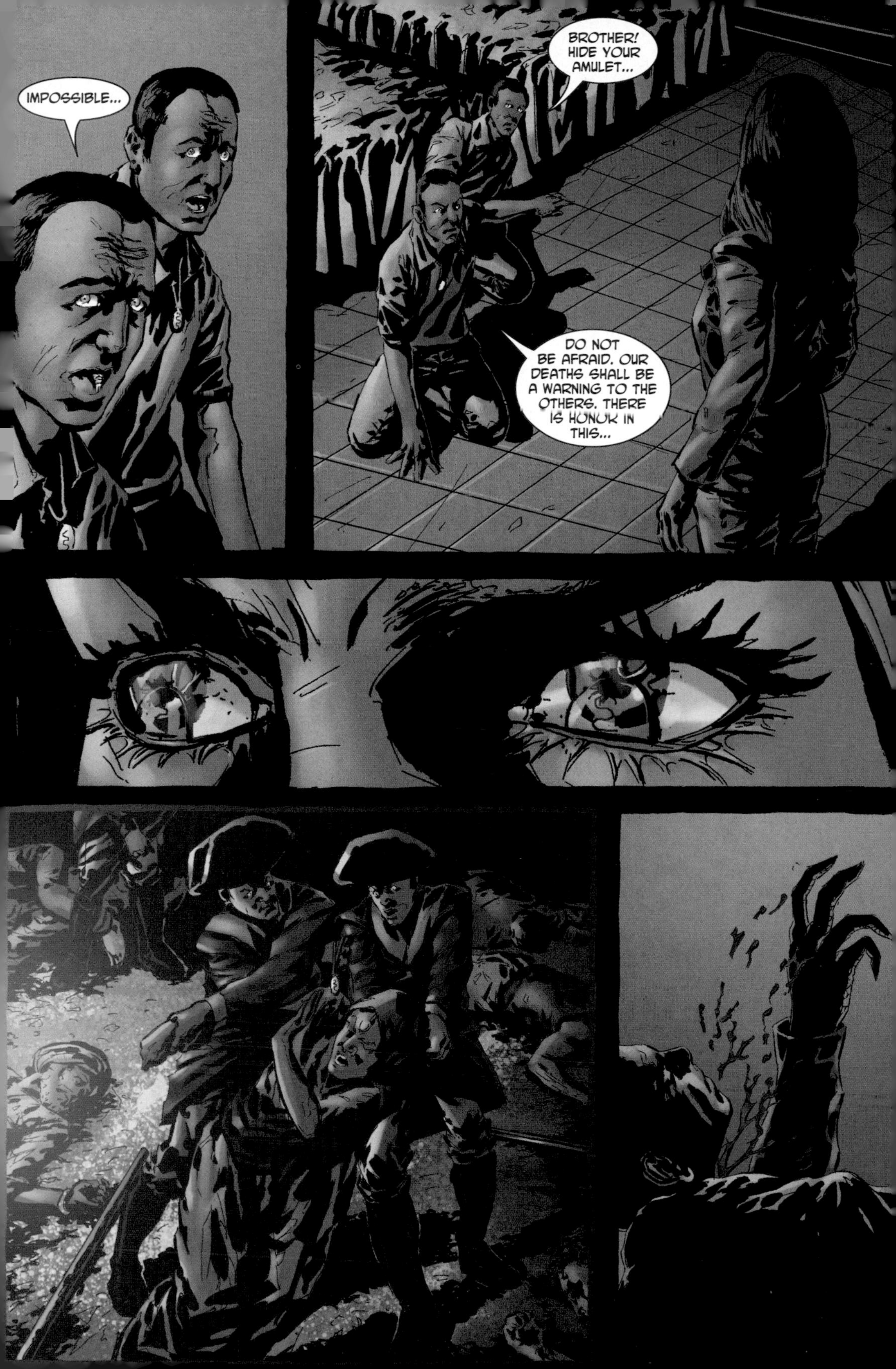
IMPOSSIBLE...
BROTHER! HIDE YOUR AMULET...
DO NOT BE AFRAID. OUR DEATHS SHALL BE A WARNING TO THE OTHERS. THERE IS HONOR IN THIS...

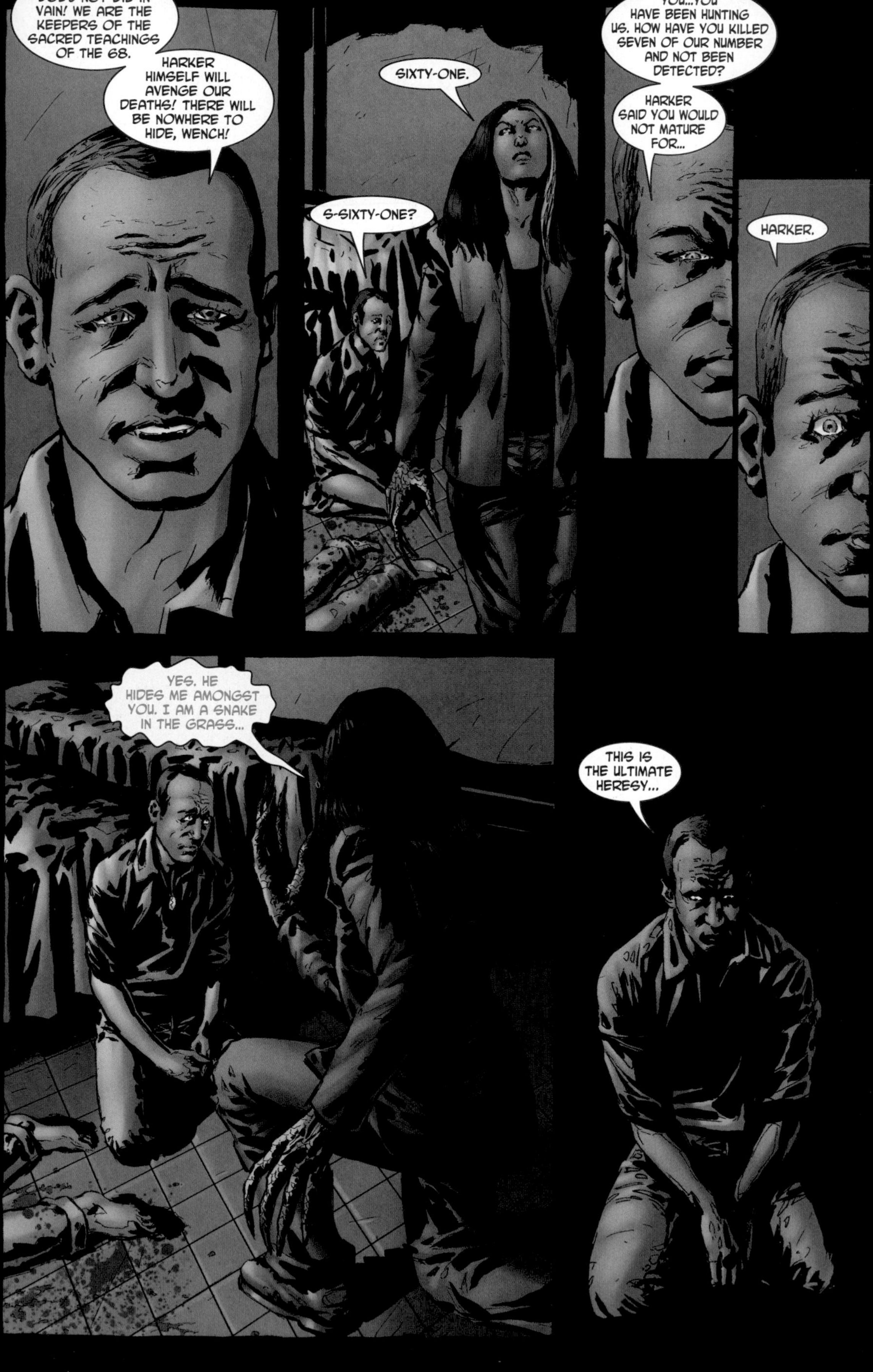
MY BROTHER DOES NOT DIE IN VAIN! WE ARE THE KEEPERS OF THE SACRED TEACHINGS OF THE 68.
HARKER HIMSELF WILL AVENGE OUR DEATHS! THERE WILL BE NOWHERE TO HIDE, WENCH!
SIXTY-ONE.
S-SIXTY-ONE?
YOU...YOU HAVE BEEN HUNTING US. HOW HAVE YOU KILLED SEVEN OF OUR NUMBER AND NOT BEEN DETECTED?
HARKER SAID YOU WOULD NOT MATURE FOR...
HARKER.
YES. HE HIDES ME AMONGST YOU. I AM A SNAKE IN THE GRASS...
THIS IS THE ULTIMATE HERESY...

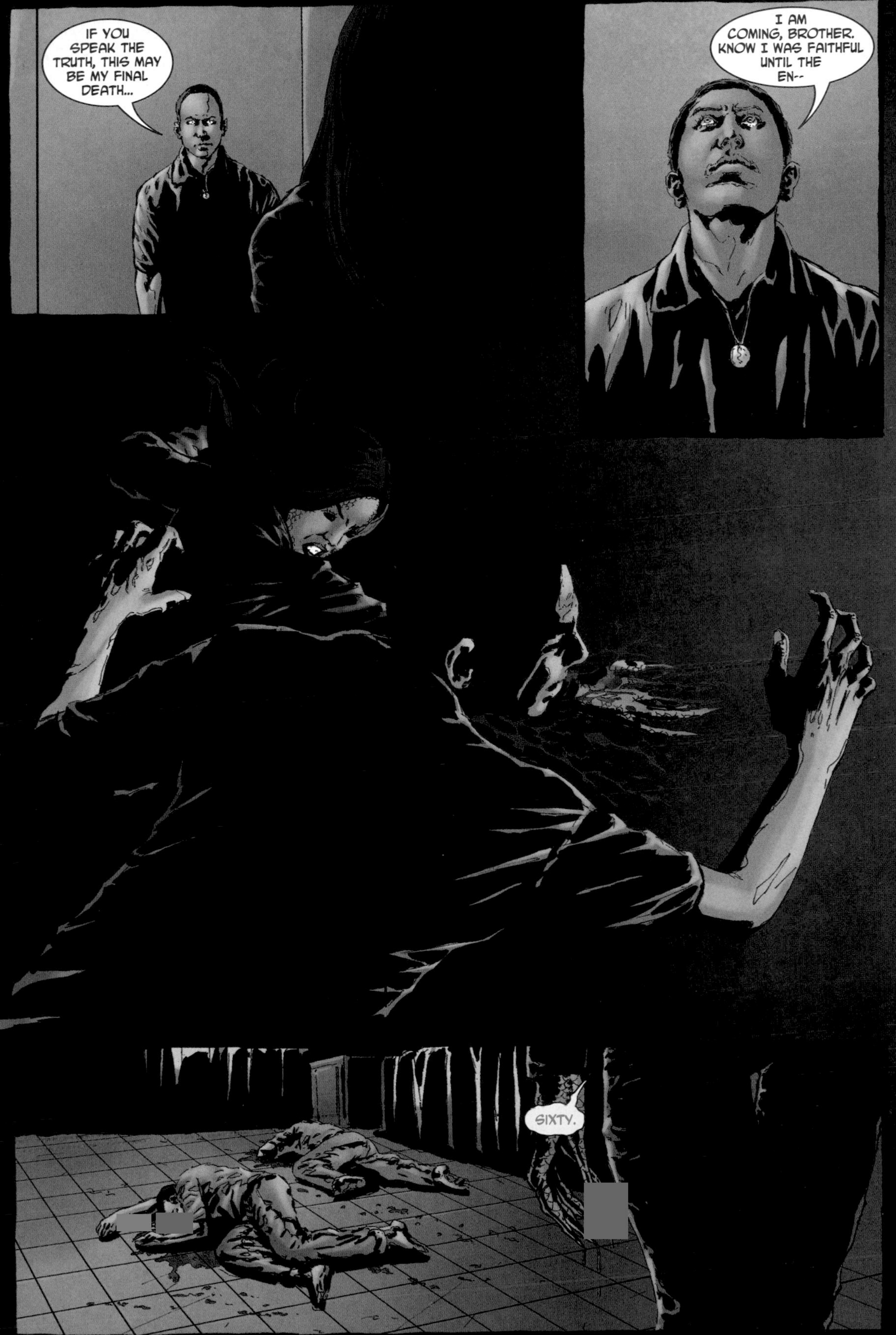
IF YOU SPEAK THE TRUTH, THIS MAY BE MY FINAL DEATH...
I AM COMING, BROTHER. KNOW I WAS FAITHFUL UNTIL THE EN--
SIXTY.

HOLY SHIT.

I THOUGHT I WAS JUST GOING TO GET SUSPENDED, BUT THEY'RE TALKING ABOUT JAIL TIME. IS HANCOCK A DETECTIVE OR THE FUCKING GOVERNOR?

I DON'T KNOW IF HANCOCK IS CHASING A PROMOTION OR WHAT, BUT THIS CASE ISN'T CLOSED. THIS GUY IS GOING TO KILL MORE PEOPLE! IT'S NOT--

SHUT UP. I'M LOOKIN' FOR SOMETHING.

WHAT?

A COUPLE OF YEARS AGO, SOME DICKHEAD AT THE *TIMES* FOUND OUT WE WERE PLANNING A STING ON A LOCAL CELEBRITY...SOME CREEP THAT WAS SLIPPING GIRLS RUFINOL. THEY PUBLISHED THE STORY BEFORE WE'D MOVED ON THE GUY AND IT BLEW THE WHOLE CASE.

I MARCHED RIGHT INTO THIS SHIT'S OFFICE AND PINNED HIM AGAINST THE WALL, AND I SAID, "WHAT IF THAT'D BEEN YOUR SISTER GETTING RAPED BY THAT SLIMEBALL"?

YOU KNOW WHAT THE LITTLE SHIT DID? HE JUST SMILED...ONE OF THOSE "I'M PROUD OF MYSELF" SMILES... AND HE SAID, "THEN I'D PRETTY MUCH BE GUARANTEED AN EXCLUSIVE INTERVIEW, WOULDN'T I"?

I ALMOST RESPECTED THE FUCKER. THE STORY WAS MORE IMPORTANT THAN ANY ETHIC... ANY REGULATION.

WHAT DOES THIS HAVE TO DO WITH--

EVERYTHING, ROOKIE. YOU COMPLAIN ABOUT POLITICS? WELL, THERE'S ALWAYS BEEN ONE THING THAT CUTS THROUGH THAT BULLSHIT.

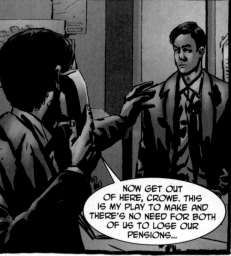

NOW GET OUT OF HERE, CROWE. THIS IS MY PLAY TO MAKE AND THERE'S NO NEED FOR BOTH OF US TO LOSE OUR PENSIONS...

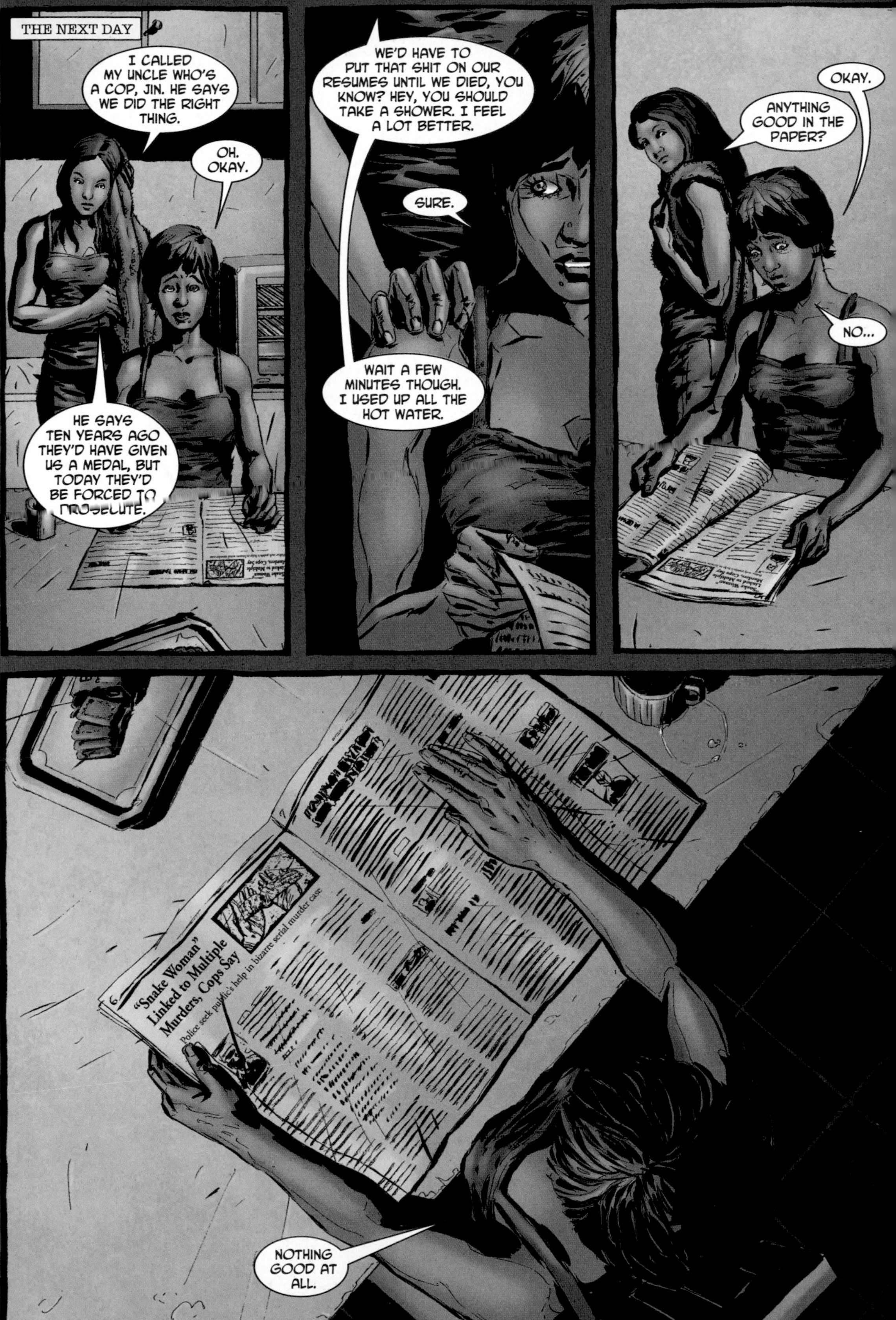
THE NEXT DAY
I CALLED MY UNCLE WHO'S A COP, JIN. HE SAYS WE DID THE RIGHT THING.
OH. OKAY.
HE SAYS TEN YEARS AGO THEY'D HAVE GIVEN US A MEDAL, BUT TODAY THEY'D BE FORCED TO PROSECUTE.
WE'D HAVE TO PUT THAT SHIT ON OUR RESUMES UNTIL WE DIED, YOU KNOW? HEY, YOU SHOULD TAKE A SHOWER. I FEEL A LOT BETTER.
SURE.
WAIT A FEW MINUTES THOUGH. I USED UP ALL THE HOT WATER.
OKAY.
ANYTHING GOOD IN THE PAPER?
NO...
"Snake Woman" Linked to Multiple Murders, Cops Say
Police seek public's help in bizarre serial murder case
NOTHING GOOD AT ALL.

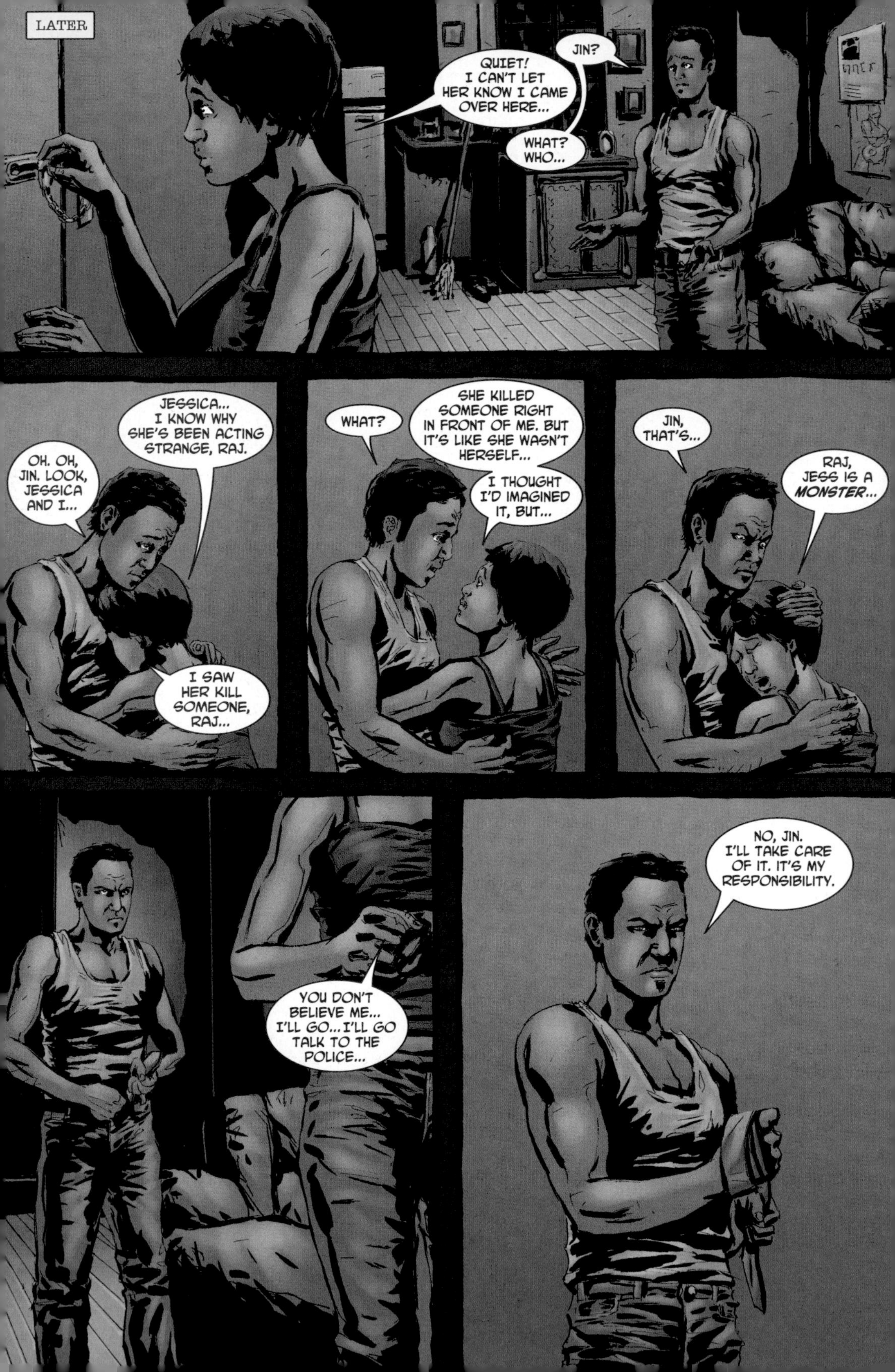
LATER
QUIET! I CAN'T LET HER KNOW I CAME OVER HERE...
JIN?
WHAT? WHO...
OH. OH, JIN. LOOK, JESSICA AND I...
JESSICA... I KNOW WHY SHE'S BEEN ACTING STRANGE, RAJ.
I SAW HER KILL SOMEONE, RAJ...
WHAT?
SHE KILLED SOMEONE RIGHT IN FRONT OF ME. BUT IT'S LIKE SHE WASN'T HERSELF...
I THOUGHT I'D IMAGINED IT, BUT...
JIN, THAT'S...
RAJ, JESS IS A *MONSTER*...
YOU DON'T BELIEVE ME... I'LL GO...I'LL GO TALK TO THE POLICE...
NO, JIN. I'LL TAKE CARE OF IT. IT'S MY RESPONSIBILITY.

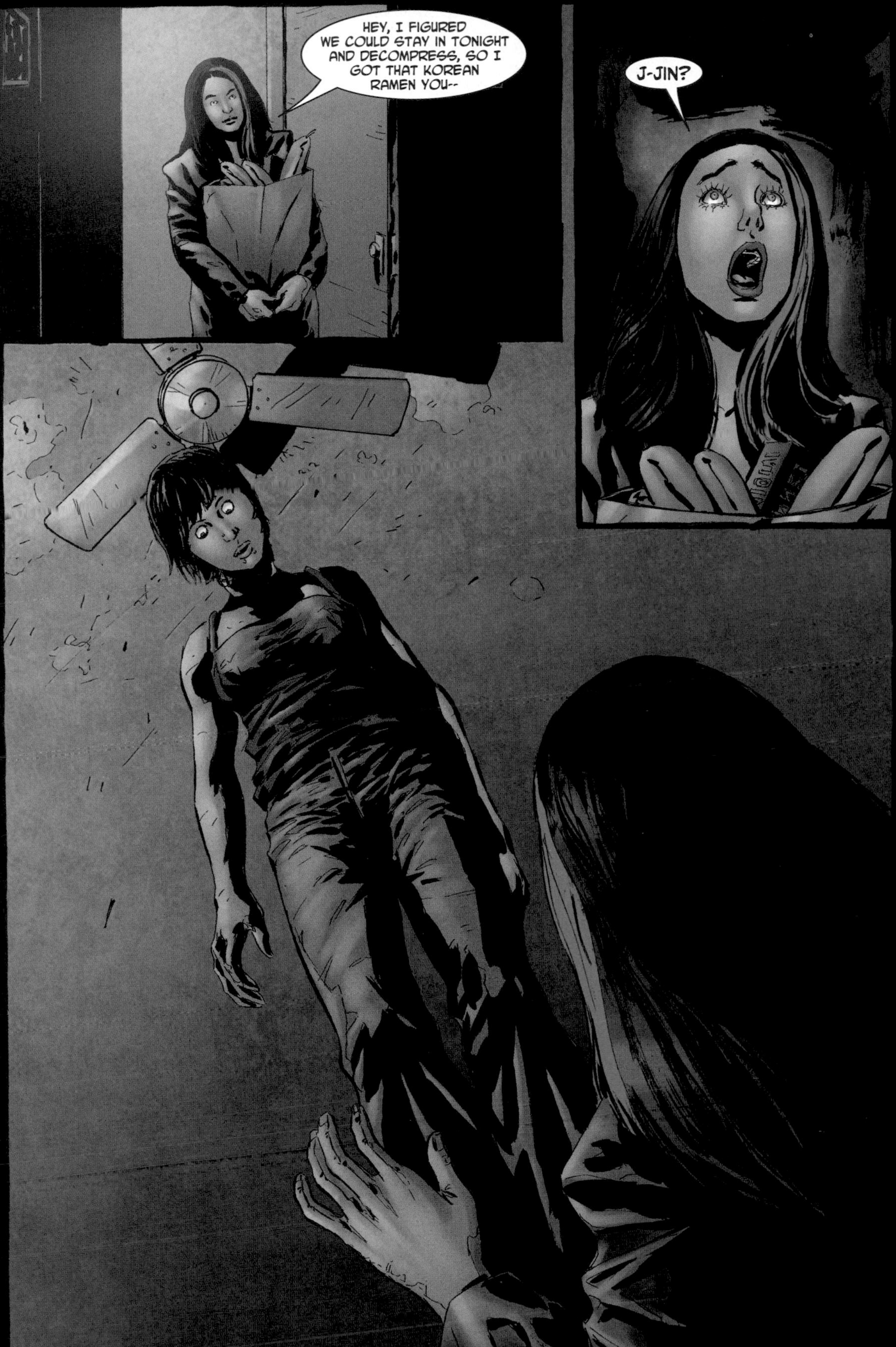
HEY, I FIGURED WE COULD STAY IN TONIGHT AND DECOMPRESS, SO I GOT THAT KOREAN RAMEN YOU--
J-JIN?

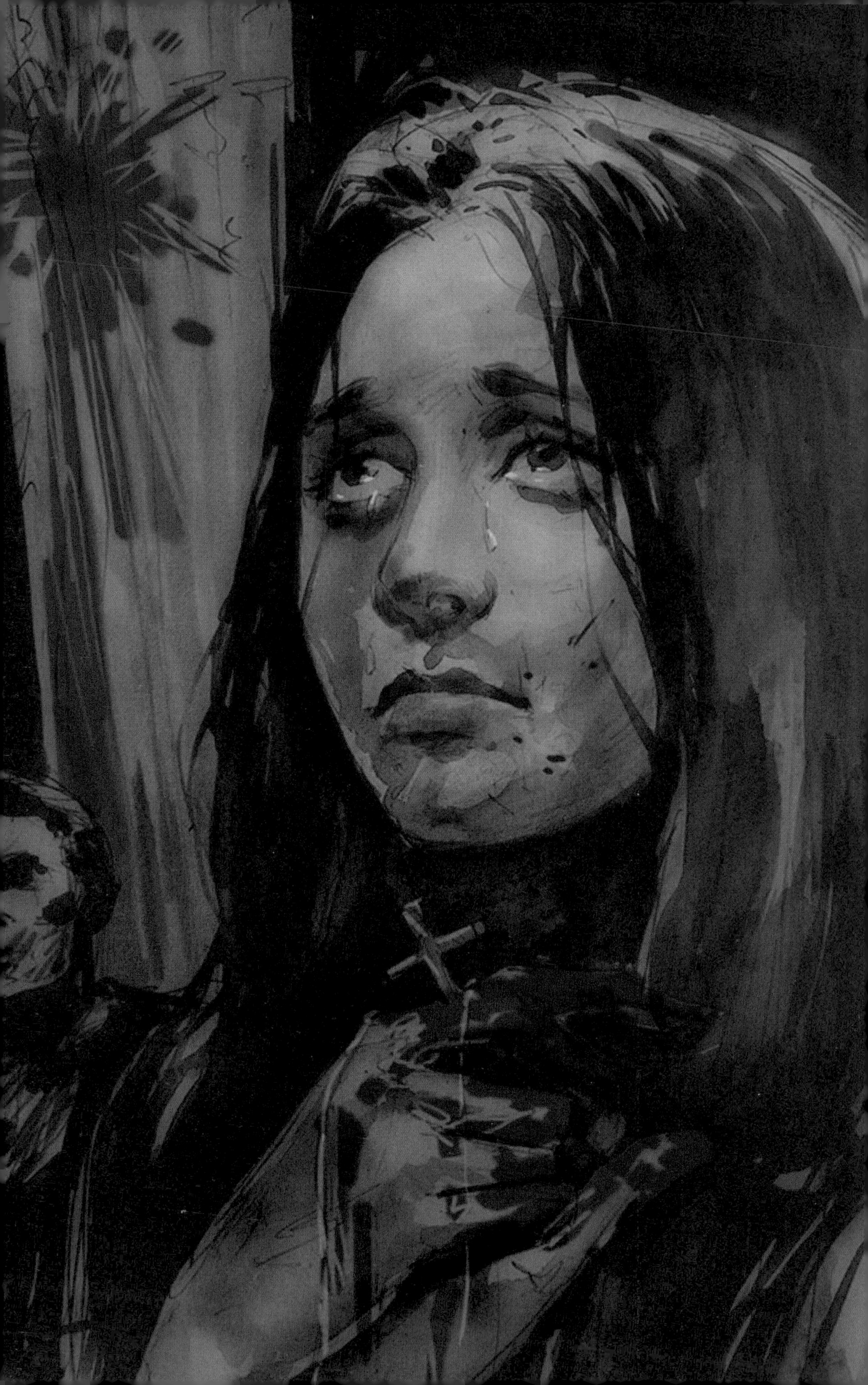

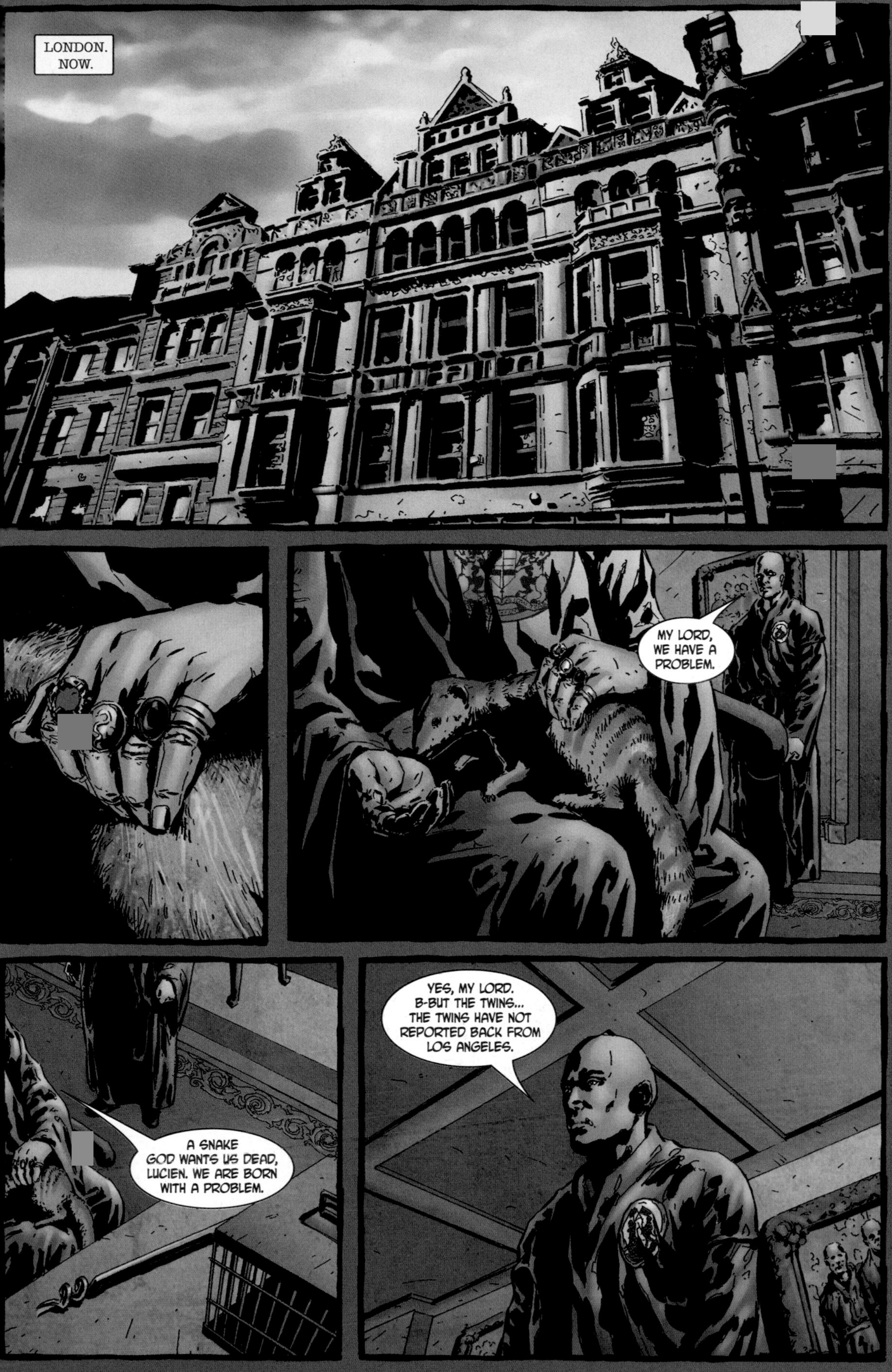
LONDON. NOW.
MY LORD, WE HAVE A PROBLEM.
A SNAKE GOD WANTS US DEAD, LUCIEN. WE ARE BORN WITH A PROBLEM.
YES, MY LORD. B-BUT THE TWINS... THE TWINS HAVE NOT REPORTED BACK FROM LOS ANGELES.

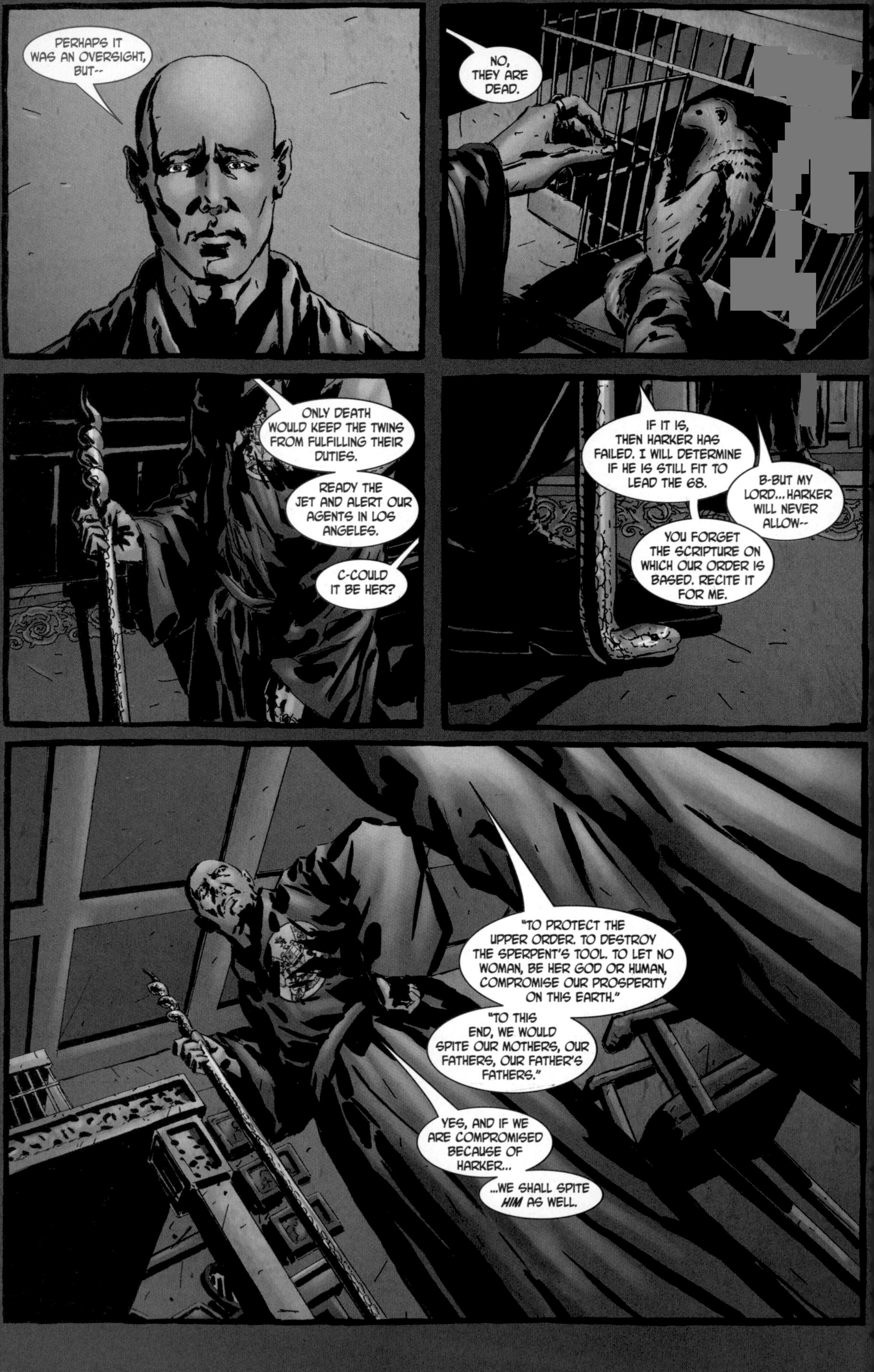
PERHAPS IT WAS AN OVERSIGHT, BUT--
NO, THEY ARE DEAD.
ONLY DEATH WOULD KEEP THE TWINS FROM FULFILLING THEIR DUTIES.
READY THE JET AND ALERT OUR AGENTS IN LOS ANGELES.
C-COULD IT BE HER?
IF IT IS, THEN HARKER HAS FAILED. I WILL DETERMINE IF HE IS STILL FIT TO LEAD THE 68.
B-BUT MY LORD...HARKER WILL NEVER ALLOW--
YOU FORGET THE SCRIPTURE ON WHICH OUR ORDER IS BASED. RECITE IT FOR ME.
"TO PROTECT THE UPPER ORDER. TO DESTROY THE SPERPENT'S TOOL. TO LET NO WOMAN, BE HER GOD OR HUMAN, COMPROMISE OUR PROSPERITY ON THIS EARTH."
"TO THIS END, WE WOULD SPITE OUR MOTHERS, OUR FATHERS, OUR FATHER'S FATHERS."
YES, AND IF WE ARE COMPROMISED BECAUSE OF HARKER...
...WE SHALL SPITE *HIM* AS WELL.

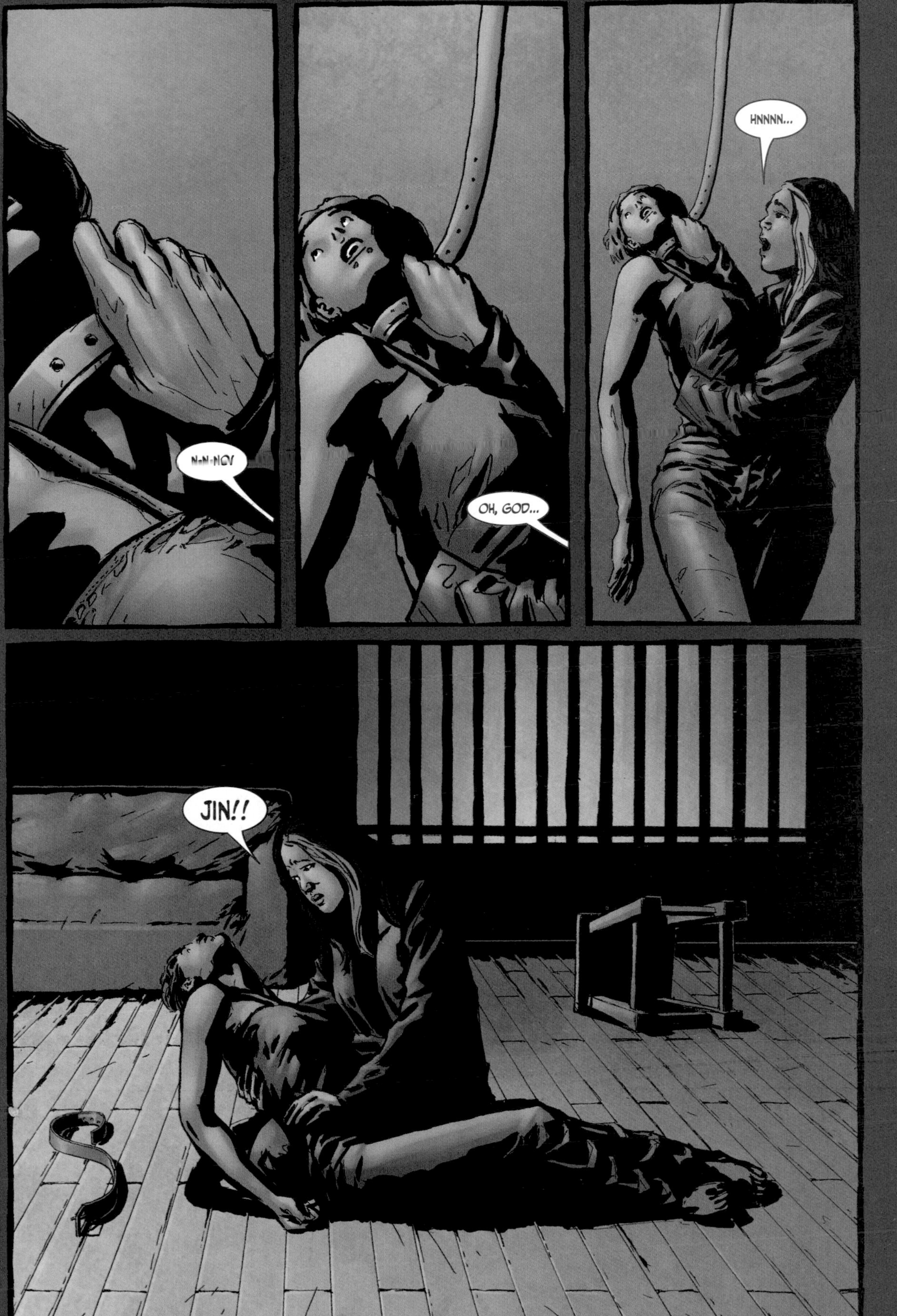
N-N-NO!
OH, GOD...
HNNNN...
JIN!!

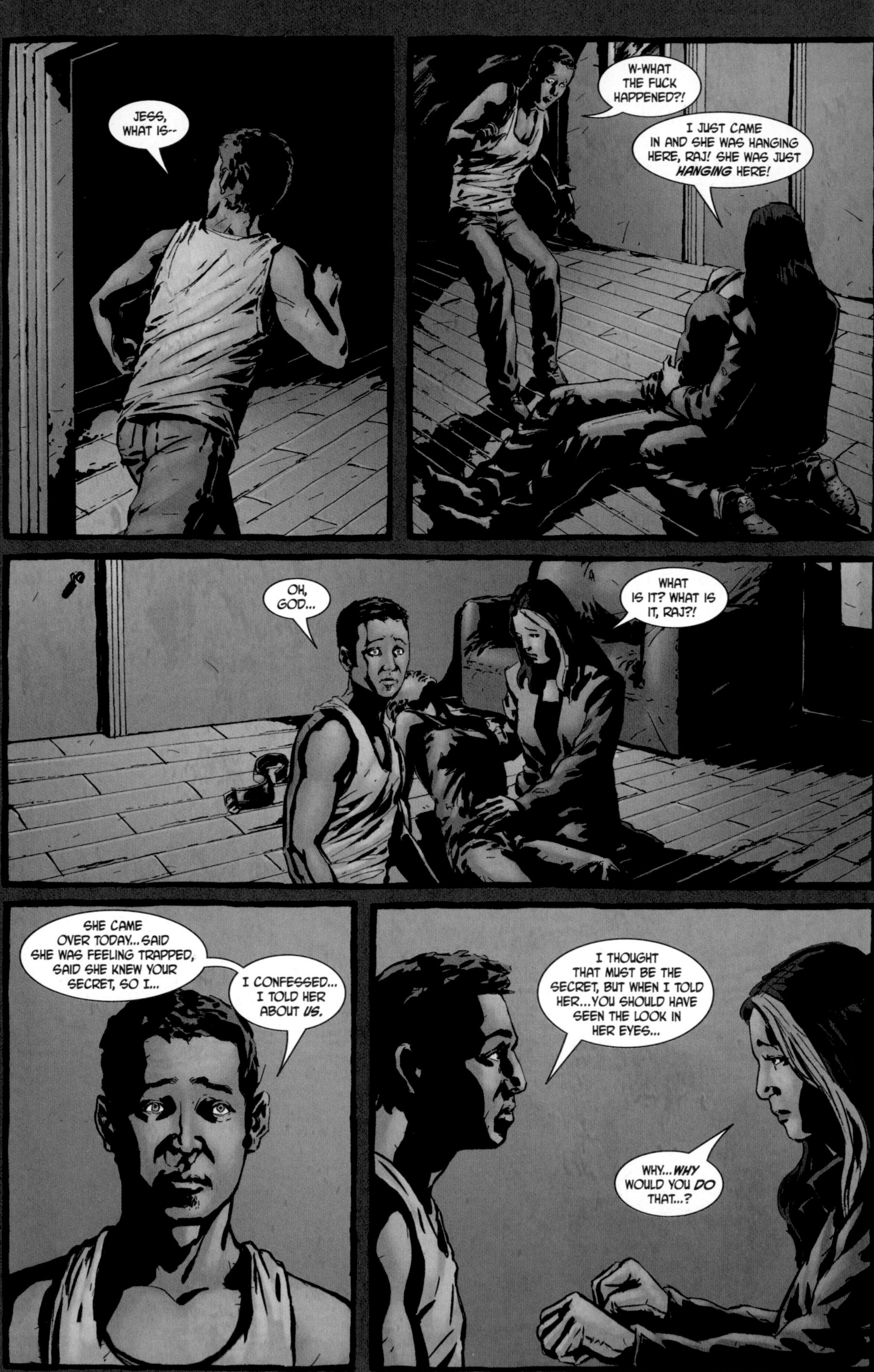
JESS, WHAT IS--
W-WHAT THE FUCK HAPPENED?!
I JUST CAME IN AND SHE WAS HANGING HERE, RAJ! SHE WAS JUST HANGING HERE!
OH, GOD...
WHAT IS IT? WHAT IS IT, RAJ?!
SHE CAME OVER TODAY... SAID SHE WAS FEELING TRAPPED, SAID SHE KNEW YOUR SECRET, SO I...
I CONFESSED... I TOLD HER ABOUT US.
I THOUGHT THAT MUST BE THE SECRET, BUT WHEN I TOLD HER... YOU SHOULD HAVE SEEN THE LOOK IN HER EYES...
WHY... WHY WOULD YOU DO THAT...?

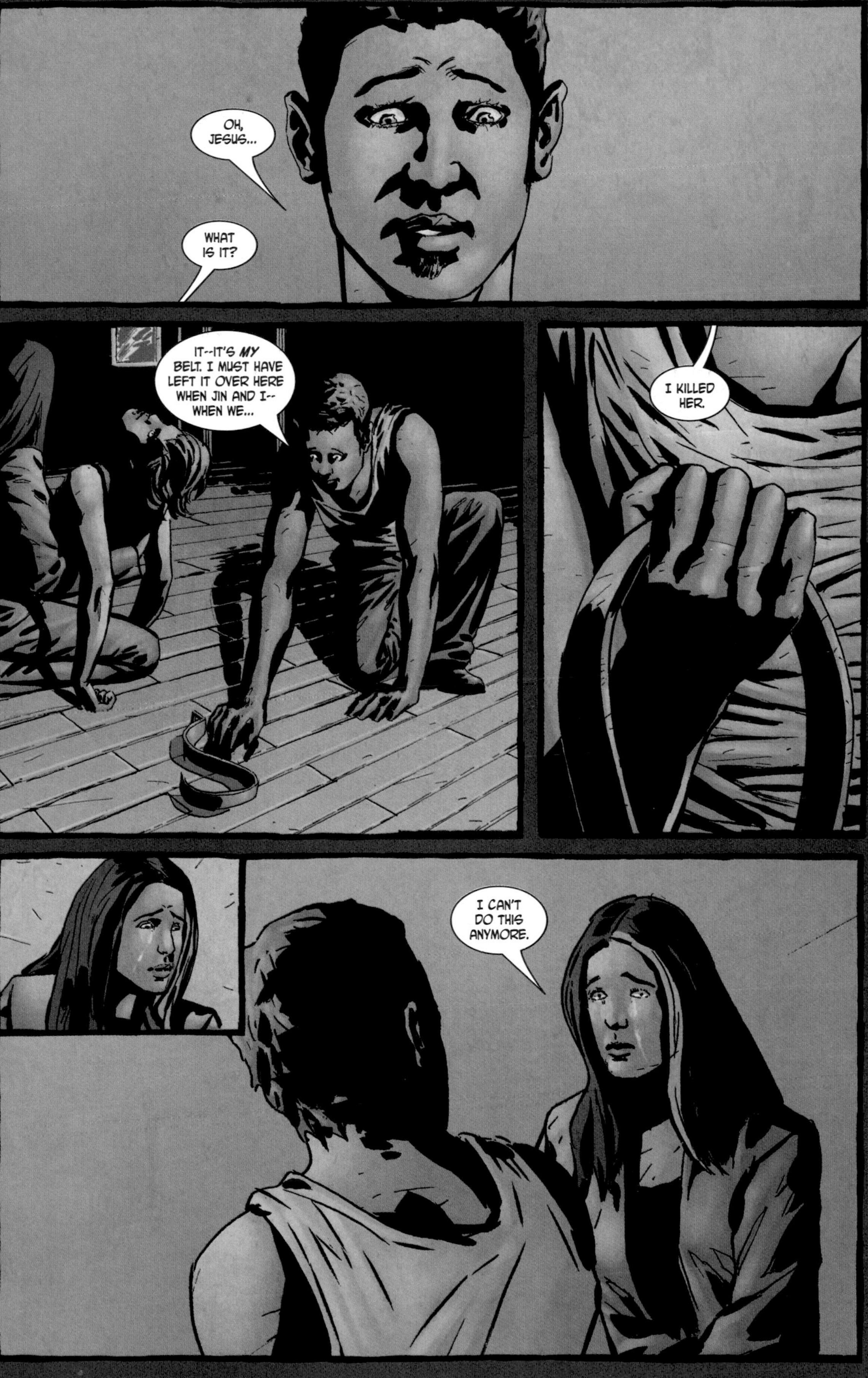
OH, JESUS...
WHAT IS IT?
IT--IT'S *MY* BELT. I MUST HAVE LEFT IT OVER HERE WHEN JIN AND I--WHEN WE...
I KILLED HER.
I CAN'T DO THIS ANYMORE.

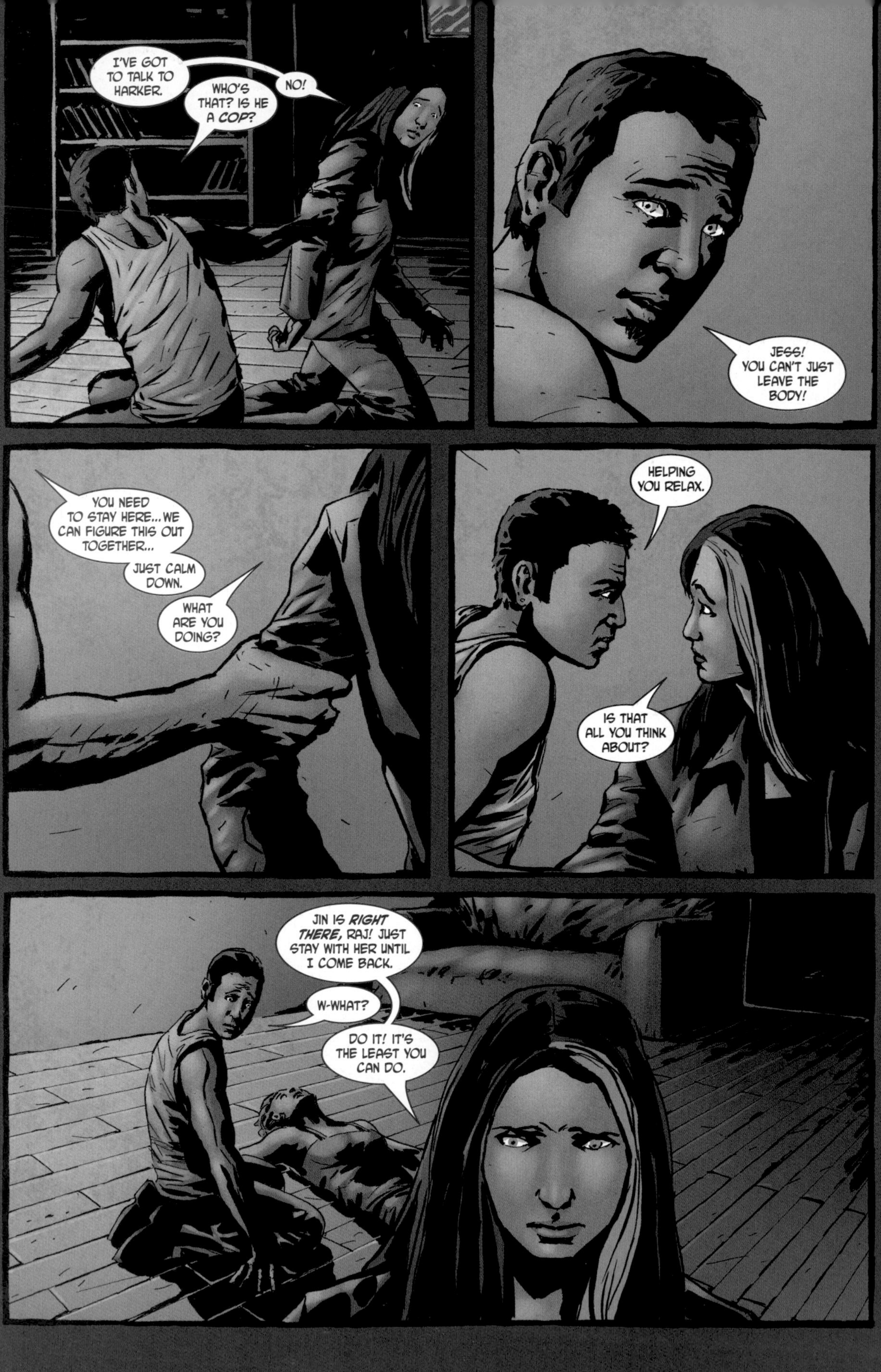
I'VE GOT TO TALK TO HARKER.
NO!
WHO'S THAT? IS HE A *COP?*
JESS! YOU CAN'T JUST LEAVE THE BODY!
YOU NEED TO STAY HERE...WE CAN FIGURE THIS OUT TOGETHER...
JUST CALM DOWN.
WHAT ARE YOU DOING?
HELPING YOU RELAX.
IS THAT ALL YOU THINK ABOUT?
JIN IS ***RIGHT THERE,*** RAJ! JUST STAY WITH HER UNTIL I COME BACK.
W-WHAT?
DO IT! IT'S THE LEAST YOU CAN DO.

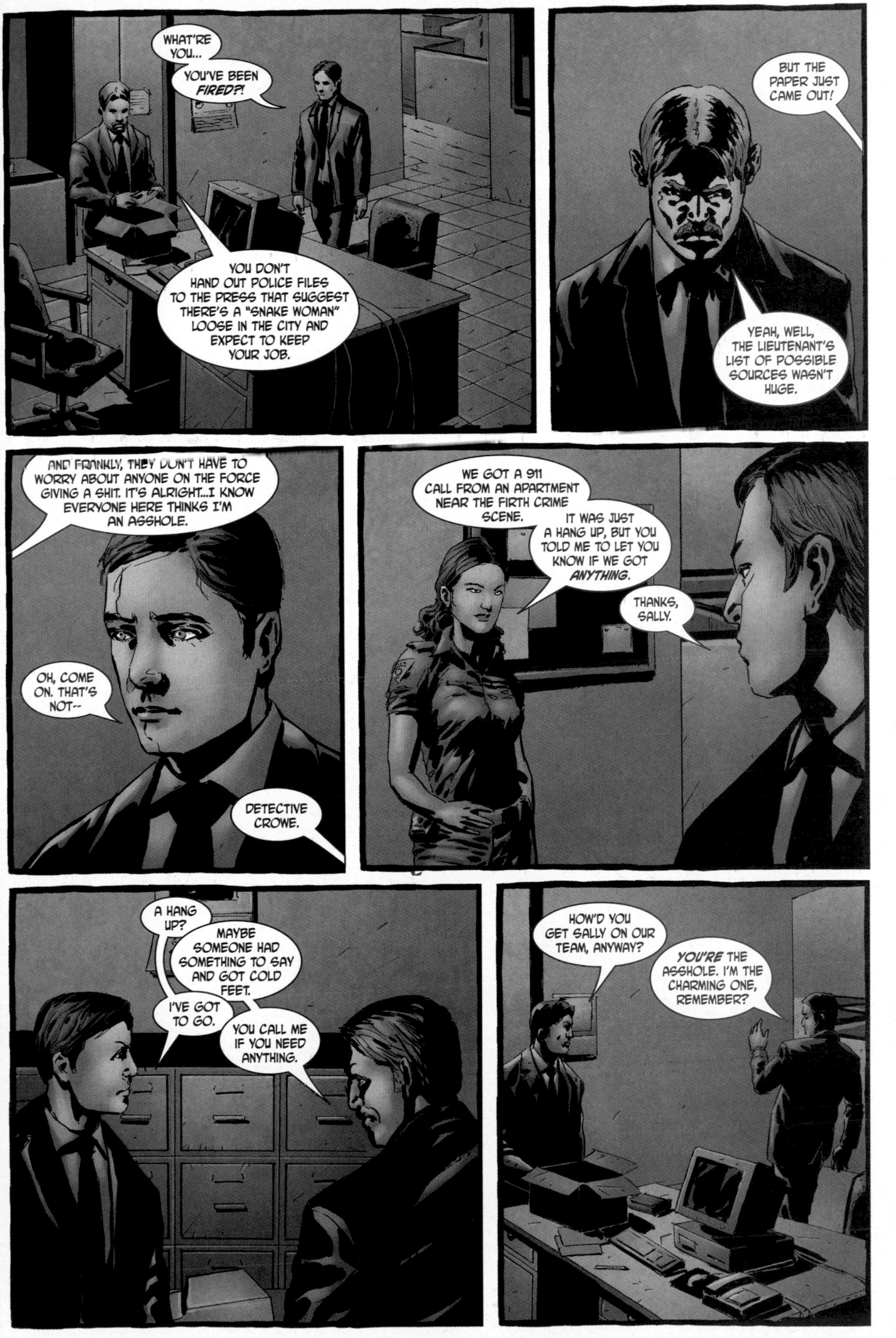
WHAT'RE YOU...
YOU'VE BEEN FIRED?!
YOU DON'T HAND OUT POLICE FILES TO THE PRESS THAT SUGGEST THERE'S A "SNAKE WOMAN" LOOSE IN THE CITY AND EXPECT TO KEEP YOUR JOB.
BUT THE PAPER JUST CAME OUT!
YEAH, WELL, THE LIEUTENANT'S LIST OF POSSIBLE SOURCES WASN'T HUGE.
AND FRANKLY, THEY DON'T HAVE TO WORRY ABOUT ANYONE ON THE FORCE GIVING A SHIT. IT'S ALRIGHT...I KNOW EVERYONE HERE THINKS I'M AN ASSHOLE.
OH, COME ON. THAT'S NOT--
DETECTIVE CROWE.
WE GOT A 911 CALL FROM AN APARTMENT NEAR THE FIRTH CRIME SCENE.
IT WAS JUST A HANG UP, BUT YOU TOLD ME TO LET YOU KNOW IF WE GOT ANYTHING.
THANKS, SALLY.
A HANG UP?
MAYBE SOMEONE HAD SOMETHING TO SAY AND GOT COLD FEET.
I'VE GOT TO GO.
YOU CALL ME IF YOU NEED ANYTHING.
HOW'D YOU GET SALLY ON OUR TEAM, ANYWAY?
YOU'RE THE ASSHOLE. I'M THE CHARMING ONE, REMEMBER?

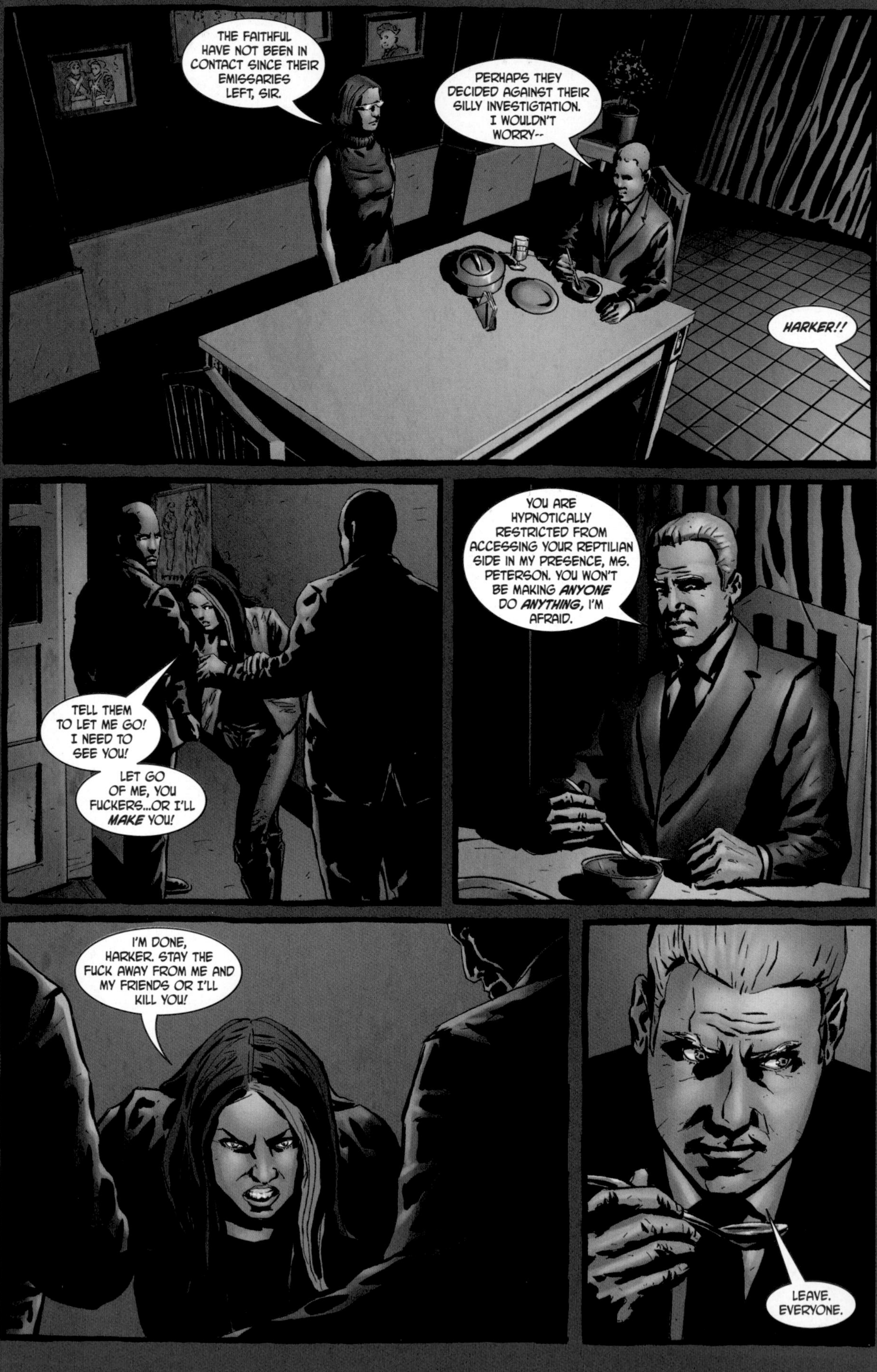
THE FAITHFUL HAVE NOT BEEN IN CONTACT SINCE THEIR EMISSARIES LEFT, SIR.
PERHAPS THEY DECIDED AGAINST THEIR SILLY INVESTIGTATION. I WOULDN'T WORRY--
HARKER!!
TELL THEM TO LET ME GO! I NEED TO SEE YOU!
LET GO OF ME, YOU FUCKERS...OR I'LL MAKE YOU!
YOU ARE HYPNOTICALLY RESTRICTED FROM ACCESSING YOUR REPTILIAN SIDE IN MY PRESENCE, MS. PETERSON. YOU WON'T BE MAKING ANYONE DO ANYTHING, I'M AFRAID.
I'M DONE, HARKER. STAY THE FUCK AWAY FROM ME AND MY FRIENDS OR I'LL KILL YOU!
LEAVE. EVERYONE.

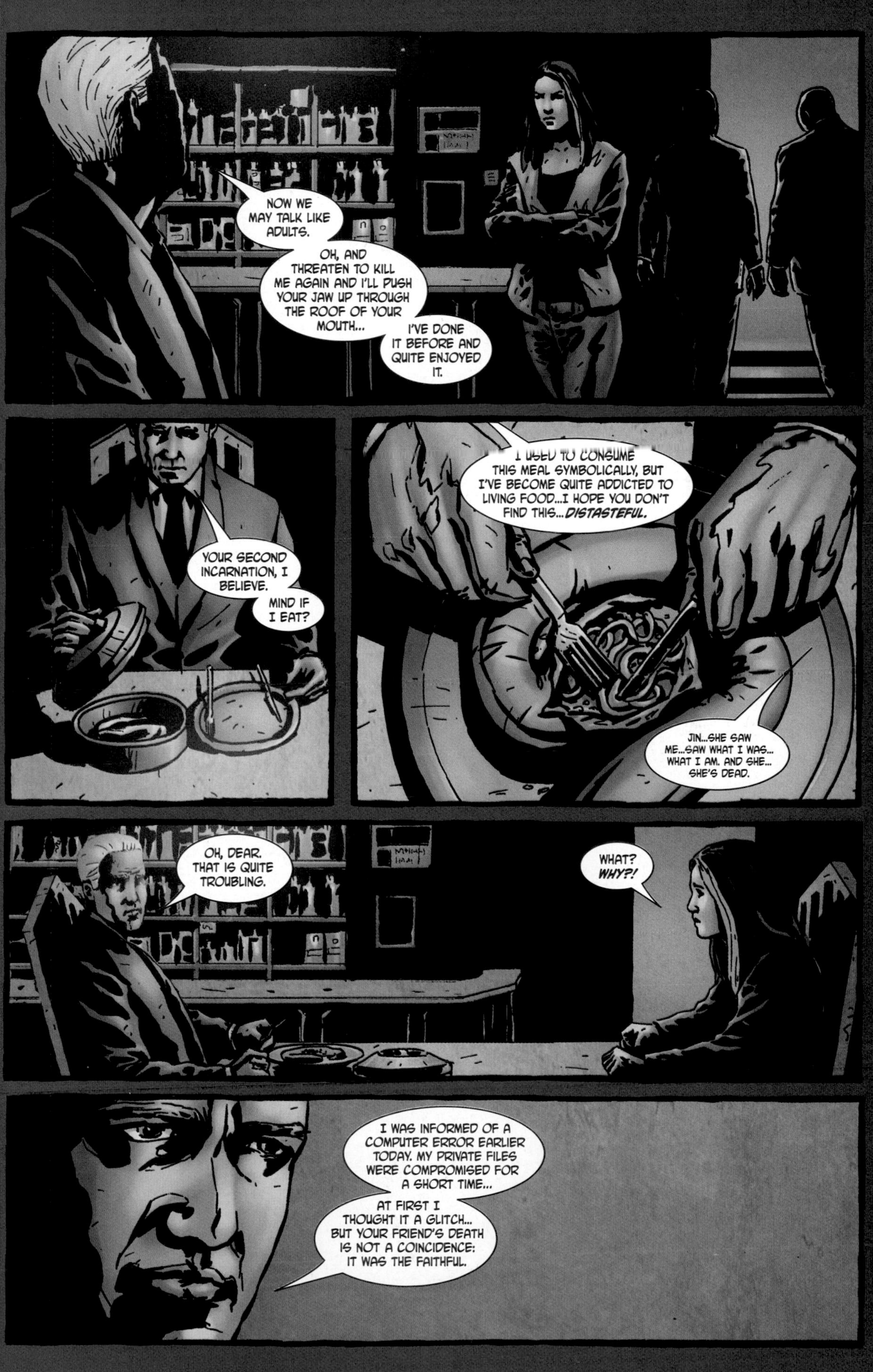
NOW WE MAY TALK LIKE ADULTS.
OH, AND THREATEN TO KILL ME AGAIN AND I'LL PUSH YOUR JAW UP THROUGH THE ROOF OF YOUR MOUTH...
I'VE DONE IT BEFORE AND QUITE ENJOYED IT.
YOUR SECOND INCARNATION, I BELIEVE.
MIND IF I EAT?
I USED TO CONSUME THIS MEAL SYMBOLICALLY, BUT I'VE BECOME QUITE ADDICTED TO LIVING FOOD...I HOPE YOU DON'T FIND THIS...DISTASTEFUL.
JIN...SHE SAW ME...SAW WHAT I WAS... WHAT I AM. AND SHE... SHE'S DEAD.
OH, DEAR. THAT IS QUITE TROUBLING.
WHAT? WHY?!
I WAS INFORMED OF A COMPUTER ERROR EARLIER TODAY. MY PRIVATE FILES WERE COMPROMISED FOR A SHORT TIME...
AT FIRST I THOUGHT IT A GLITCH... BUT YOUR FRIEND'S DEATH IS NOT A COINCIDENCE: IT WAS THE FAITHFUL.

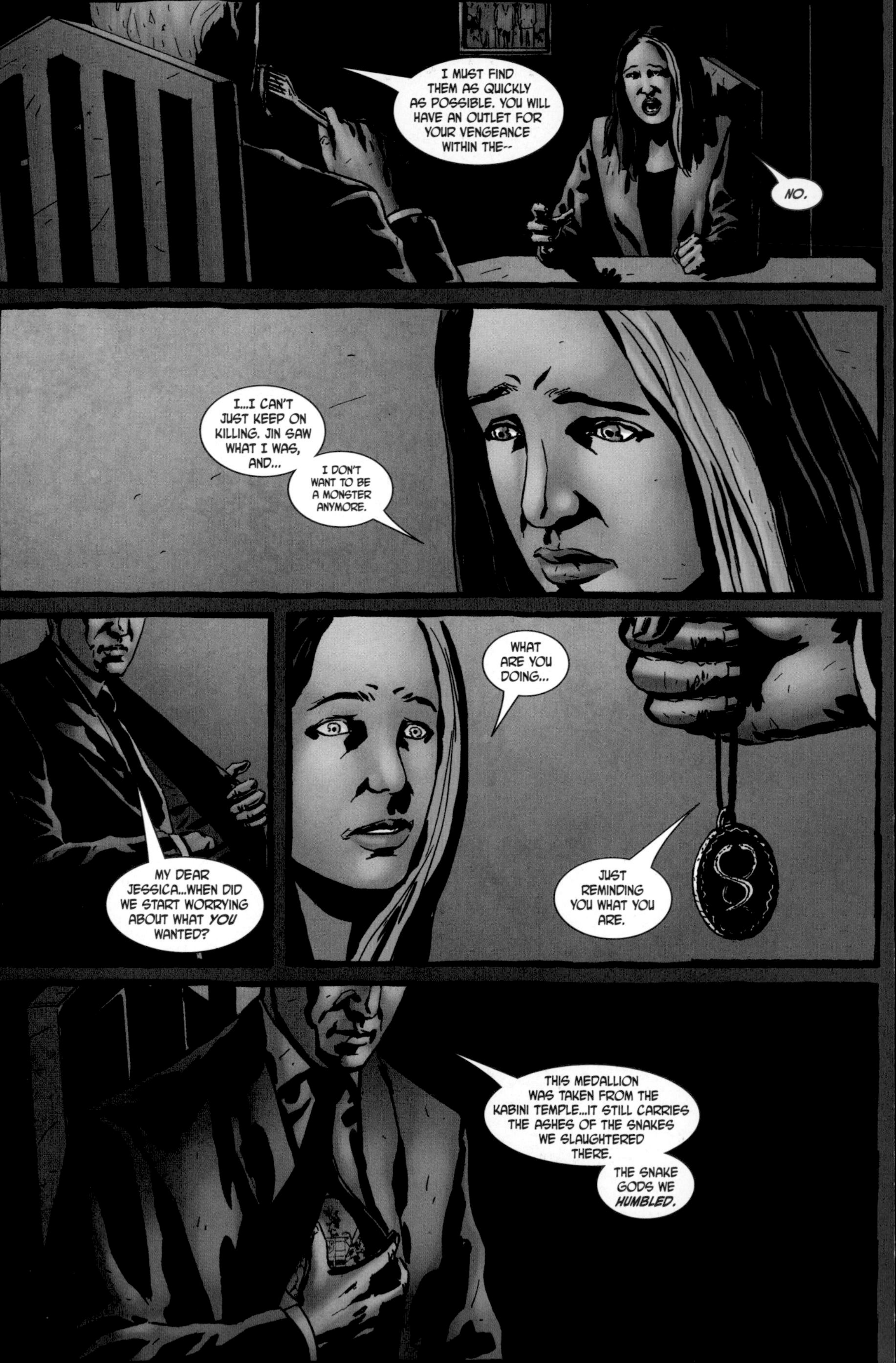
I MUST FIND THEM AS QUICKLY AS POSSIBLE. YOU WILL HAVE AN OUTLET FOR YOUR VENGEANCE WITHIN THE--
NO.
I...I CAN'T JUST KEEP ON KILLING. JIN SAW WHAT I WAS, AND...
I DON'T WANT TO BE A MONSTER ANYMORE.
MY DEAR JESSICA...WHEN DID WE START WORRYING ABOUT WHAT *YOU* WANTED?
WHAT ARE YOU DOING...
JUST REMINDING YOU WHAT YOU ARE.
THIS MEDALLION WAS TAKEN FROM THE KABINI TEMPLE...IT STILL CARRIES THE ASHES OF THE SNAKES WE SLAUGHTERED THERE.
THE SNAKE GODS WE *HUMBLED*.

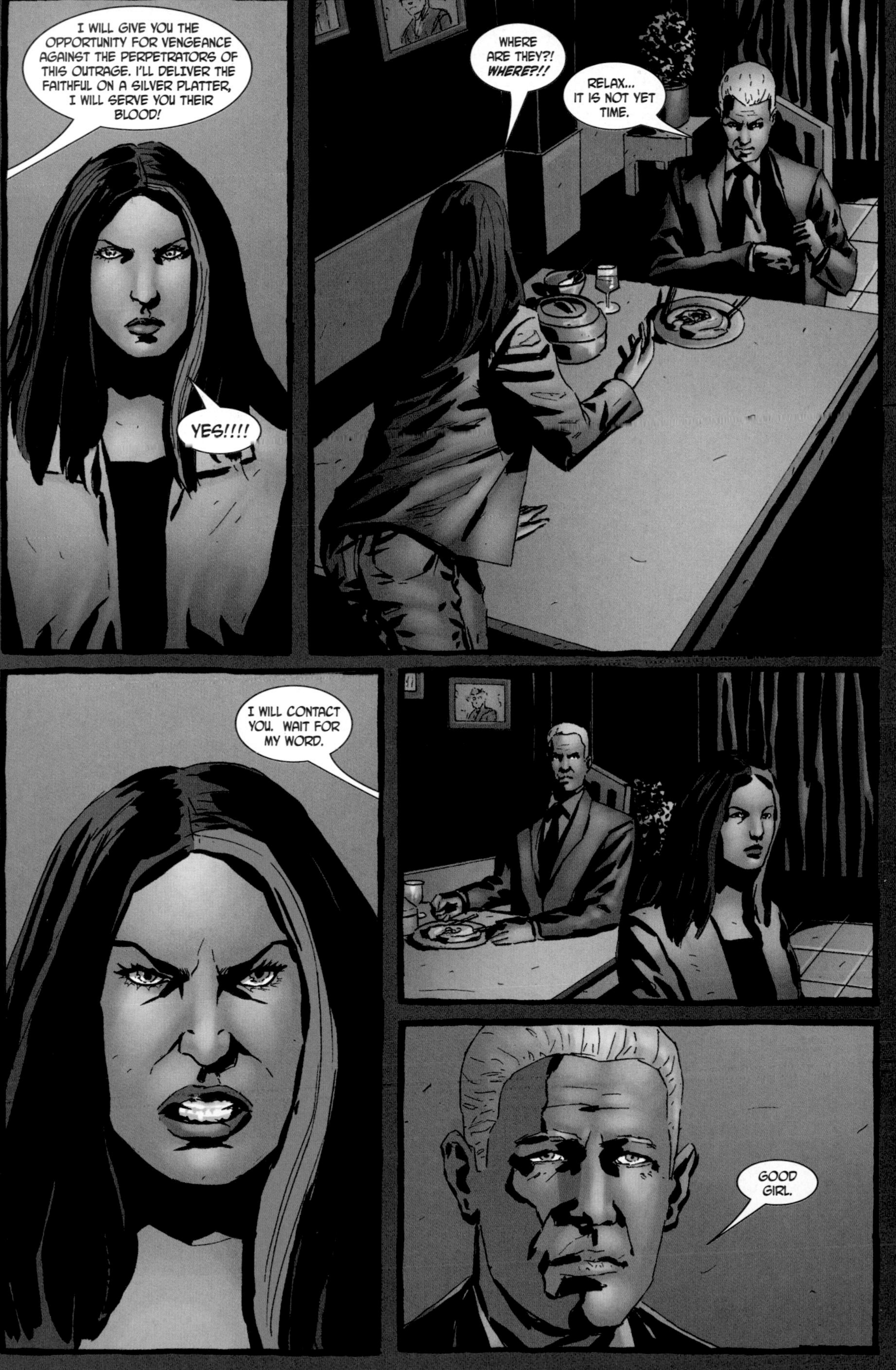
I WILL GIVE YOU THE OPPORTUNITY FOR VENGEANCE AGAINST THE PERPETRATORS OF THIS OUTRAGE. I'LL DELIVER THE FAITHFUL ON A SILVER PLATTER, I WILL SERVE YOU THEIR BLOOD!
YES!!!!
WHERE ARE THEY?! *WHERE?!!*
RELAX... IT IS NOT YET TIME.
I WILL CONTACT YOU. WAIT FOR MY WORD.
GOOD GIRL.

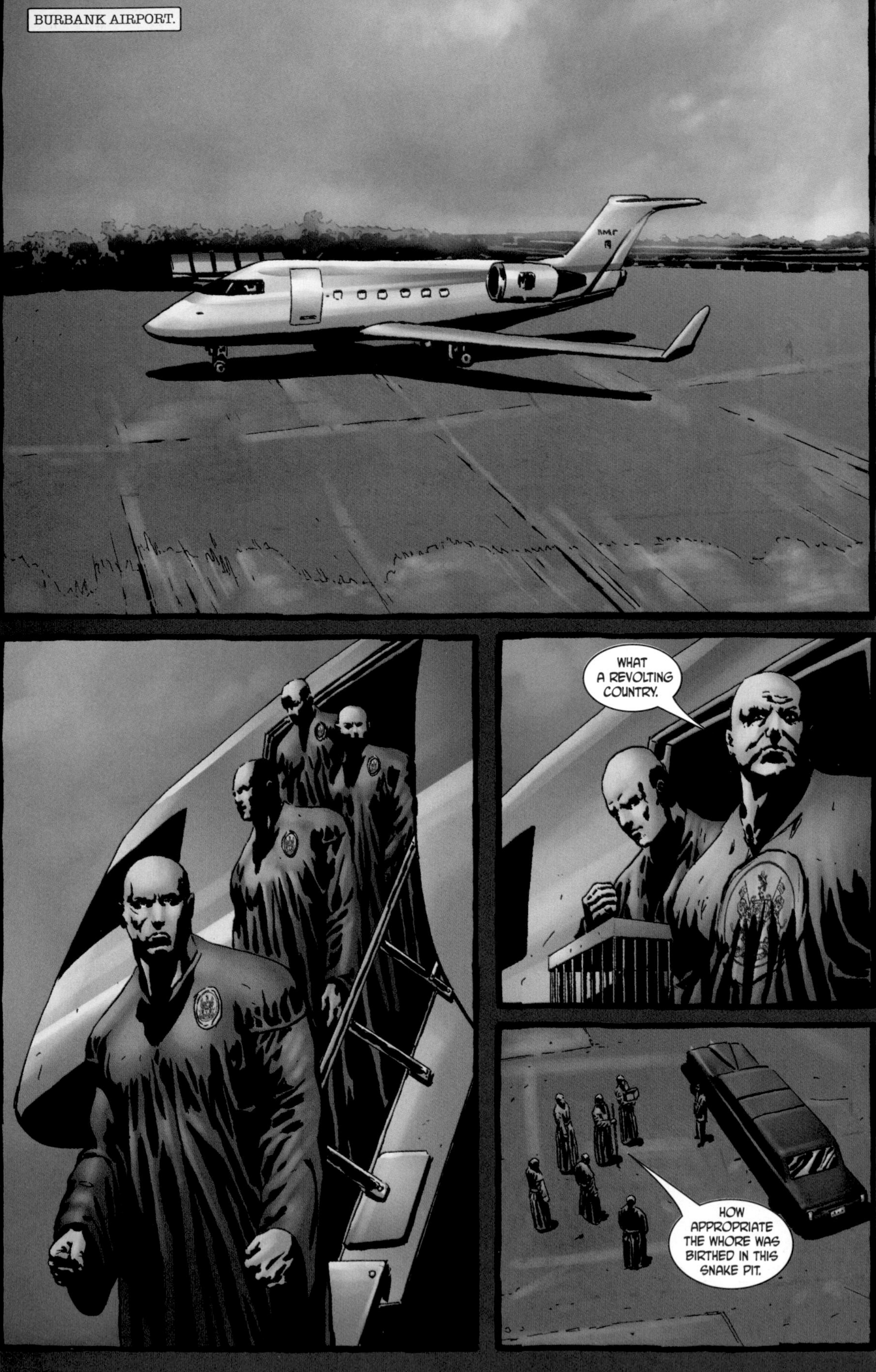
BURBANK AIRPORT.
WHAT A REVOLTING COUNTRY.
HOW APPROPRIATE THE WHORE WAS BIRTHED IN THIS SNAKE PIT.

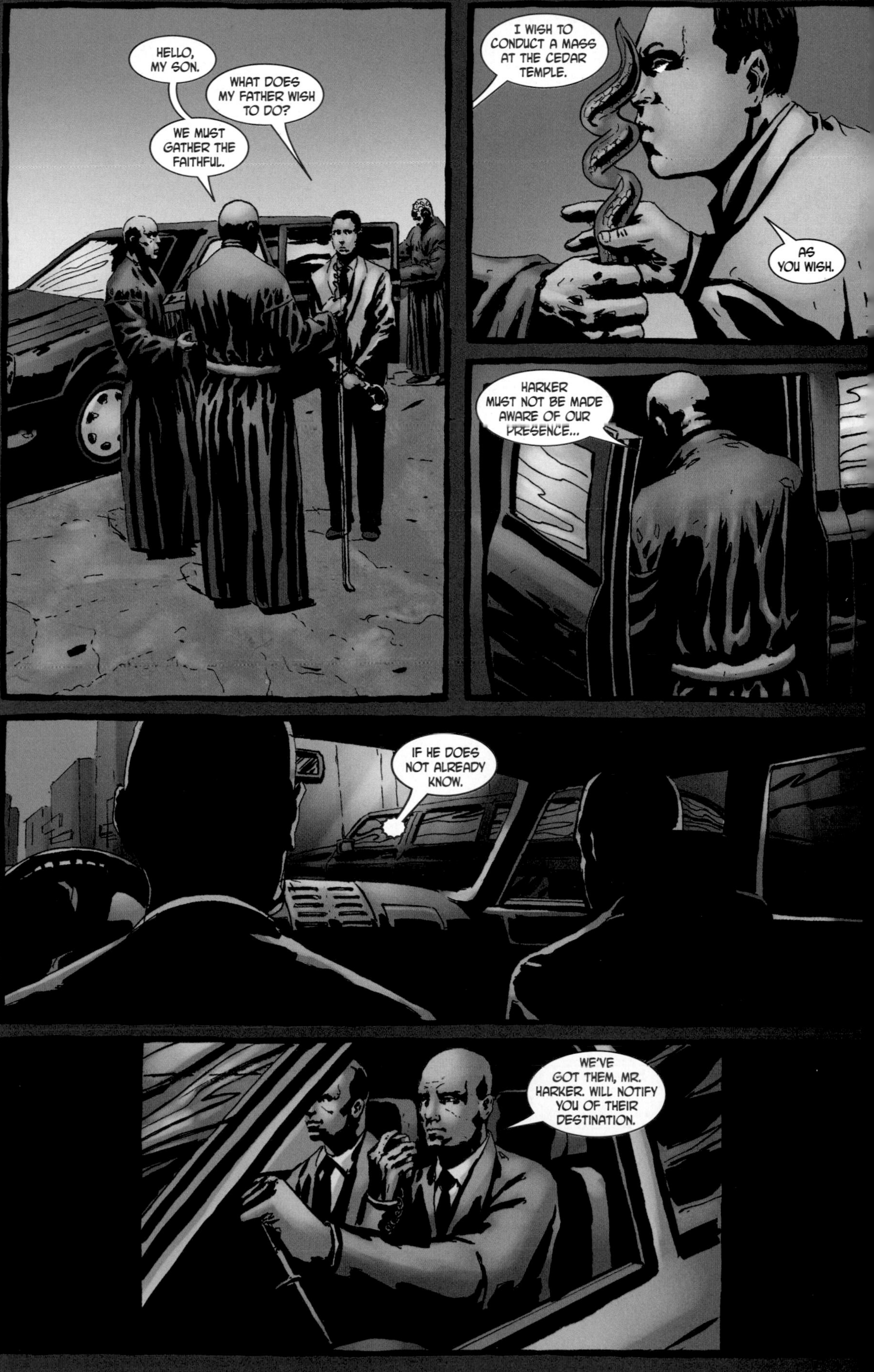
HELLO, MY SON.
WHAT DOES MY FATHER WISH TO DO?
WE MUST GATHER THE FAITHFUL.
I WISH TO CONDUCT A MASS AT THE CEDAR TEMPLE.
AS YOU WISH.
HARKER MUST NOT BE MADE AWARE OF OUR PRESENCE...
IF HE DOES NOT ALREADY KNOW.
WE'VE GOT THEM, MR. HARKER. WILL NOTIFY YOU OF THEIR DESTINATION.

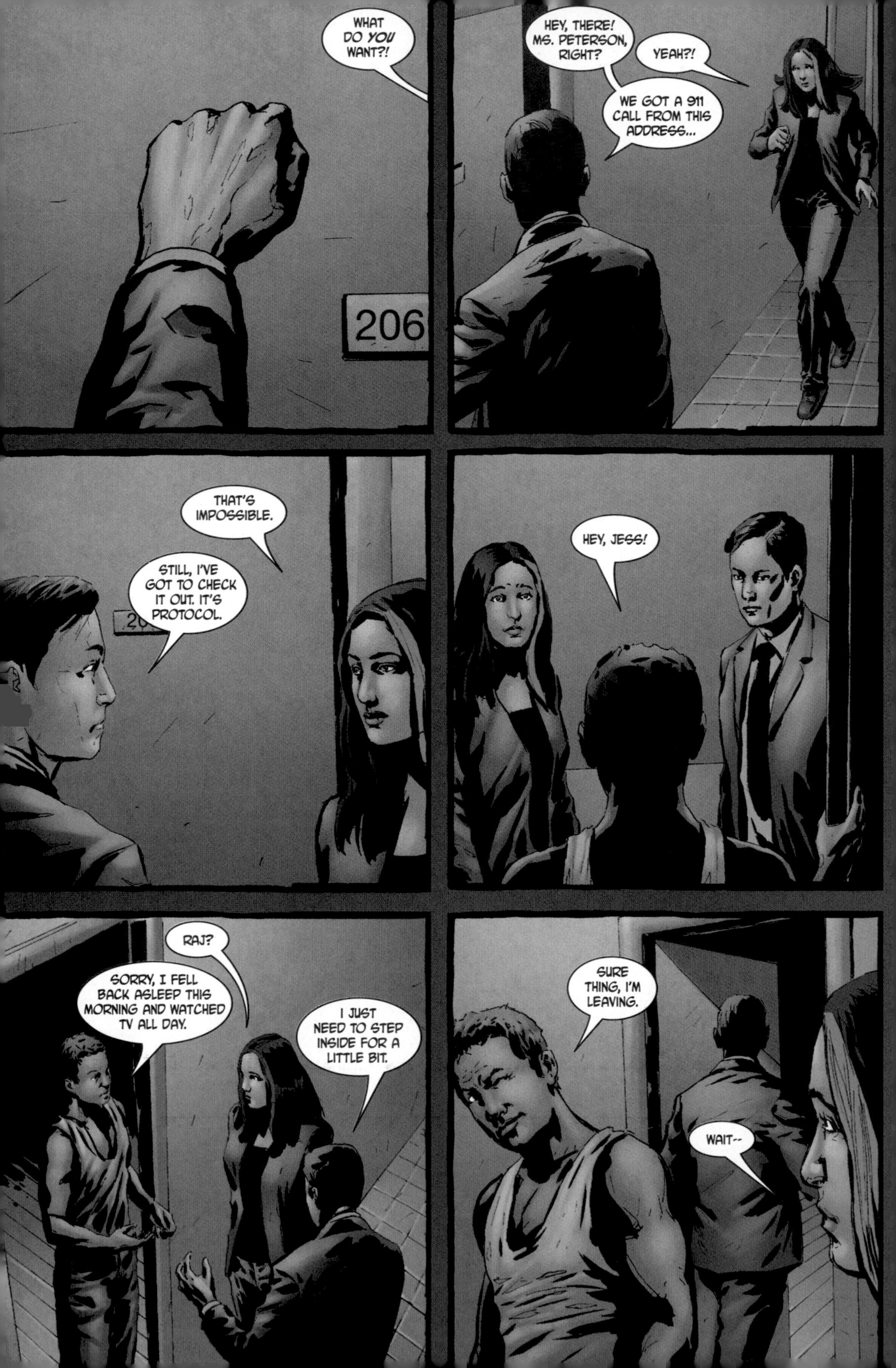
WHAT DO YOU WANT?!
206
HEY, THERE! MS. PETERSON, RIGHT?
YEAH?!
WE GOT A 911 CALL FROM THIS ADDRESS...
THAT'S IMPOSSIBLE.
STILL, I'VE GOT TO CHECK IT OUT. IT'S PROTOCOL.
HEY, JESS!
RAJ?
SORRY, I FELL BACK ASLEEP THIS MORNING AND WATCHED TV ALL DAY.
I JUST NEED TO STEP INSIDE FOR A LITTLE BIT.
SURE THING, I'M LEAVING.
WAIT--

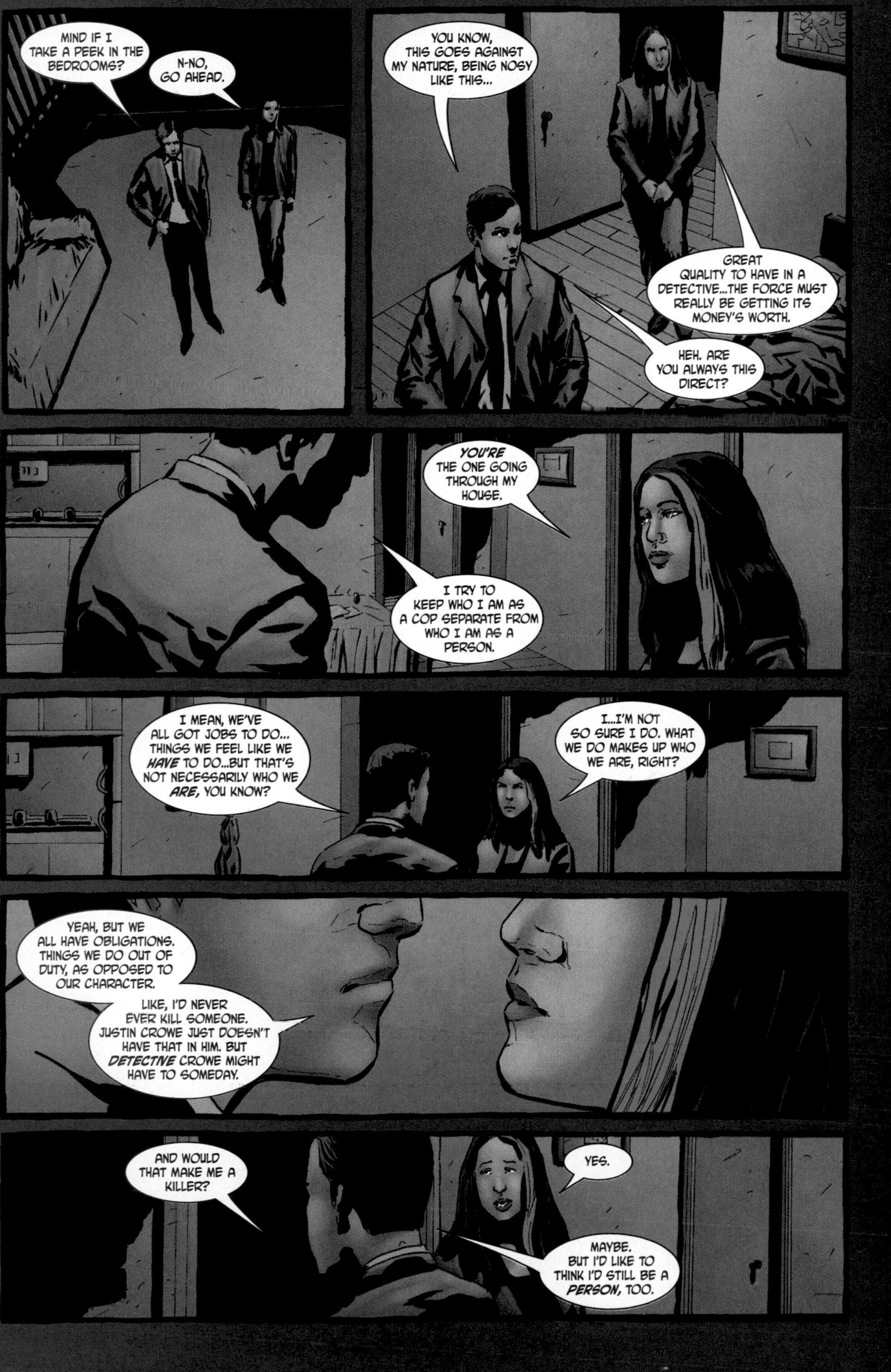
MIND IF I TAKE A PEEK IN THE BEDROOMS?
N-NO, GO AHEAD.
YOU KNOW, THIS GOES AGAINST MY NATURE, BEING NOSY LIKE THIS...
GREAT QUALITY TO HAVE IN A DETECTIVE...THE FORCE MUST REALLY BE GETTING ITS MONEY'S WORTH.
HEH. ARE YOU ALWAYS THIS DIRECT?
YOU'RE THE ONE GOING THROUGH MY HOUSE.
I TRY TO KEEP WHO I AM AS A COP SEPARATE FROM WHO I AM AS A PERSON.
I MEAN, WE'VE ALL GOT JOBS TO DO... THINGS WE FEEL LIKE WE *HAVE* TO DO...BUT THAT'S NOT NECESSARILY WHO WE *ARE,* YOU KNOW?
I...I'M NOT SO SURE I DO. WHAT WE DO MAKES UP WHO WE ARE, RIGHT?
YEAH, BUT WE ALL HAVE OBLIGATIONS. THINGS WE DO OUT OF DUTY, AS OPPOSED TO OUR CHARACTER.
LIKE, I'D NEVER EVER KILL SOMEONE. JUSTIN CROWE JUST DOESN'T HAVE THAT IN HIM. BUT *DETECTIVE* CROWE MIGHT HAVE TO SOMEDAY.
AND WOULD THAT MAKE ME A KILLER?
YES.
MAYBE. BUT I'D LIKE TO THINK I'D STILL BE A *PERSON,* TOO.

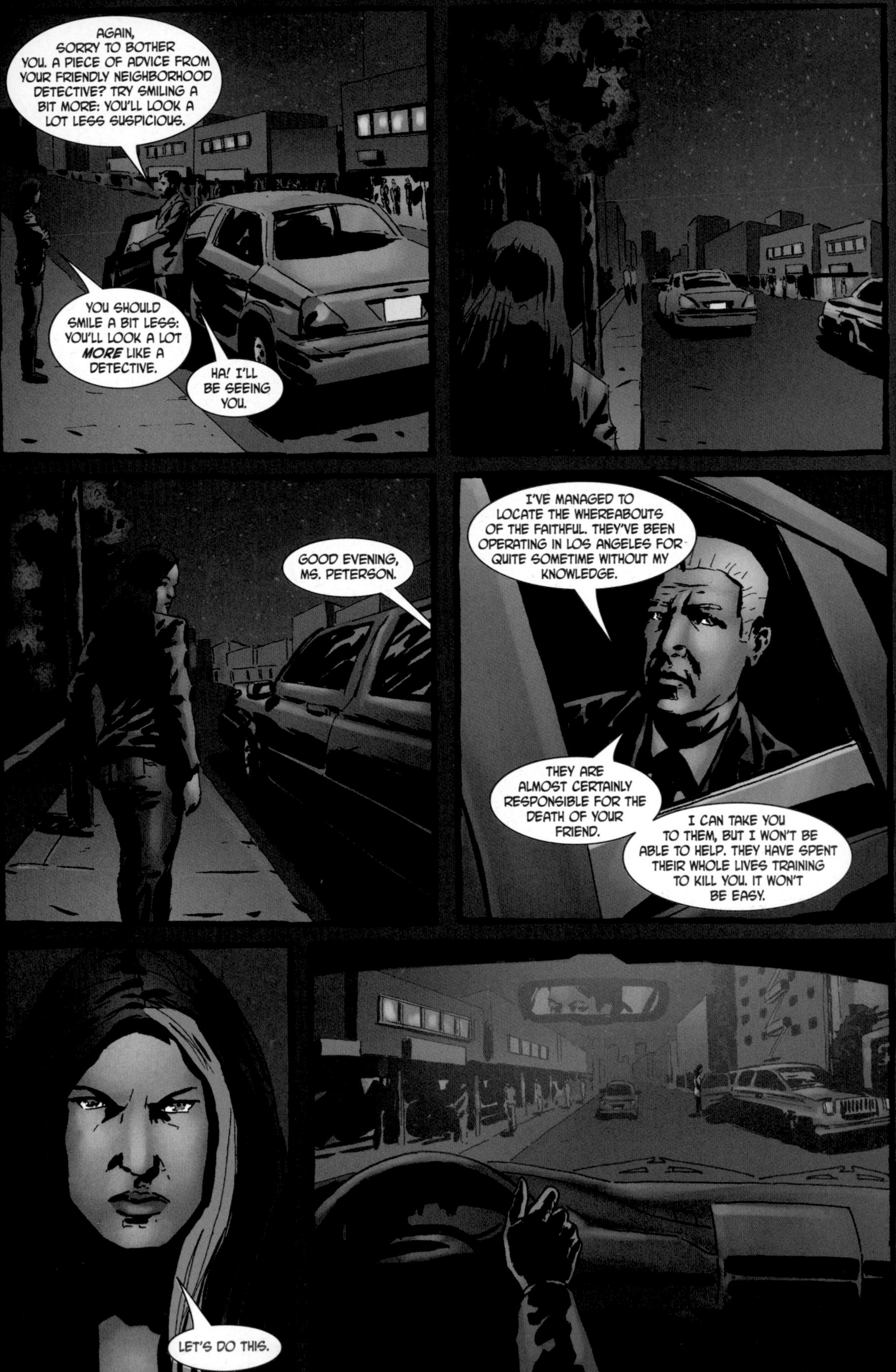
AGAIN, SORRY TO BOTHER YOU. A PIECE OF ADVICE FROM YOUR FRIENDLY NEIGHBORHOOD DETECTIVE? TRY SMILING A BIT MORE: YOU'LL LOOK A LOT LESS SUSPICIOUS.
YOU SHOULD SMILE A BIT LESS: YOU'LL LOOK A LOT *MORE* LIKE A DETECTIVE.
HA! I'LL BE SEEING YOU.
GOOD EVENING, MS. PETERSON.
I'VE MANAGED TO LOCATE THE WHEREABOUTS OF THE FAITHFUL. THEY'VE BEEN OPERATING IN LOS ANGELES FOR QUITE SOMETIME WITHOUT MY KNOWLEDGE.
THEY ARE ALMOST CERTAINLY RESPONSIBLE FOR THE DEATH OF YOUR FRIEND.
I CAN TAKE YOU TO THEM, BUT I WON'T BE ABLE TO HELP. THEY HAVE SPENT THEIR WHOLE LIVES TRAINING TO KILL YOU. IT WON'T BE EASY.
LET'S DO THIS.

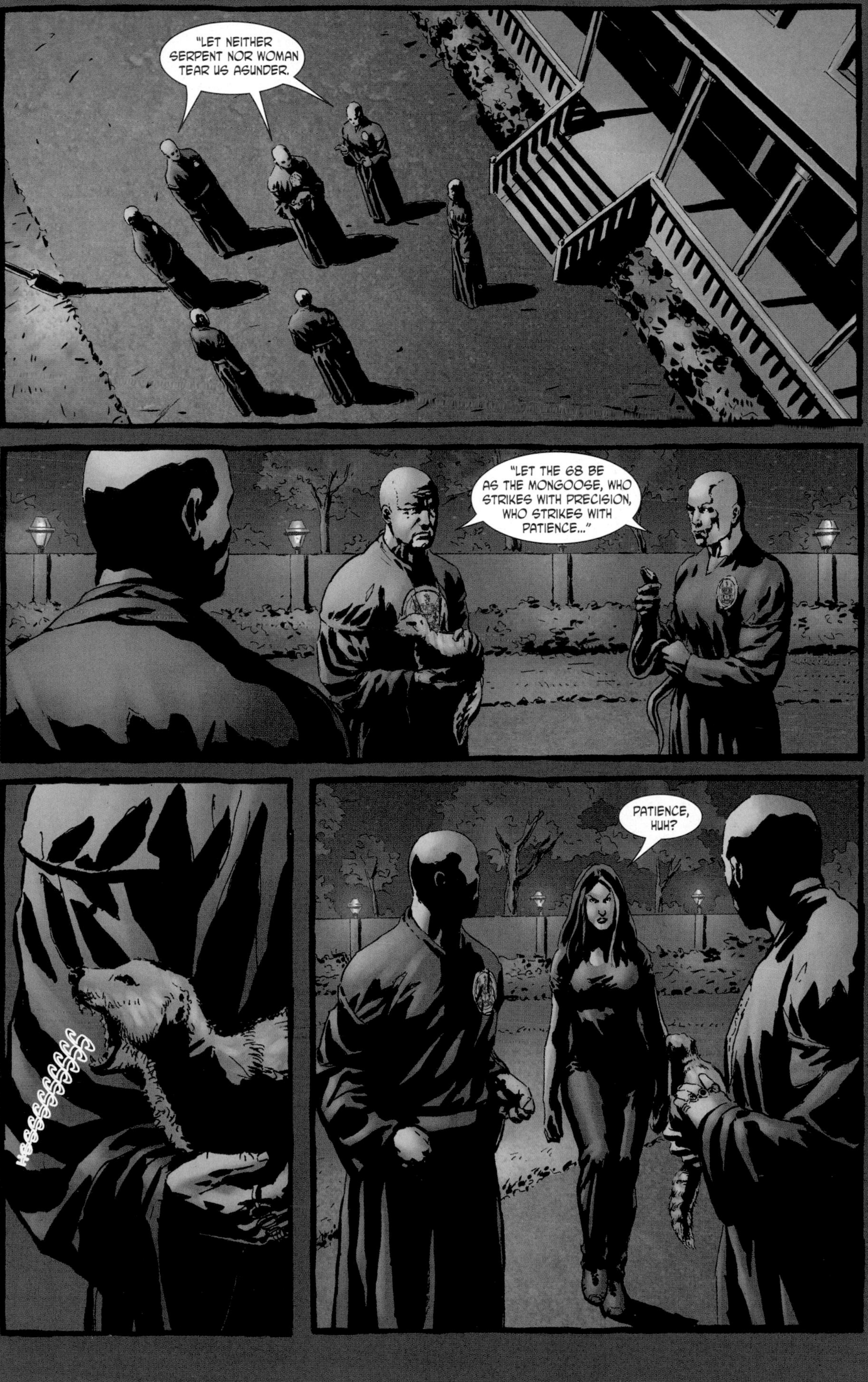
"LET NEITHER SERPENT NOR WOMAN TEAR US ASUNDER.
"LET THE 68 BE AS THE MONGOOSE, WHO STRIKES WITH PRECISION, WHO STRIKES WITH PATIENCE..."
HSSSSSSSSSS
PATIENCE, HUH?

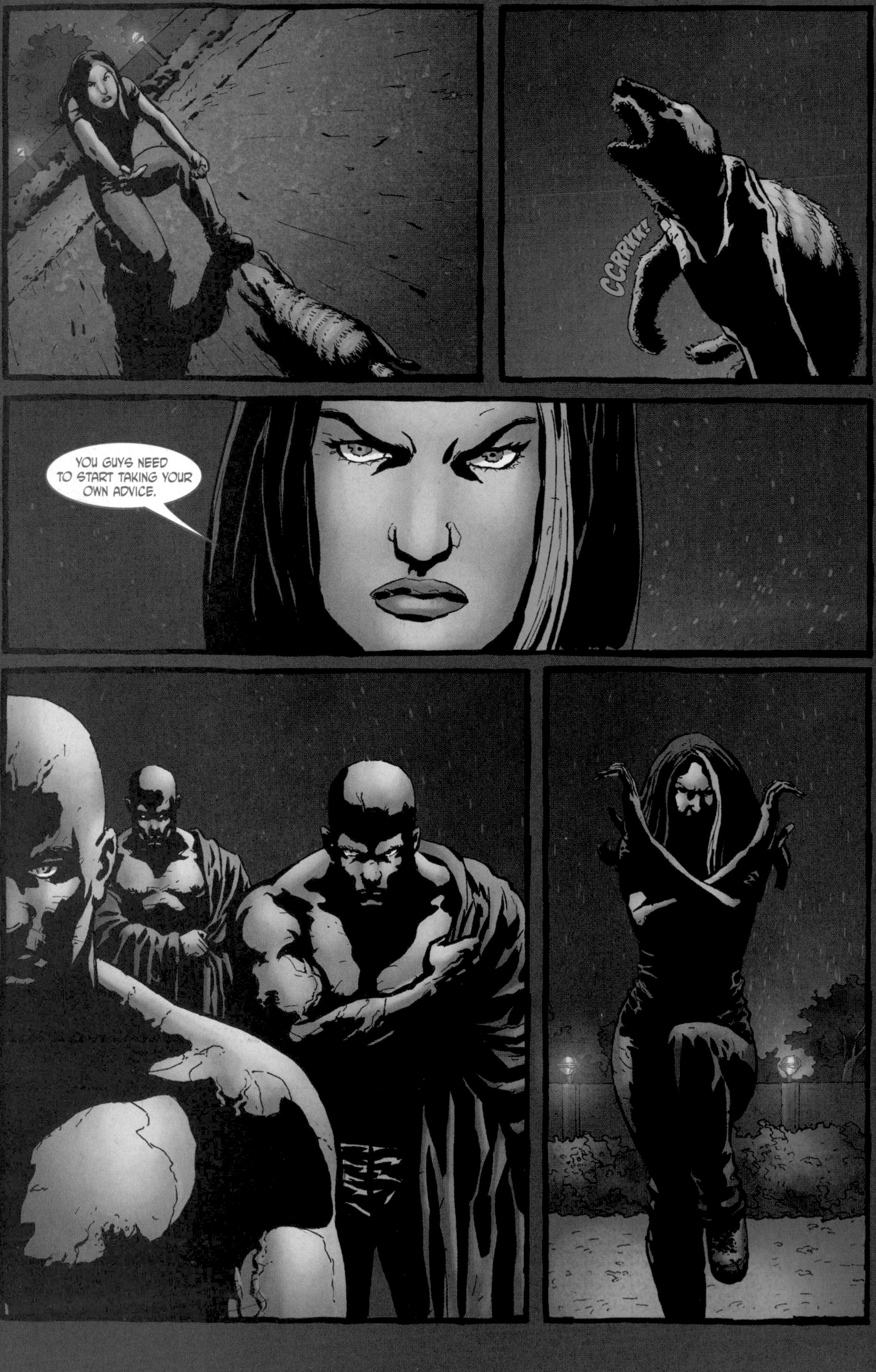
CCRRKK!
YOU GUYS NEED TO START TAKING YOUR OWN ADVICE.

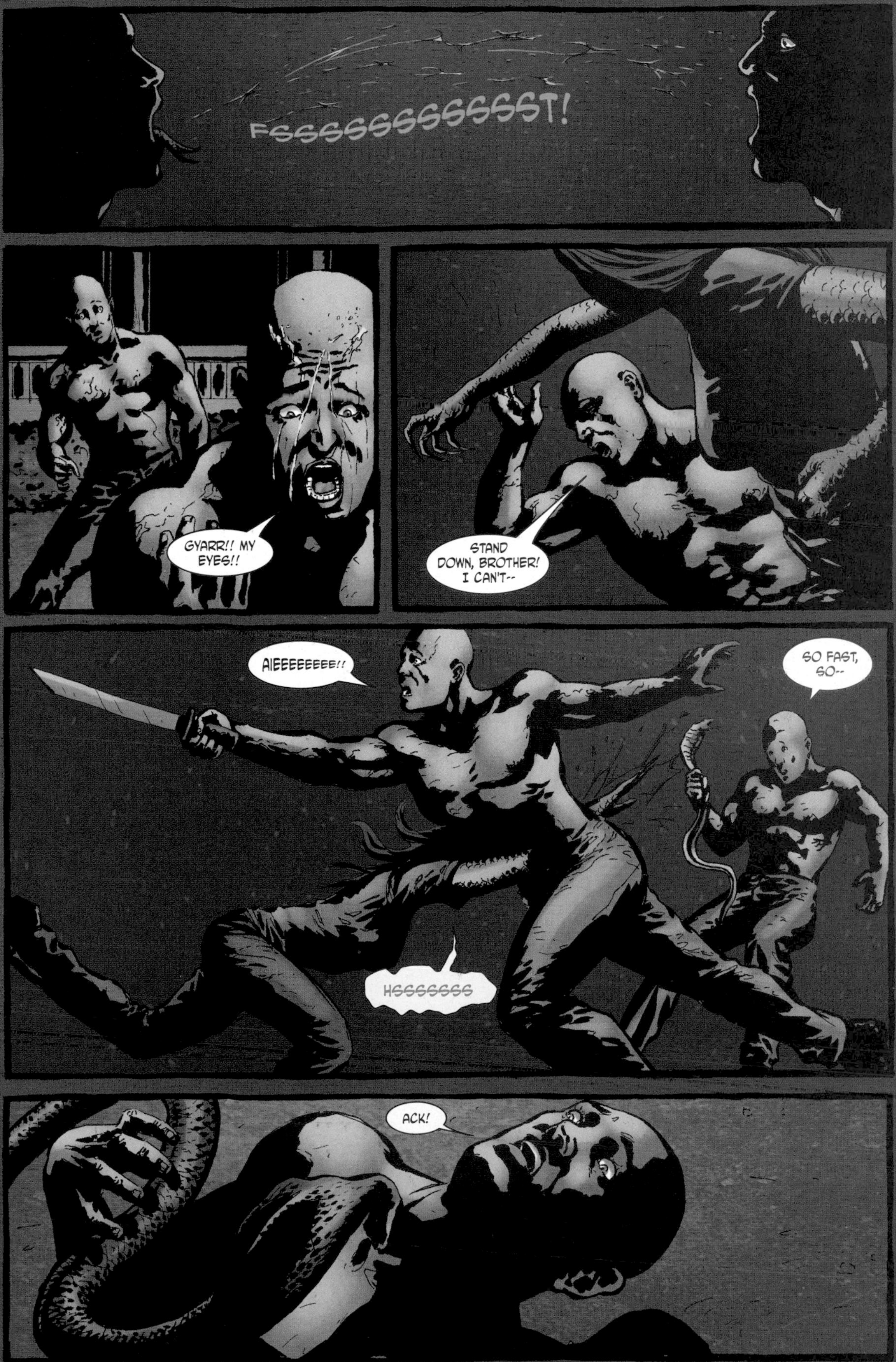
FSSSSSSSSSSSST!
GYARR!! MY EYES!!
STAND DOWN, BROTHER! I CAN'T--
AIEEEEEEEE!!
SO FAST, SO--
HSSSSSSS
ACK!

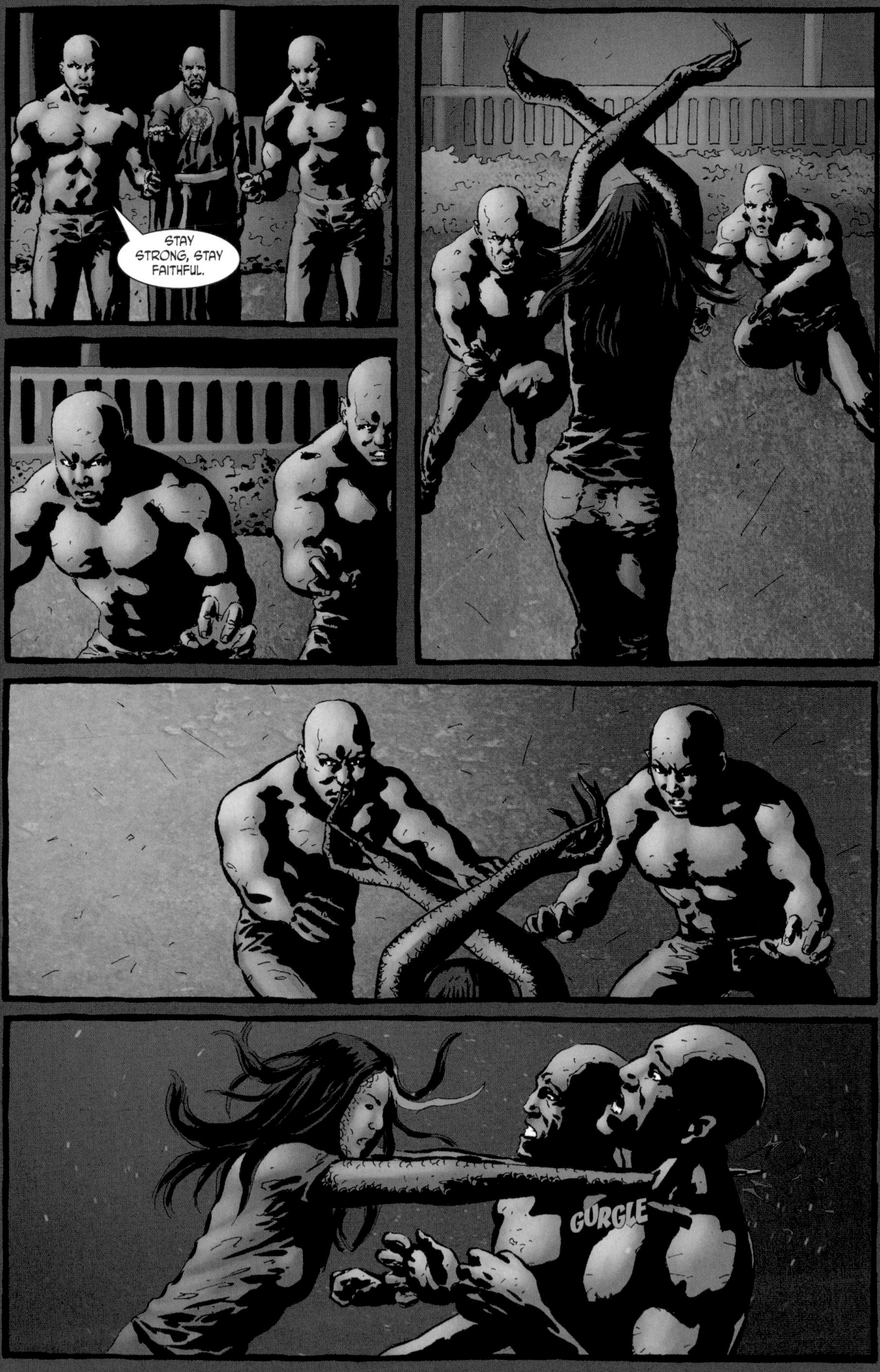

STAY STRONG, STAY FAITHFUL.
GURGLE

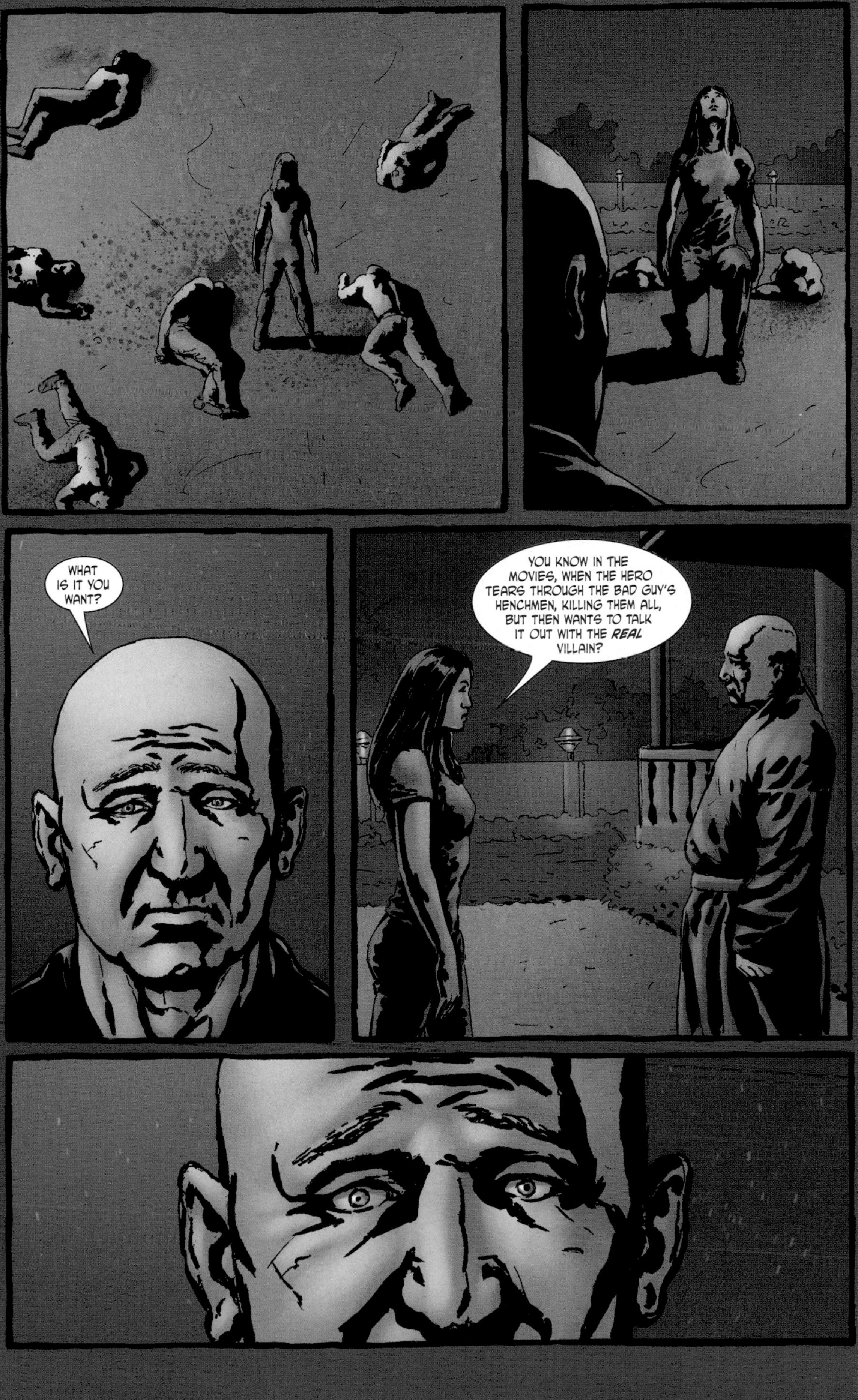
WHAT IS IT YOU WANT?
YOU KNOW IN THE MOVIES, WHEN THE HERO TEARS THROUGH THE BAD GUY'S HENCHMEN, KILLING THEM ALL, BUT THEN WANTS TO TALK IT OUT WITH THE *REAL* VILLAIN?

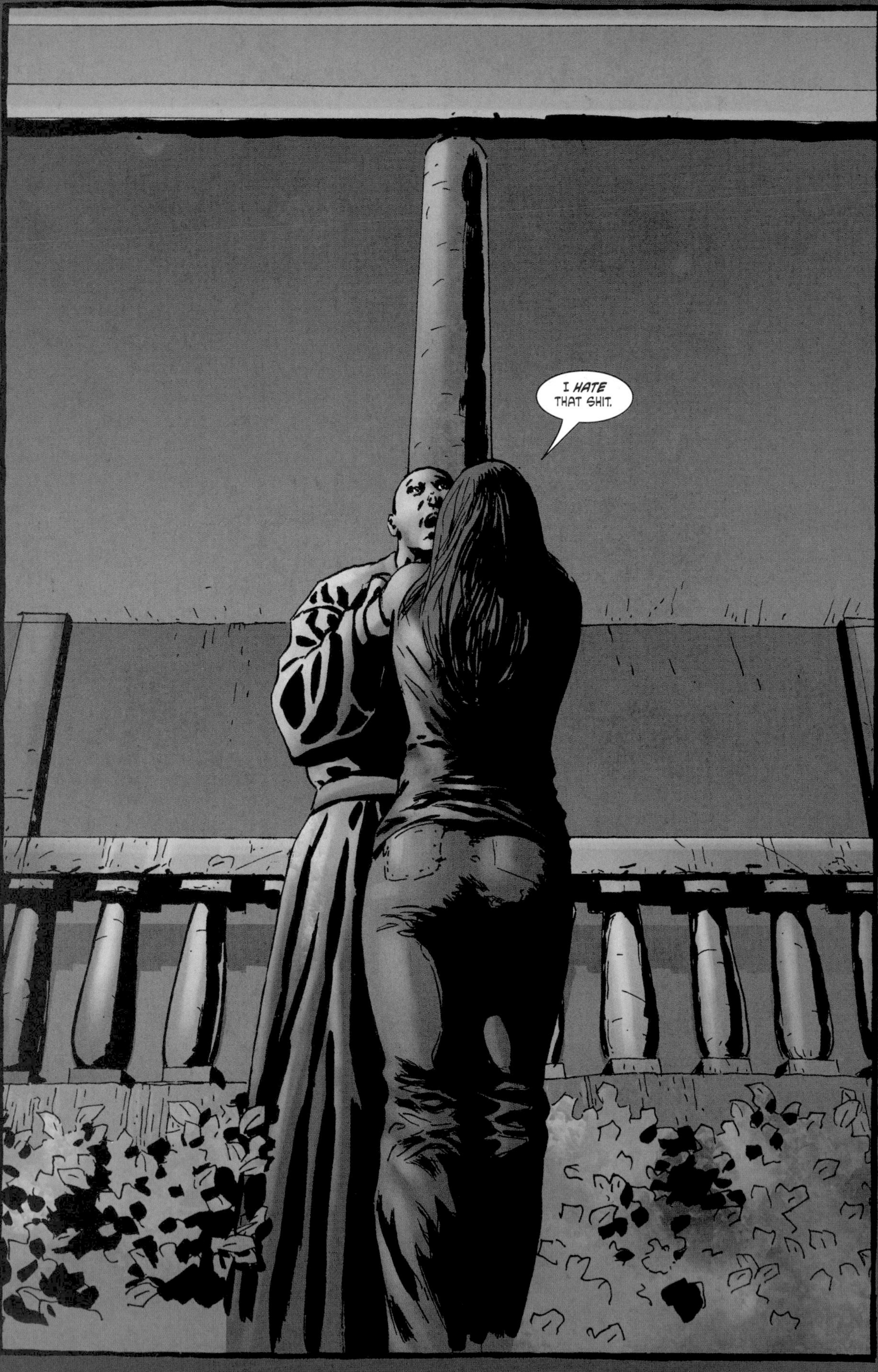
I *HATE* THAT SHIT.

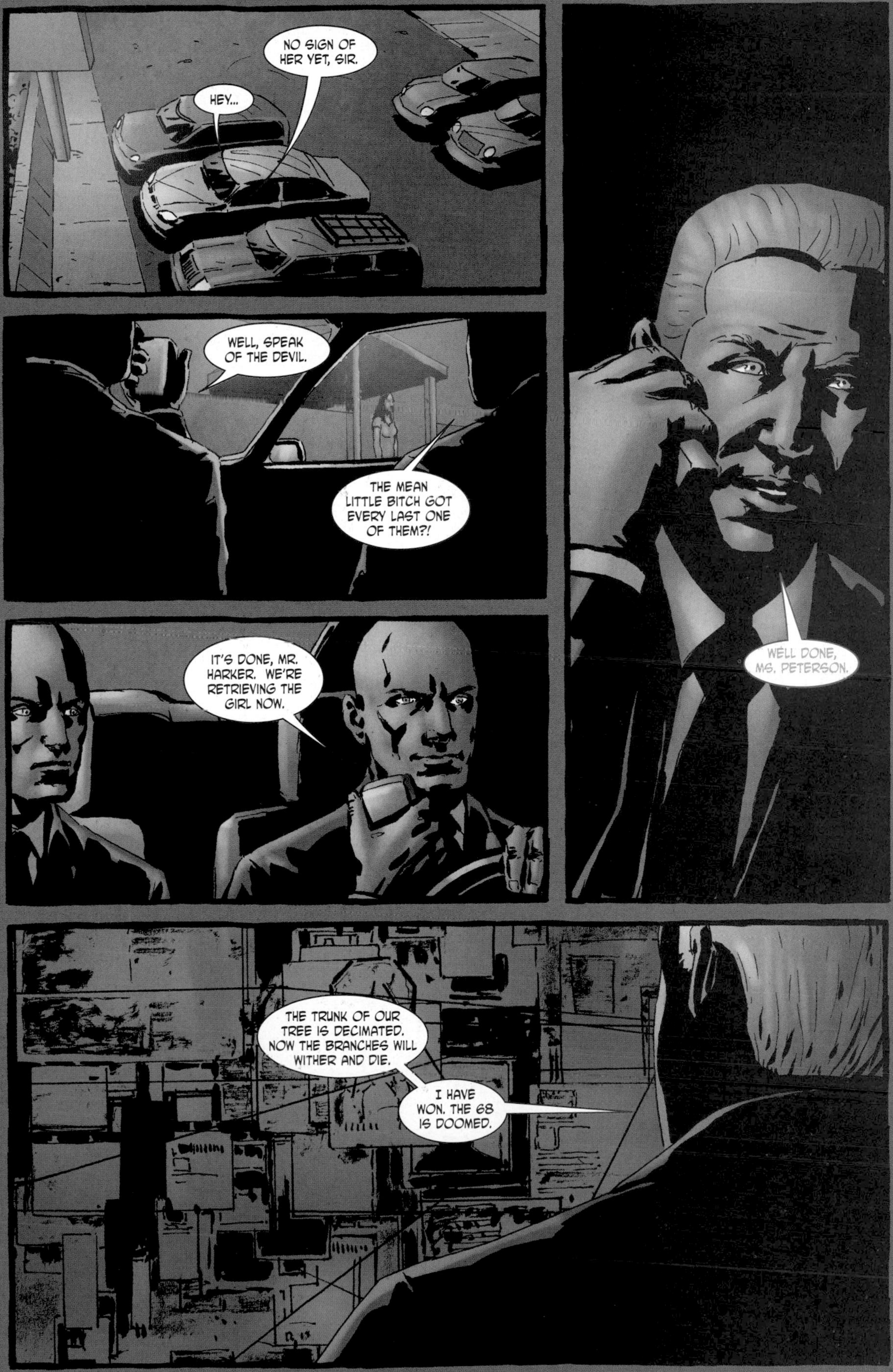
NO SIGN OF HER YET, SIR.
HEY...
WELL, SPEAK OF THE DEVIL.
THE MEAN LITTLE BITCH GOT EVERY LAST ONE OF THEM?!
IT'S DONE, MR. HARKER. WE'RE RETRIEVING THE GIRL NOW.
WELL DONE, MS. PETERSON.
THE TRUNK OF OUR TREE IS DECIMATED. NOW THE BRANCHES WILL WITHER AND DIE.
I HAVE WON. THE 68 IS DOOMED.

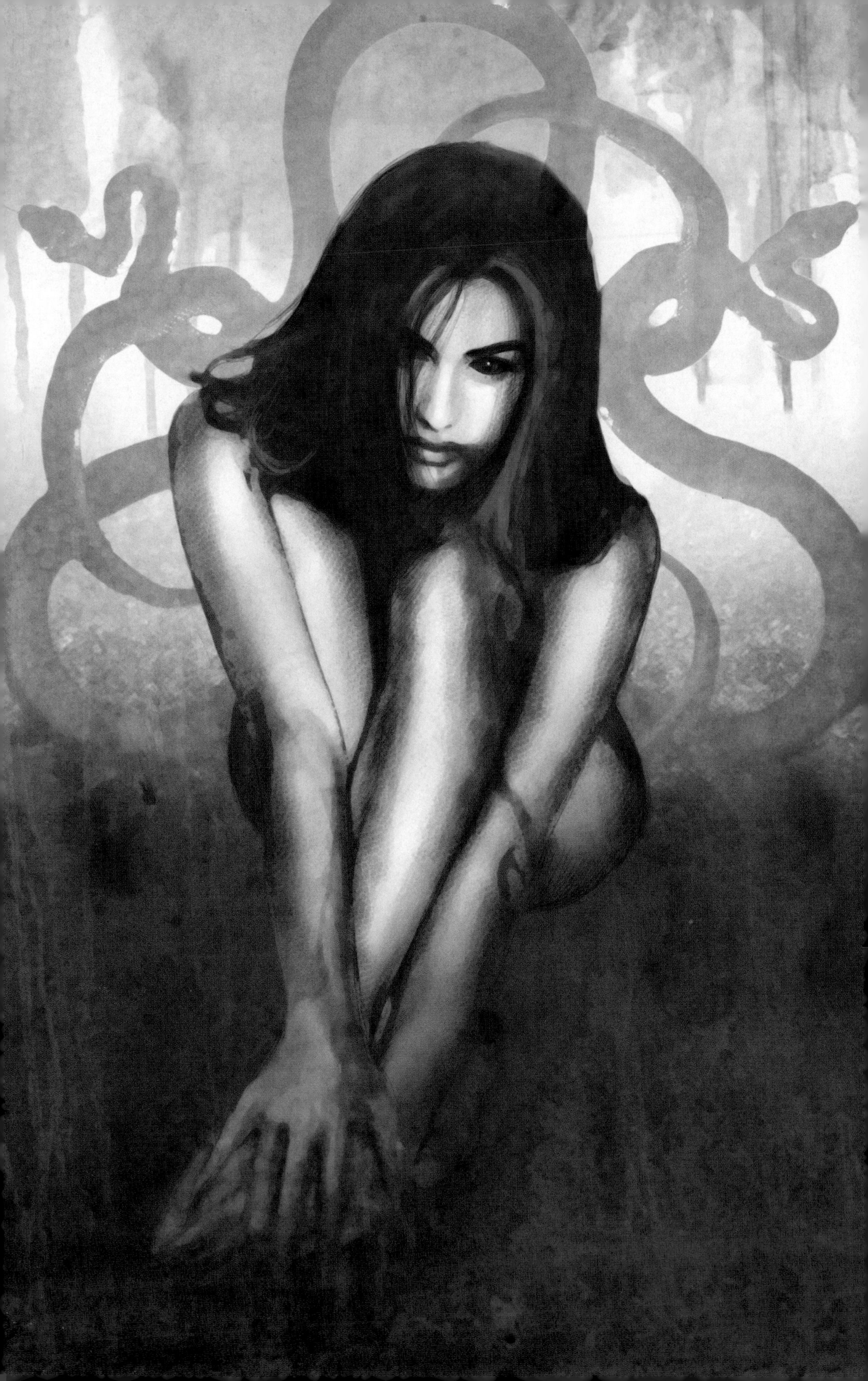

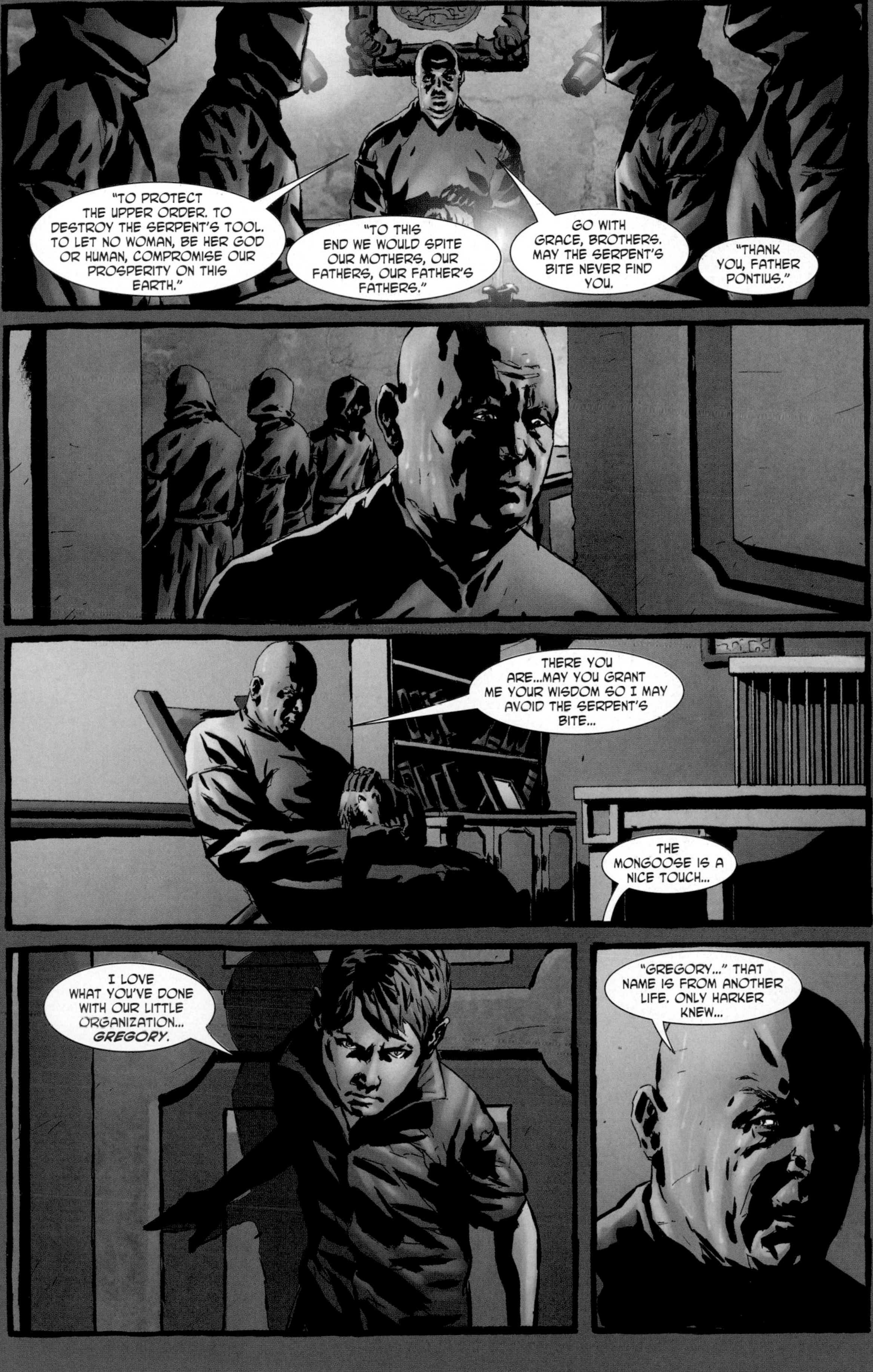
"TO PROTECT THE UPPER ORDER. TO DESTROY THE SERPENT'S TOOL. TO LET NO WOMAN, BE HER GOD OR HUMAN, COMPROMISE OUR PROSPERITY ON THIS EARTH."
"TO THIS END WE WOULD SPITE OUR MOTHERS, OUR FATHERS, OUR FATHER'S FATHERS."
GO WITH GRACE, BROTHERS. MAY THE SERPENT'S BITE NEVER FIND YOU.
"THANK YOU, FATHER PONTIUS."
THERE YOU ARE...MAY YOU GRANT ME YOUR WISDOM SO I MAY AVOID THE SERPENT'S BITE...
THE MONGOOSE IS A NICE TOUCH...
I LOVE WHAT YOU'VE DONE WITH OUR LITTLE ORGANIZATION... ***GREGORY***.
"GREGORY..." THAT NAME IS FROM ANOTHER LIFE. ONLY HARKER KNEW...

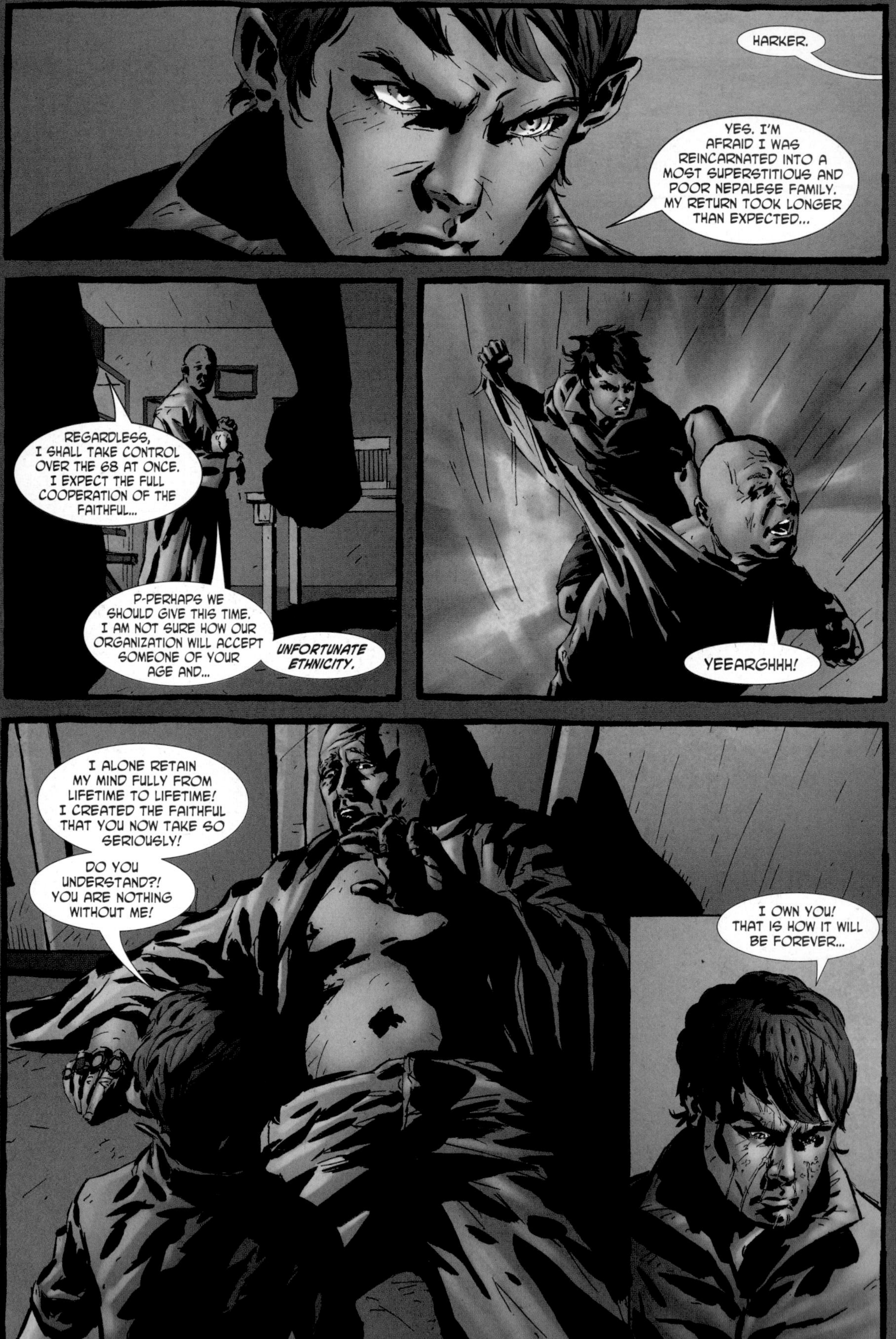
HARKER.
YES. I'M AFRAID I WAS REINCARNATED INTO A MOST SUPERSTITIOUS AND POOR NEPALESE FAMILY. MY RETURN TOOK LONGER THAN EXPECTED...
REGARDLESS, I SHALL TAKE CONTROL OVER THE 68 AT ONCE. I EXPECT THE FULL COOPERATION OF THE FAITHFUL...
P-PERHAPS WE SHOULD GIVE THIS TIME. I AM NOT SURE HOW OUR ORGANIZATION WILL ACCEPT SOMEONE OF YOUR AGE AND...
UNFORTUNATE ETHNICITY.
YEEARGHHH!
I ALONE RETAIN MY MIND FULLY FROM LIFETIME TO LIFETIME! I CREATED THE FAITHFUL THAT YOU NOW TAKE SO SERIOUSLY!
DO YOU UNDERSTAND?! YOU ARE NOTHING WITHOUT ME!
I OWN YOU! THAT IS HOW IT WILL BE FOREVER...

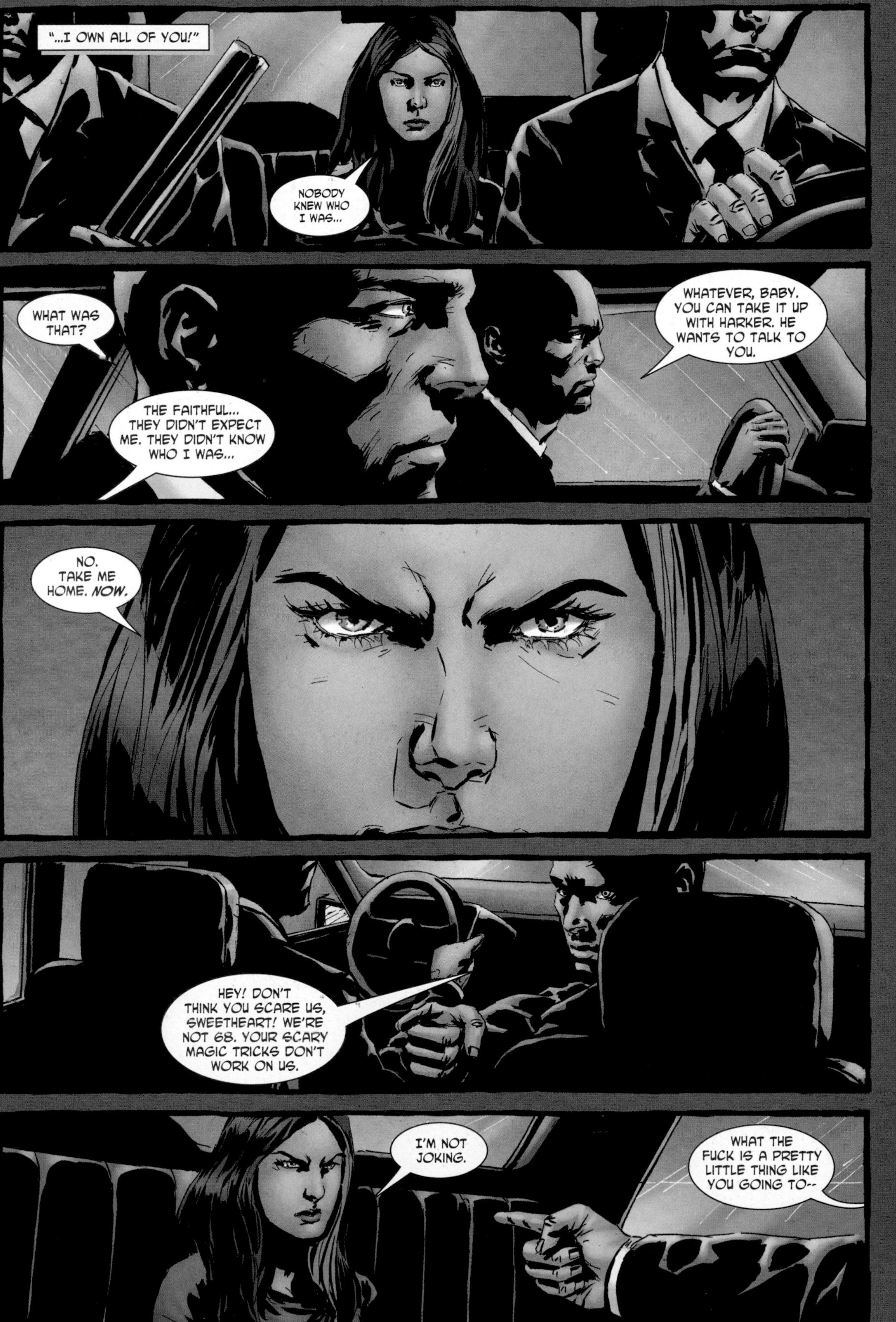
"...I OWN ALL OF YOU!"
NOBODY KNEW WHO I WAS...
WHAT WAS THAT?
THE FAITHFUL... THEY DIDN'T EXPECT ME. THEY DIDN'T KNOW WHO I WAS...
WHATEVER, BABY. YOU CAN TAKE IT UP WITH HARKER. HE WANTS TO TALK TO YOU.
NO. TAKE ME HOME. *NOW.*
HEY! DON'T THINK YOU SCARE US, SWEETHEART! WE'RE NOT 68. YOUR SCARY MAGIC TRICKS DON'T WORK ON US.
I'M NOT JOKING.
WHAT THE FUCK IS A PRETTY LITTLE THING LIKE YOU GOING TO--

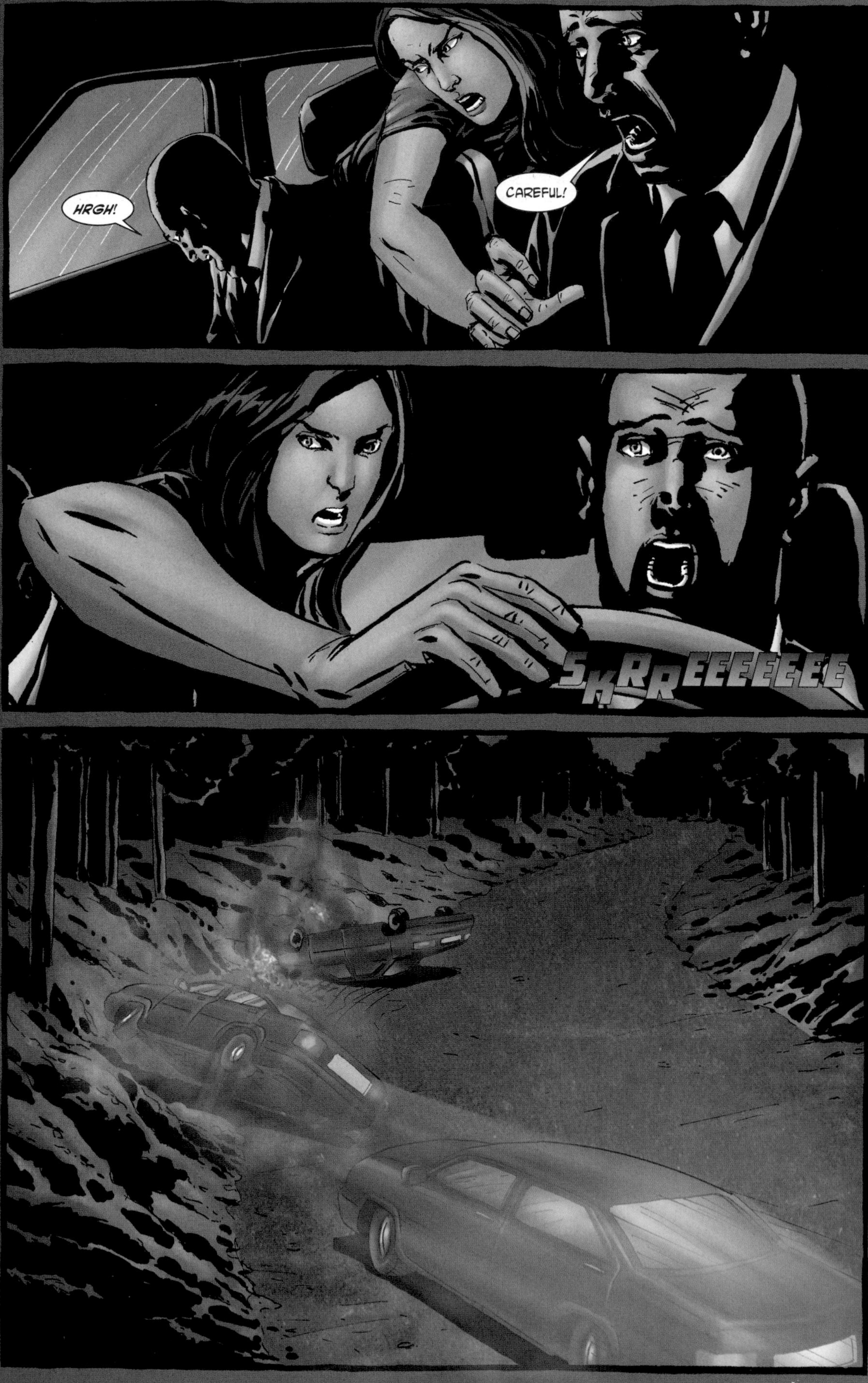
HRGH!
CAREFUL!
SKRREEEEEEE

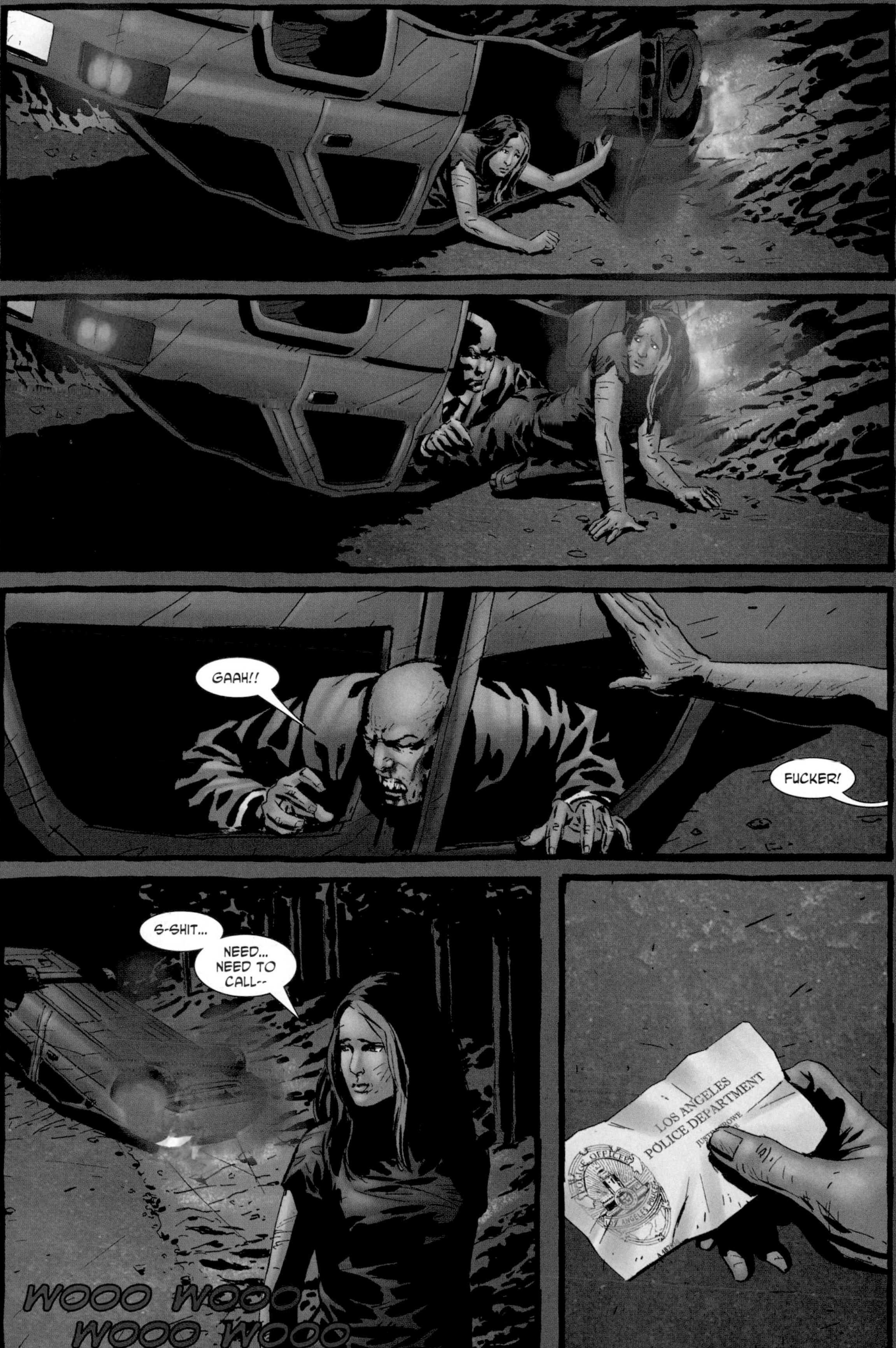
GAAH!!
FUCKER!
S-SHIT...
NEED... NEED TO CALL--
WOOO WOOO
WOOO WOOO
LOS ANGELES
POLICE DEPARTMENT

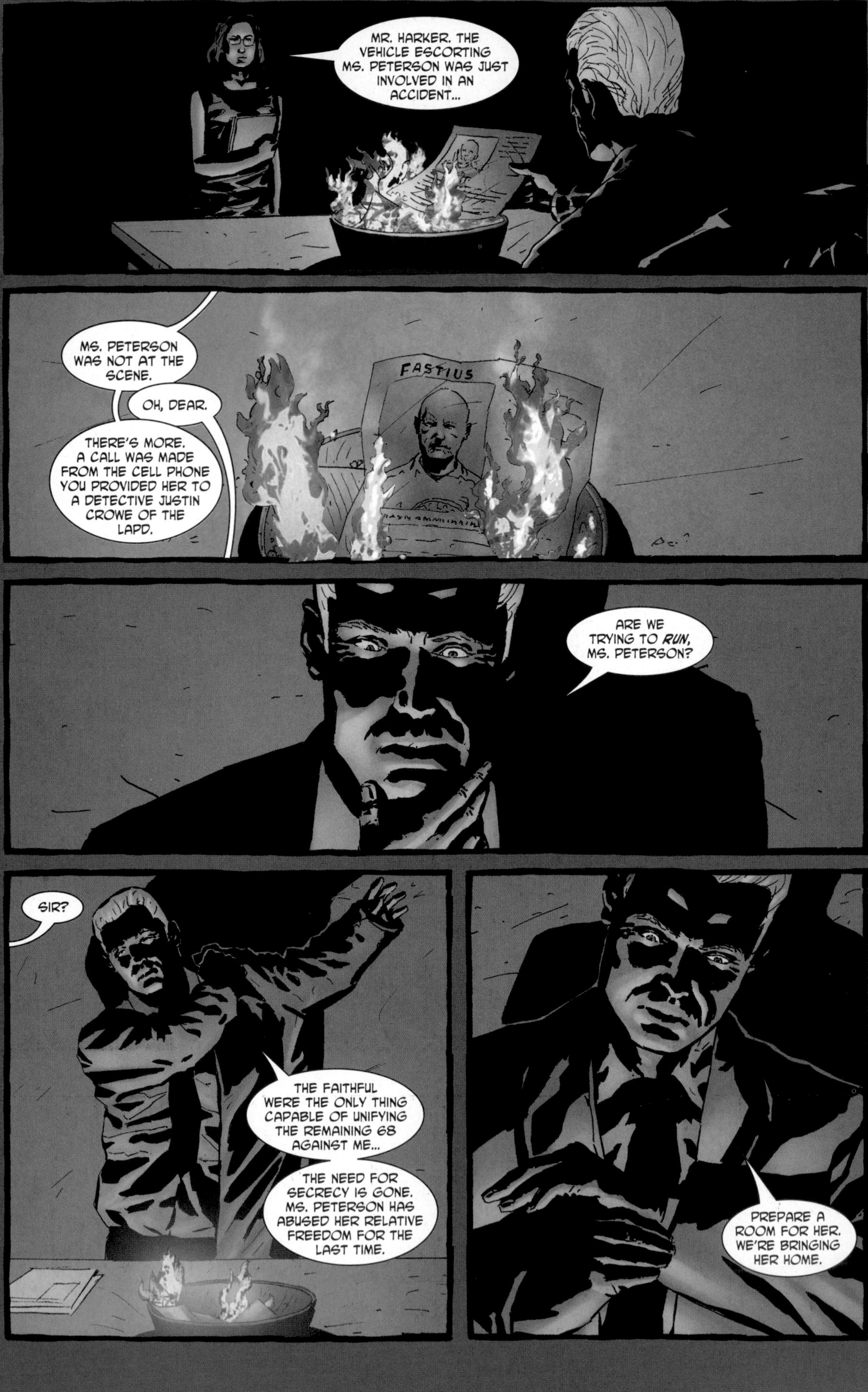
MR. HARKER. THE VEHICLE ESCORTING MS. PETERSON WAS JUST INVOLVED IN AN ACCIDENT...
MS. PETERSON WAS NOT AT THE SCENE.
OH, DEAR.
THERE'S MORE. A CALL WAS MADE FROM THE CELL PHONE YOU PROVIDED HER TO A DETECTIVE JUSTIN CROWE OF THE LAPD.
FASTIUS
ARE WE TRYING TO *RUN*, MS. PETERSON?
SIR?
THE FAITHFUL WERE THE ONLY THING CAPABLE OF UNIFYING THE REMAINING 68 AGAINST ME...
THE NEED FOR SECRECY IS GONE. MS. PETERSON HAS ABUSED HER RELATIVE FREEDOM FOR THE LAST TIME.
PREPARE A ROOM FOR HER. WE'RE BRINGING HER HOME.

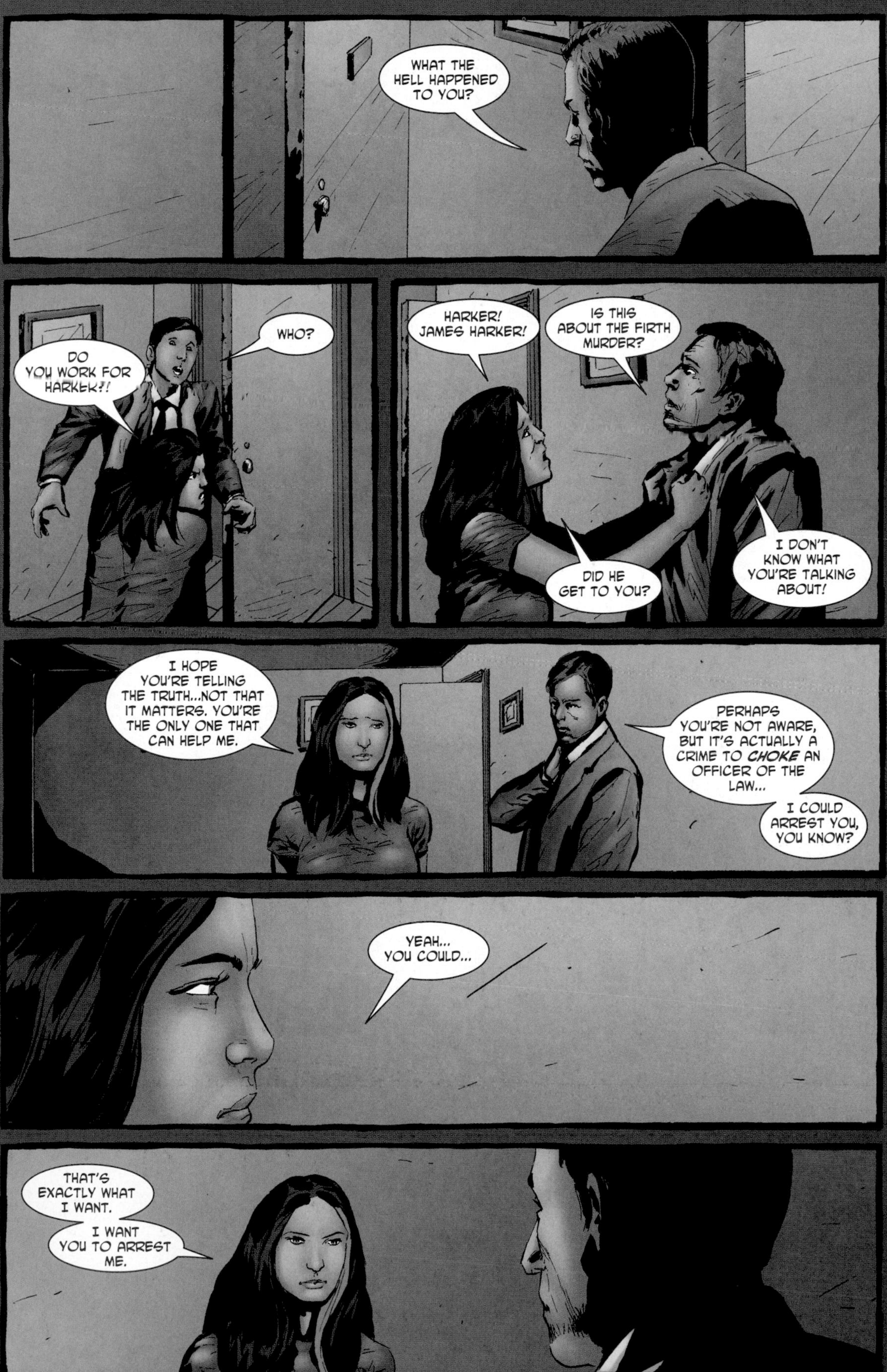
WHAT THE HELL HAPPENED TO YOU?
DO YOU WORK FOR HARKER?!
WHO?
HARKER! JAMES HARKER!
IS THIS ABOUT THE FIRTH MURDER?
DID HE GET TO YOU?
I DON'T KNOW WHAT YOU'RE TALKING ABOUT!
I HOPE YOU'RE TELLING THE TRUTH...NOT THAT IT MATTERS. YOU'RE THE ONLY ONE THAT CAN HELP ME.
PERHAPS YOU'RE NOT AWARE, BUT IT'S ACTUALLY A CRIME TO *CHOKE* AN OFFICER OF THE LAW...
I COULD ARREST YOU, YOU KNOW?
YEAH... YOU COULD...
THAT'S EXACTLY WHAT I WANT.
I WANT YOU TO ARREST ME.

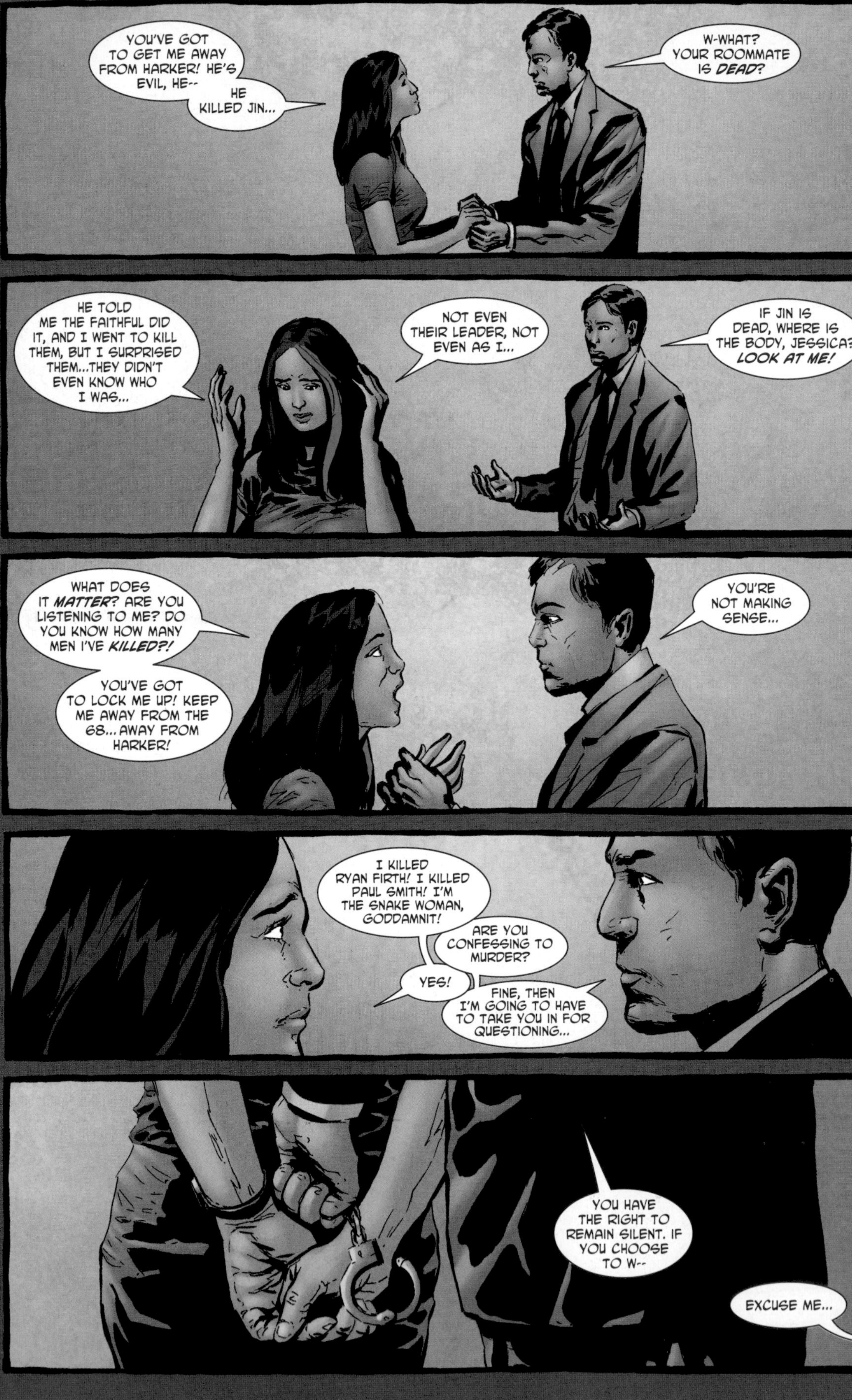
YOU'VE GOT TO GET ME AWAY FROM HARKER! HE'S EVIL, HE--
HE KILLED JIN...
W-WHAT? YOUR ROOMMATE IS *DEAD*?
HE TOLD ME THE FAITHFUL DID IT, AND I WENT TO KILL THEM, BUT I SURPRISED THEM...THEY DIDN'T EVEN KNOW WHO I WAS...
NOT EVEN THEIR LEADER, NOT EVEN AS I...
IF JIN IS DEAD, WHERE IS THE BODY, JESSICA? *LOOK AT ME!*
WHAT DOES IT *MATTER*? ARE YOU LISTENING TO ME? DO YOU KNOW HOW MANY MEN I'VE *KILLED?!*
YOU'VE GOT TO LOCK ME UP! KEEP ME AWAY FROM THE 68... AWAY FROM HARKER!
YOU'RE NOT MAKING SENSE...
I KILLED RYAN FIRTH! I KILLED PAUL SMITH! I'M THE SNAKE WOMAN, GODDAMNIT!
ARE YOU CONFESSING TO MURDER?
YES!
FINE, THEN I'M GOING TO HAVE TO TAKE YOU IN FOR QUESTIONING...
YOU HAVE THE RIGHT TO REMAIN SILENT. IF YOU CHOOSE TO W--
EXCUSE ME...

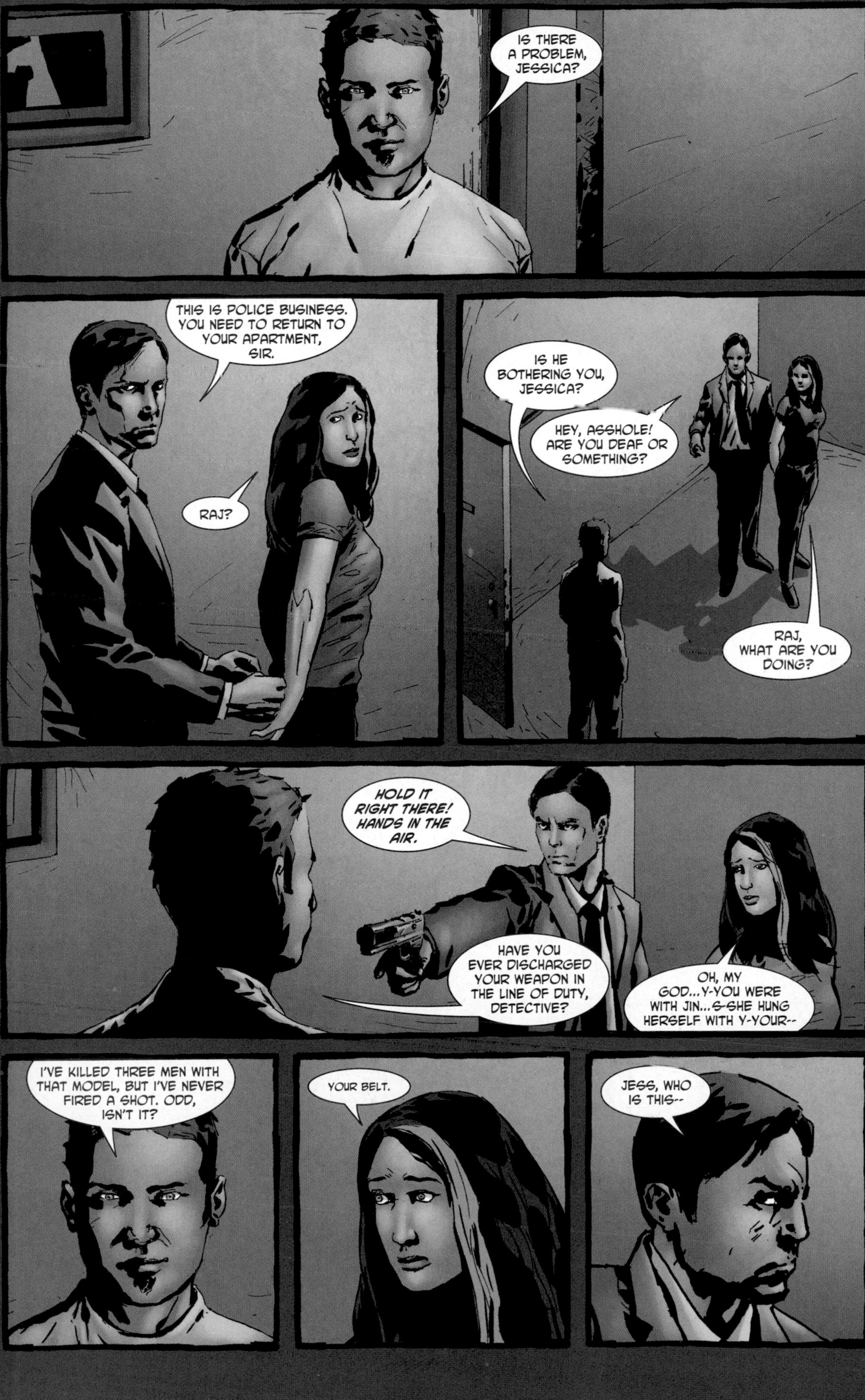
IS THERE A PROBLEM, JESSICA?
THIS IS POLICE BUSINESS. YOU NEED TO RETURN TO YOUR APARTMENT, SIR.
RAJ?
IS HE BOTHERING YOU, JESSICA?
HEY, ASSHOLE! ARE YOU DEAF OR SOMETHING?
RAJ, WHAT ARE YOU DOING?
HOLD IT RIGHT THERE! HANDS IN THE AIR.
HAVE YOU EVER DISCHARGED YOUR WEAPON IN THE LINE OF DUTY, DETECTIVE?
OH, MY GOD...Y-YOU WERE WITH JIN...S-SHE HUNG HERSELF WITH Y-YOUR--
I'VE KILLED THREE MEN WITH THAT MODEL, BUT I'VE NEVER FIRED A SHOT. ODD, ISN'T IT?
YOUR BELT.
JESS, WHO IS THIS--

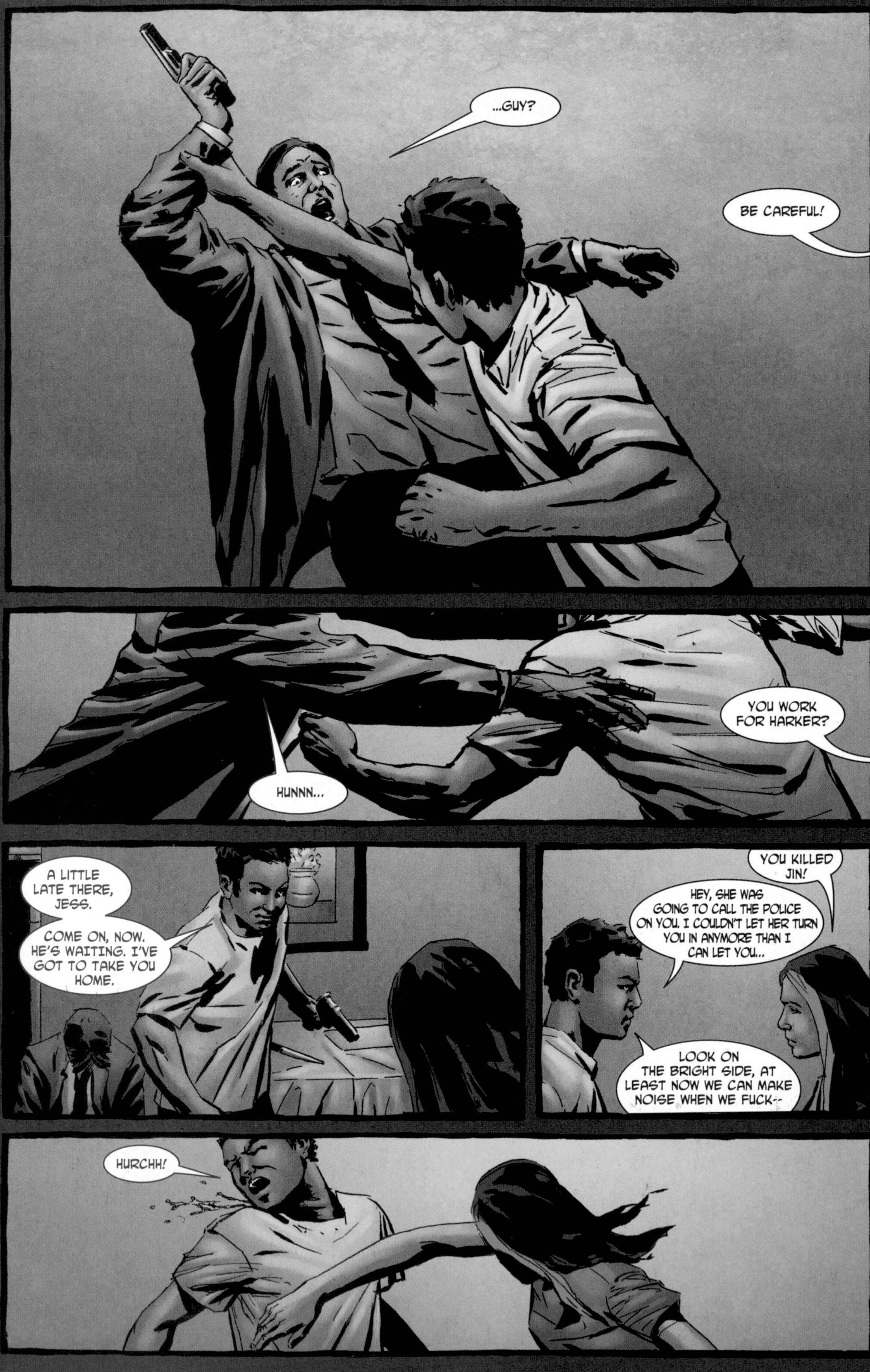
...GUY?
BE CAREFUL!
YOU WORK FOR HARKER?
HUNNN...
A LITTLE LATE THERE, JESS.
COME ON, NOW. HE'S WAITING. I'VE GOT TO TAKE YOU HOME.
YOU KILLED JIN!
HEY, SHE WAS GOING TO CALL THE POLICE ON YOU. I COULDN'T LET HER TURN YOU IN ANYMORE THAN I CAN LET YOU...
LOOK ON THE BRIGHT SIDE, AT LEAST NOW WE CAN MAKE NOISE WHEN WE FUCK--
HURCHH!

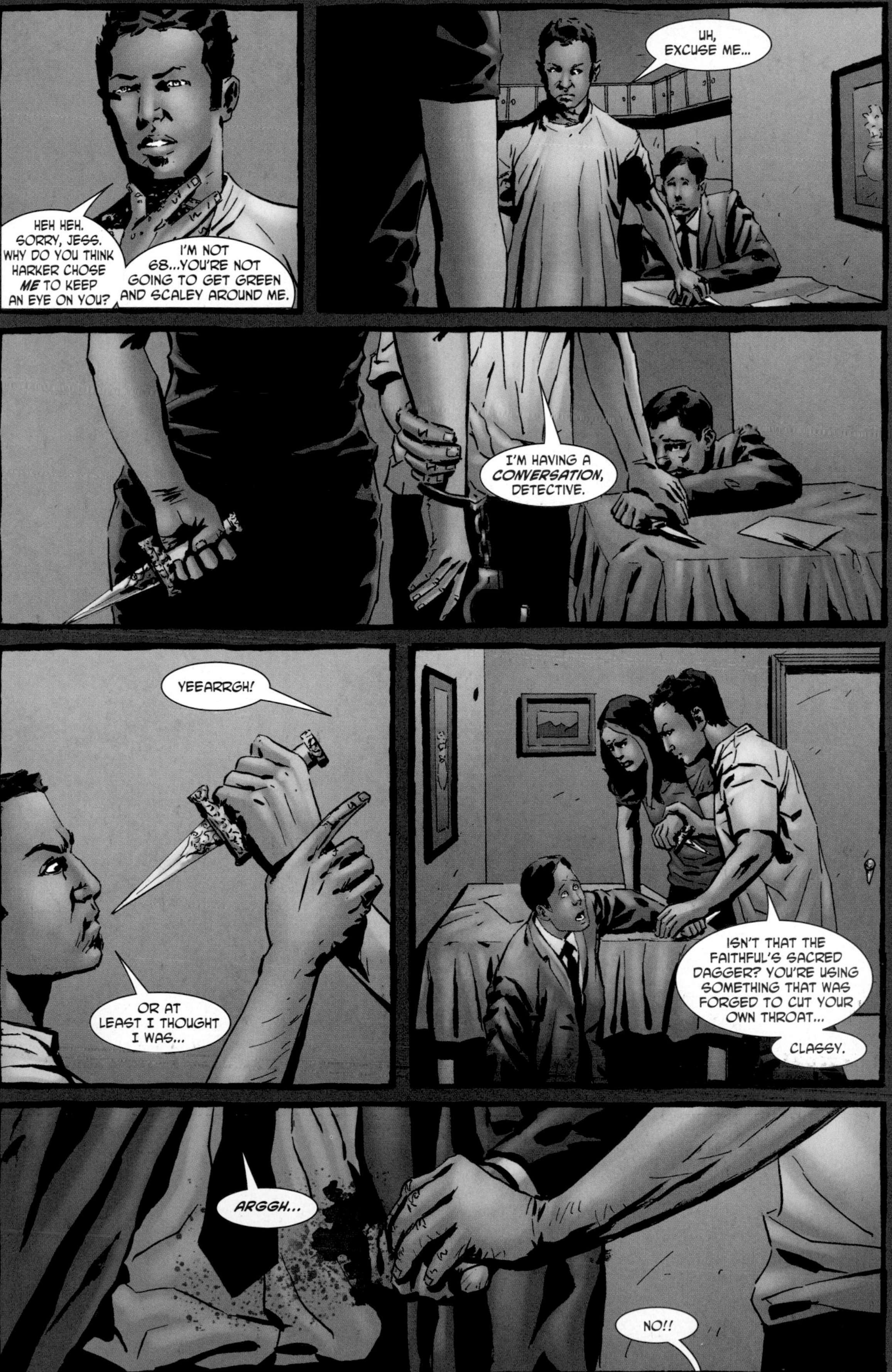
HEH HEH. SORRY, JESS. WHY DO YOU THINK HARKER CHOSE *ME* TO KEEP AN EYE ON YOU?
I'M NOT 68...YOU'RE NOT GOING TO GET GREEN AND SCALEY AROUND ME.
UH, EXCUSE ME...
I'M HAVING A *CONVERSATION*, DETECTIVE.
YEEARRGH!
OR AT LEAST I THOUGHT I WAS...
ISN'T THAT THE FAITHFUL'S SACRED DAGGER? YOU'RE USING SOMETHING THAT WAS FORGED TO CUT YOUR OWN THROAT...
CLASSY.
ARGGH...
NO!!

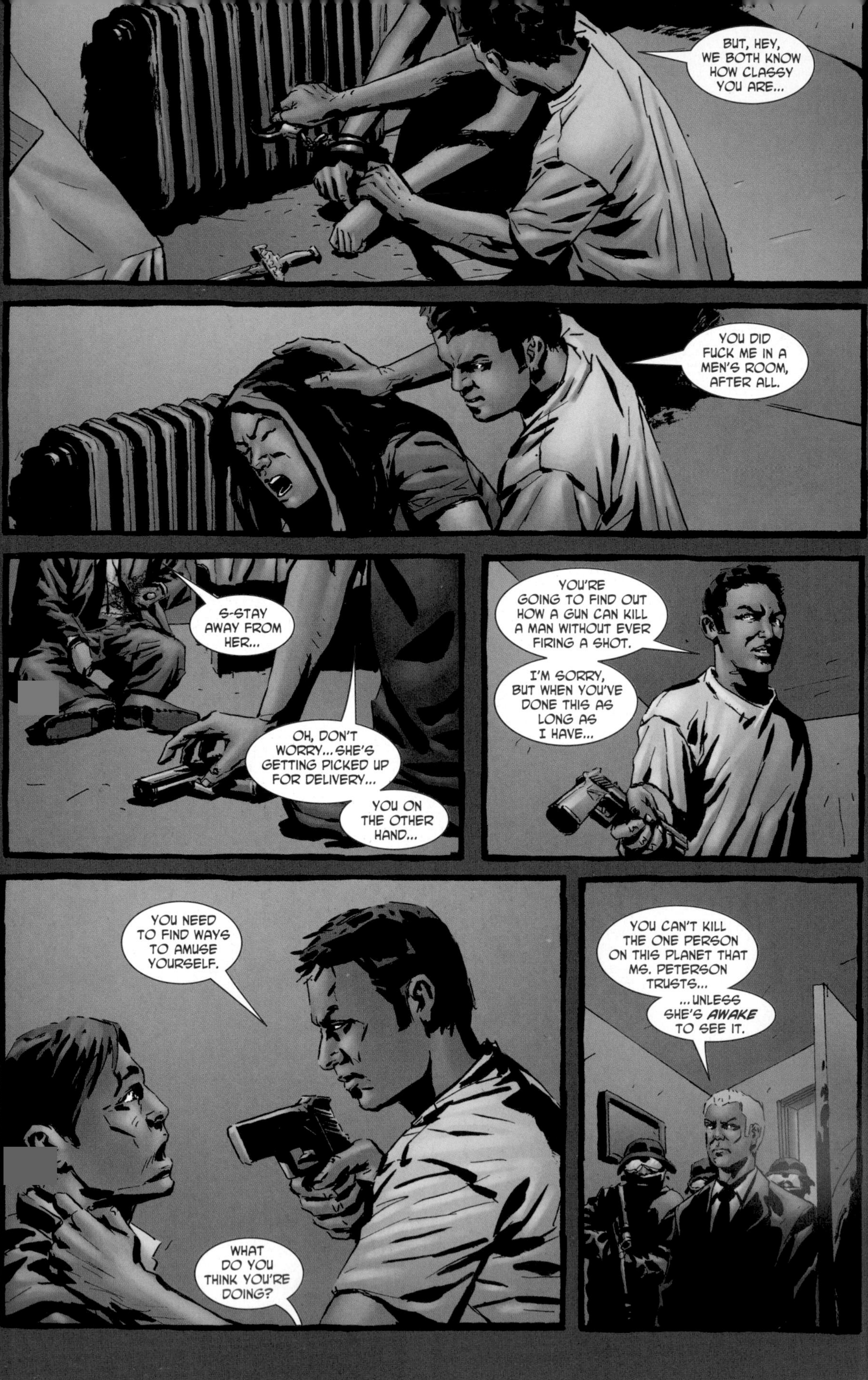
BUT, HEY, WE BOTH KNOW HOW CLASSY YOU ARE...
YOU DID FUCK ME IN A MEN'S ROOM, AFTER ALL.
S-STAY AWAY FROM HER...
OH, DON'T WORRY... SHE'S GETTING PICKED UP FOR DELIVERY...
YOU ON THE OTHER HAND...
YOU'RE GOING TO FIND OUT HOW A GUN CAN KILL A MAN WITHOUT EVER FIRING A SHOT.
I'M SORRY, BUT WHEN YOU'VE DONE THIS AS LONG AS I HAVE...
YOU NEED TO FIND WAYS TO AMUSE YOURSELF.
WHAT DO YOU THINK YOU'RE DOING?
YOU CAN'T KILL THE ONE PERSON ON THIS PLANET THAT MS. PETERSON TRUSTS...
...UNLESS SHE'S *AWAKE* TO SEE IT.

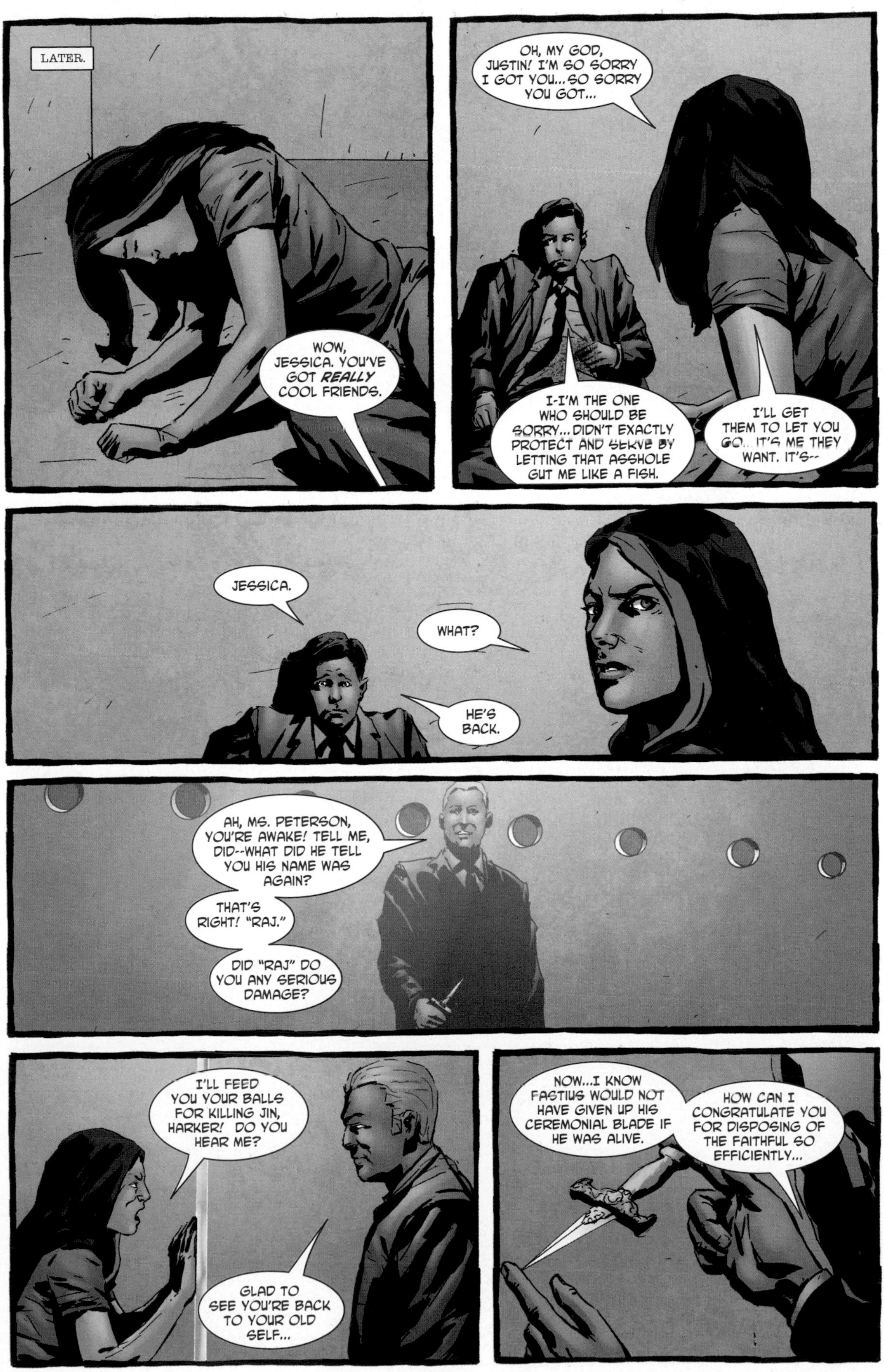
LATER.
WOW, JESSICA. YOU'VE GOT *REALLY* COOL FRIENDS.
OH, MY GOD, JUSTIN! I'M SO SORRY I GOT YOU...SO SORRY YOU GOT...
I-I'M THE ONE WHO SHOULD BE SORRY...DIDN'T EXACTLY PROTECT AND SERVE BY LETTING THAT ASSHOLE GUT ME LIKE A FISH.
I'LL GET THEM TO LET YOU GO... IT'S ME THEY WANT. IT'S--
JESSICA.
WHAT?
HE'S BACK.
AH, MS. PETERSON, YOU'RE AWAKE! TELL ME, DID--WHAT DID HE TELL YOU HIS NAME WAS AGAIN?
THAT'S RIGHT! "RAJ."
DID "RAJ" DO YOU ANY SERIOUS DAMAGE?
I'LL FEED YOU YOUR BALLS FOR KILLING JIN, HARKER! DO YOU HEAR ME?
GLAD TO SEE YOU'RE BACK TO YOUR OLD SELF...
NOW...I KNOW FASTIUS WOULD NOT HAVE GIVEN UP HIS CEREMONIAL BLADE IF HE WAS ALIVE.
HOW CAN I CONGRATULATE YOU FOR DISPOSING OF THE FAITHFUL SO EFFICIENTLY...

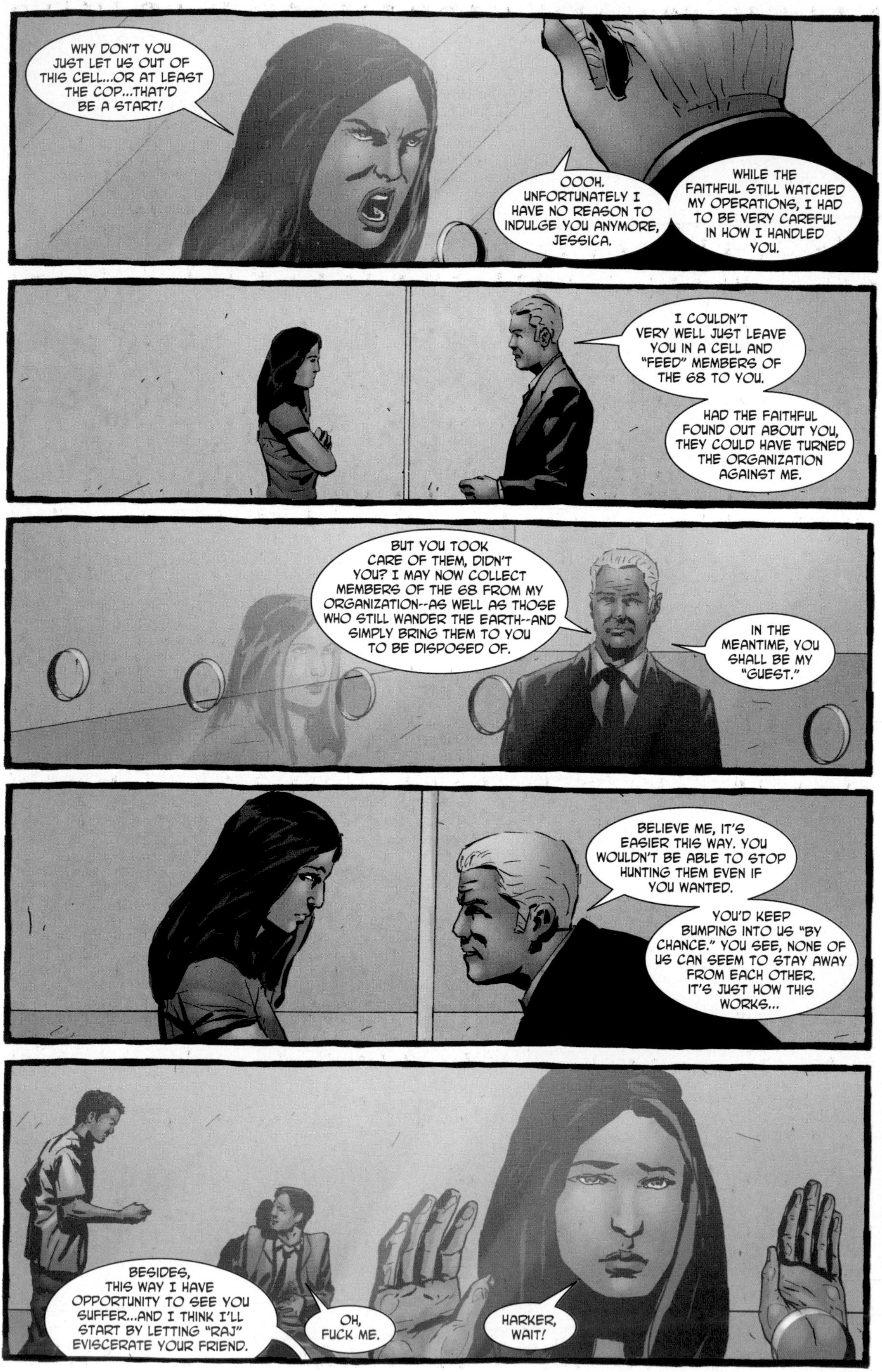

WHY DON'T YOU JUST LET US OUT OF THIS CELL...OR AT LEAST THE COP...THAT'D BE A START!
OOOH. UNFORTUNATELY I HAVE NO REASON TO INDULGE YOU ANYMORE, JESSICA.
WHILE THE FAITHFUL STILL WATCHED MY OPERATIONS, I HAD TO BE VERY CAREFUL IN HOW I HANDLED YOU.
I COULDN'T VERY WELL JUST LEAVE YOU IN A CELL AND "FEED" MEMBERS OF THE 68 TO YOU.
HAD THE FAITHFUL FOUND OUT ABOUT YOU, THEY COULD HAVE TURNED THE ORGANIZATION AGAINST ME.
BUT YOU TOOK CARE OF THEM, DIDN'T YOU? I MAY NOW COLLECT MEMBERS OF THE 68 FROM MY ORGANIZATION--AS WELL AS THOSE WHO STILL WANDER THE EARTH--AND SIMPLY BRING THEM TO YOU TO BE DISPOSED OF.
IN THE MEANTIME, YOU SHALL BE MY "GUEST."
BELIEVE ME, IT'S EASIER THIS WAY. YOU WOULDN'T BE ABLE TO STOP HUNTING THEM EVEN IF YOU WANTED.
YOU'D KEEP BUMPING INTO US "BY CHANCE." YOU SEE, NONE OF US CAN SEEM TO STAY AWAY FROM EACH OTHER. IT'S JUST HOW THIS WORKS...
BESIDES, THIS WAY I HAVE OPPORTUNITY TO SEE YOU SUFFER...AND I THINK I'LL START BY LETTING "RAJ" EVISCERATE YOUR FRIEND.
OH, FUCK ME.
HARKER, WAIT!

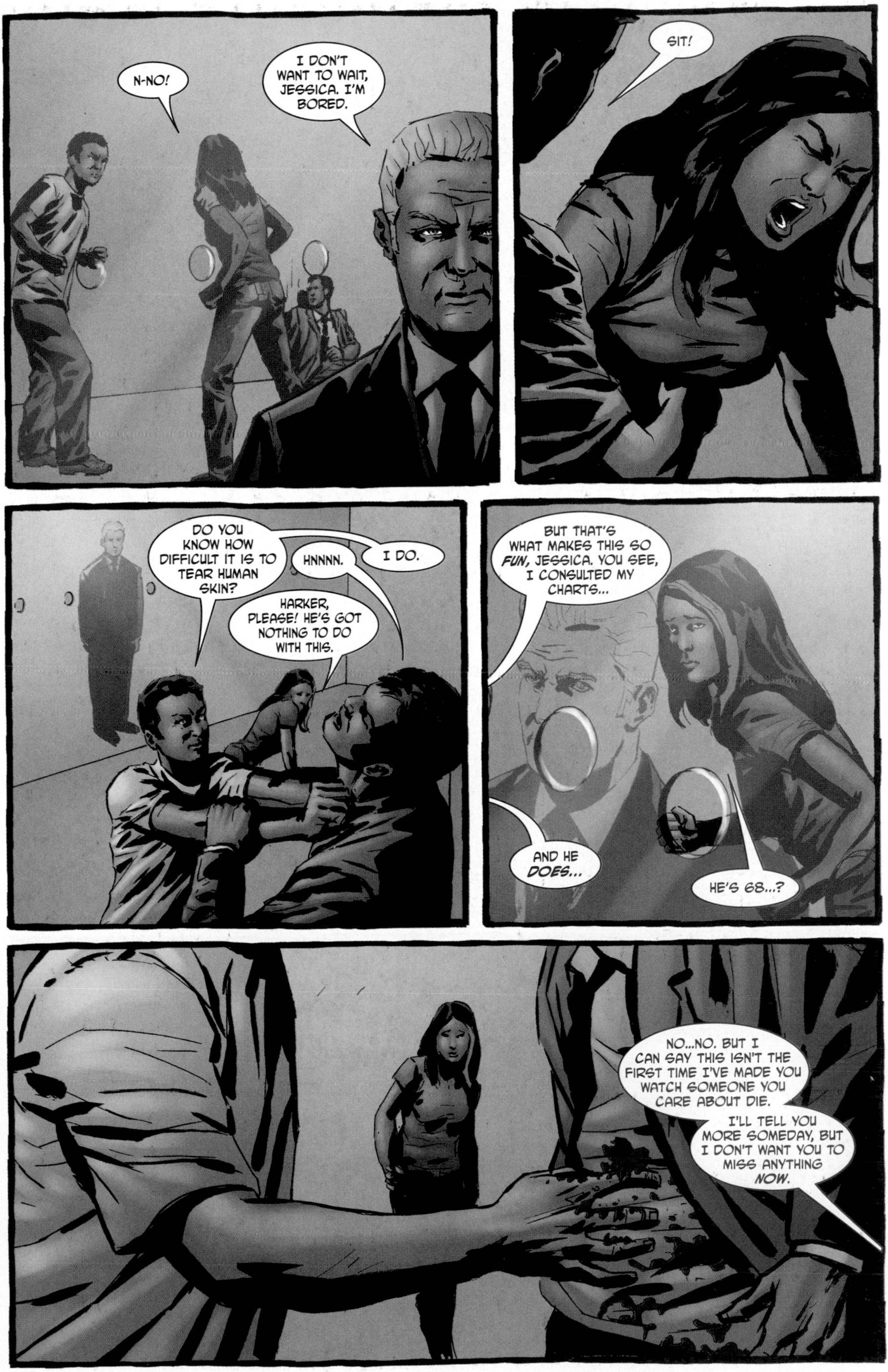
N-NO!
I DON'T WANT TO WAIT, JESSICA. I'M BORED.
SIT!
DO YOU KNOW HOW DIFFICULT IT IS TO TEAR HUMAN SKIN?
I DO.
HNNNN.
HARKER, PLEASE! HE'S GOT NOTHING TO DO WITH THIS.
BUT THAT'S WHAT MAKES THIS SO *FUN*, JESSICA. YOU SEE, I CONSULTED MY CHARTS...
AND HE *DOES*...
HE'S 68...?
NO...NO. BUT I CAN SAY THIS ISN'T THE FIRST TIME I'VE MADE YOU WATCH SOMEONE YOU CARE ABOUT DIE.
I'LL TELL YOU MORE SOMEDAY, BUT I DON'T WANT YOU TO MISS ANYTHING *NOW*.

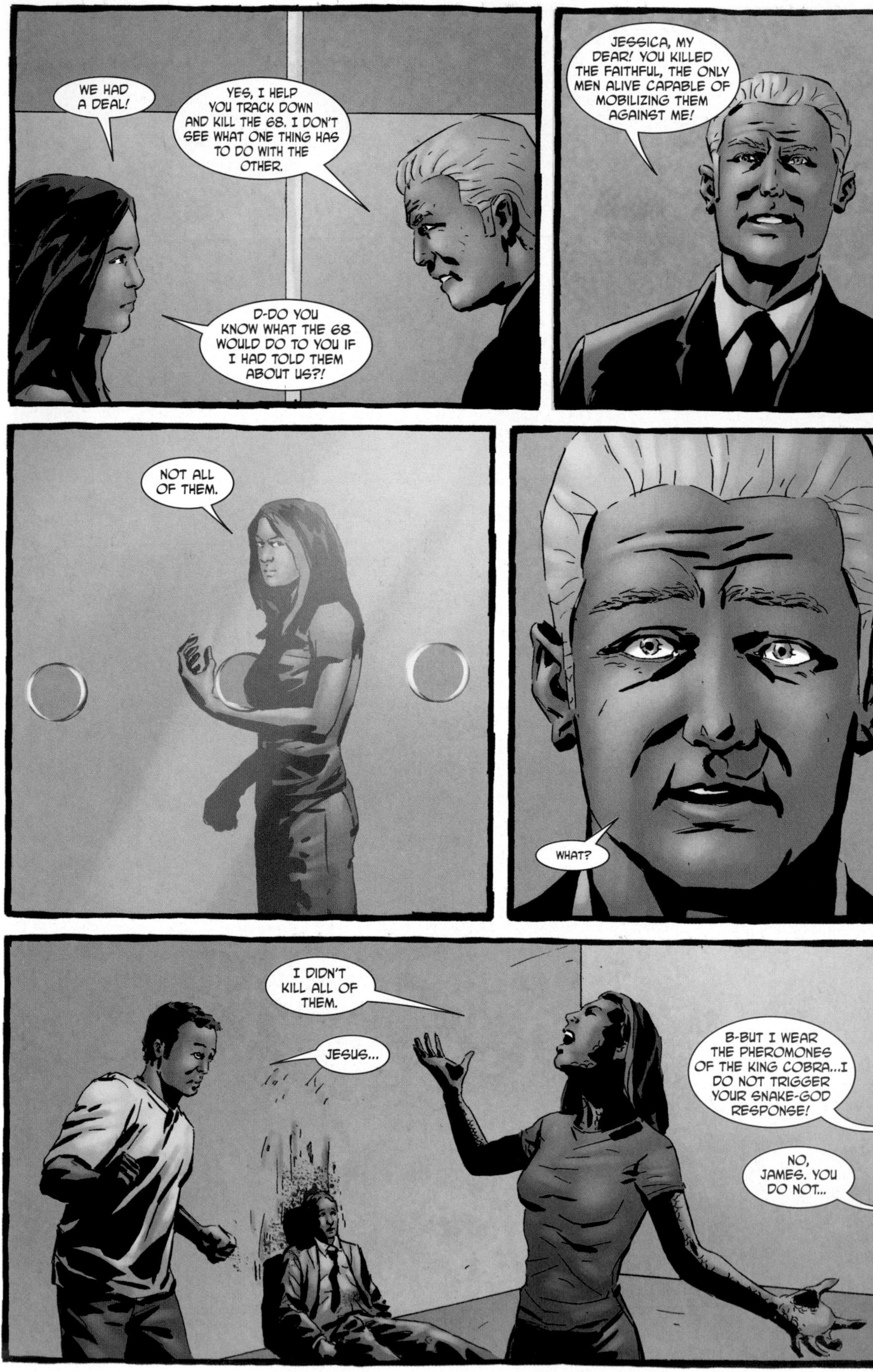
WE HAD A DEAL!
YES, I HELP YOU TRACK DOWN AND KILL THE 68. I DON'T SEE WHAT ONE THING HAS TO DO WITH THE OTHER.
D-DO YOU KNOW WHAT THE 68 WOULD DO TO YOU IF I HAD TOLD THEM ABOUT US?!
JESSICA, MY DEAR! YOU KILLED THE FAITHFUL, THE ONLY MEN ALIVE CAPABLE OF MOBILIZING THEM AGAINST ME!
NOT ALL OF THEM.
WHAT?
I DIDN'T KILL ALL OF THEM.
JESUS...
B-BUT I WEAR THE PHEROMONES OF THE KING COBRA...I DO NOT TRIGGER YOUR SNAKE-GOD RESPONSE!
NO, JAMES. YOU DO NOT...

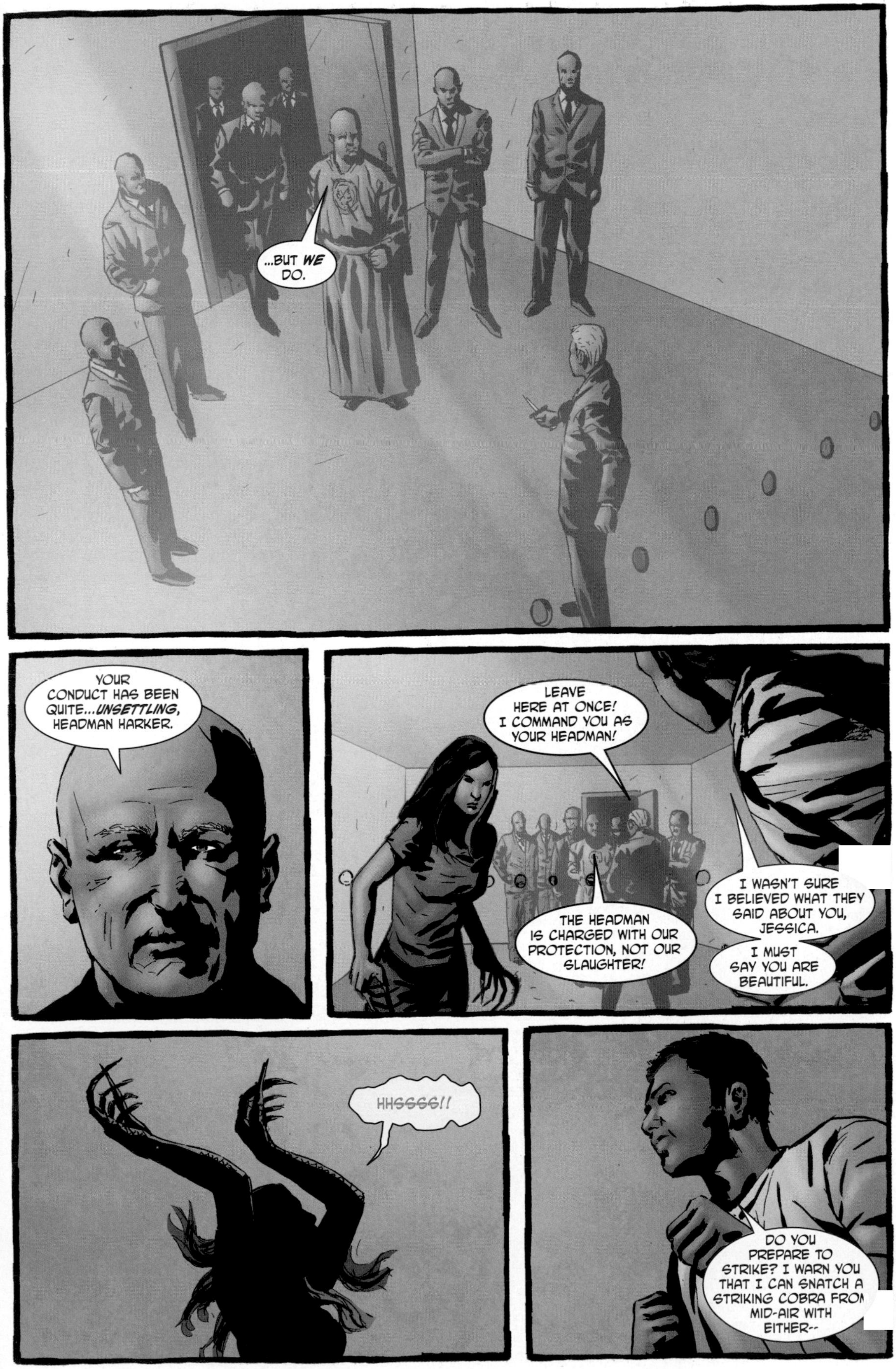
...BUT WE DO.
YOUR CONDUCT HAS BEEN QUITE...UNSETTLING, HEADMAN HARKER.
LEAVE HERE AT ONCE! I COMMAND YOU AS YOUR HEADMAN!
THE HEADMAN IS CHARGED WITH OUR PROTECTION, NOT OUR SLAUGHTER!
I WASN'T SURE I BELIEVED WHAT THEY SAID ABOUT YOU, JESSICA.
I MUST SAY YOU ARE BEAUTIFUL.
HHSSSS!!
DO YOU PREPARE TO STRIKE? I WARN YOU THAT I CAN SNATCH A STRIKING COBRA FROM MID-AIR WITH EITHER--

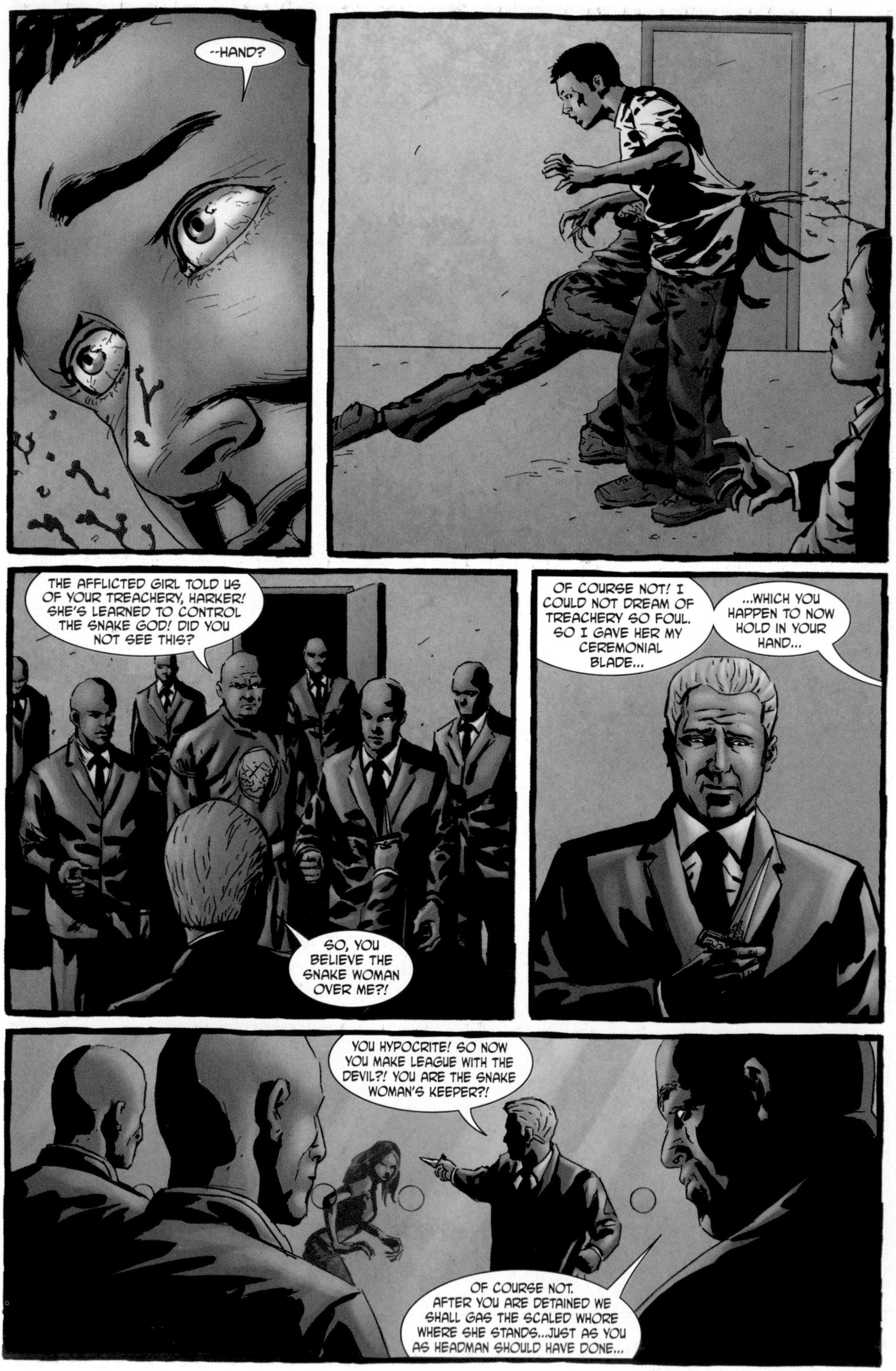
--HAND?
THE AFFLICTED GIRL TOLD US OF YOUR TREACHERY, HARKER! SHE'S LEARNED TO CONTROL THE SNAKE GOD! DID YOU NOT SEE THIS?
SO, YOU BELIEVE THE SNAKE WOMAN OVER ME?!
OF COURSE NOT! I COULD NOT DREAM OF TREACHERY SO FOUL. SO I GAVE HER MY CEREMONIAL BLADE...
...WHICH YOU HAPPEN TO NOW HOLD IN YOUR HAND...
YOU HYPOCRITE! SO NOW YOU MAKE LEAGUE WITH THE DEVIL?! YOU ARE THE SNAKE WOMAN'S KEEPER?!
OF COURSE NOT. AFTER YOU ARE DETAINED WE SHALL GAS THE SCALED WHORE WHERE SHE STANDS...JUST AS YOU AS HEADMAN SHOULD HAVE DONE...

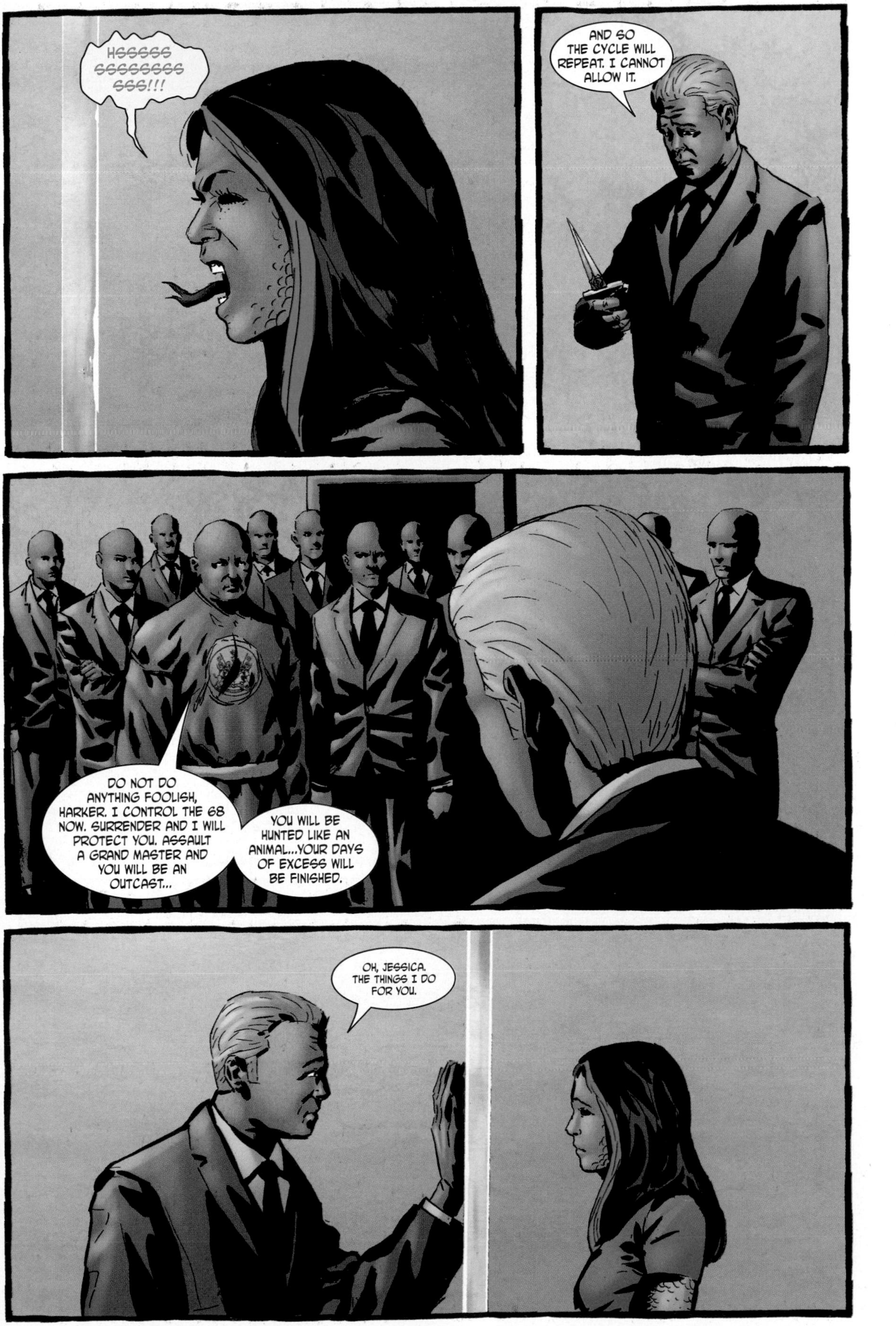
HSSSSS SSSSSSSS SSS!!!
AND SO THE CYCLE WILL REPEAT. I CANNOT ALLOW IT.
DO NOT DO ANYTHING FOOLISH, HARKER. I CONTROL THE 68 NOW. SURRENDER AND I WILL PROTECT YOU. ASSAULT A GRAND MASTER AND YOU WILL BE AN OUTCAST...
YOU WILL BE HUNTED LIKE AN ANIMAL...YOUR DAYS OF EXCESS WILL BE FINISHED.
OH, JESSICA. THE THINGS I DO FOR YOU.

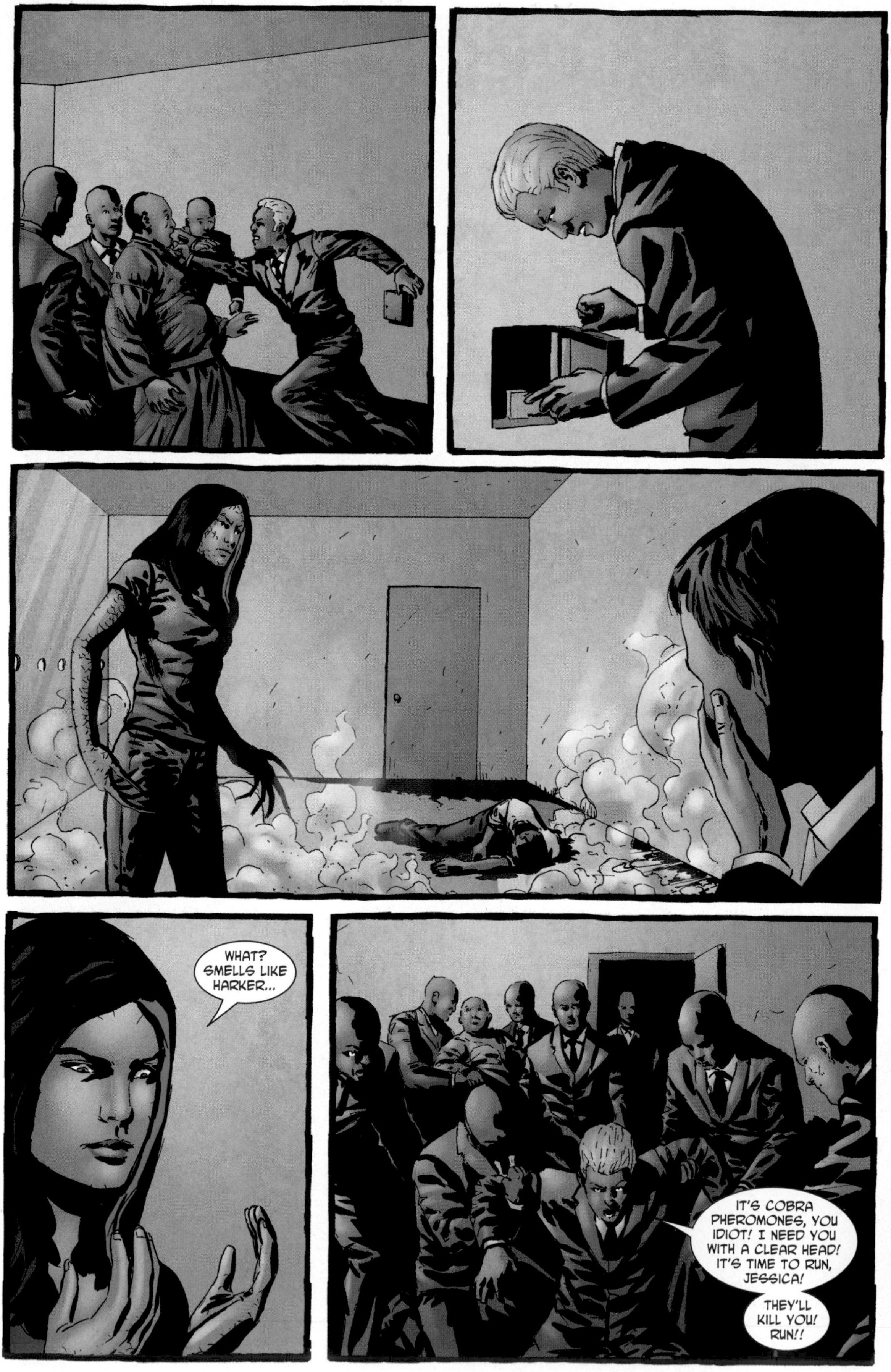
WHAT? SMELLS LIKE HARKER...
IT'S COBRA PHEROMONES, YOU IDIOT! I NEED YOU WITH A CLEAR HEAD! IT'S TIME TO RUN, JESSICA!
THEY'LL KILL YOU! RUN!!

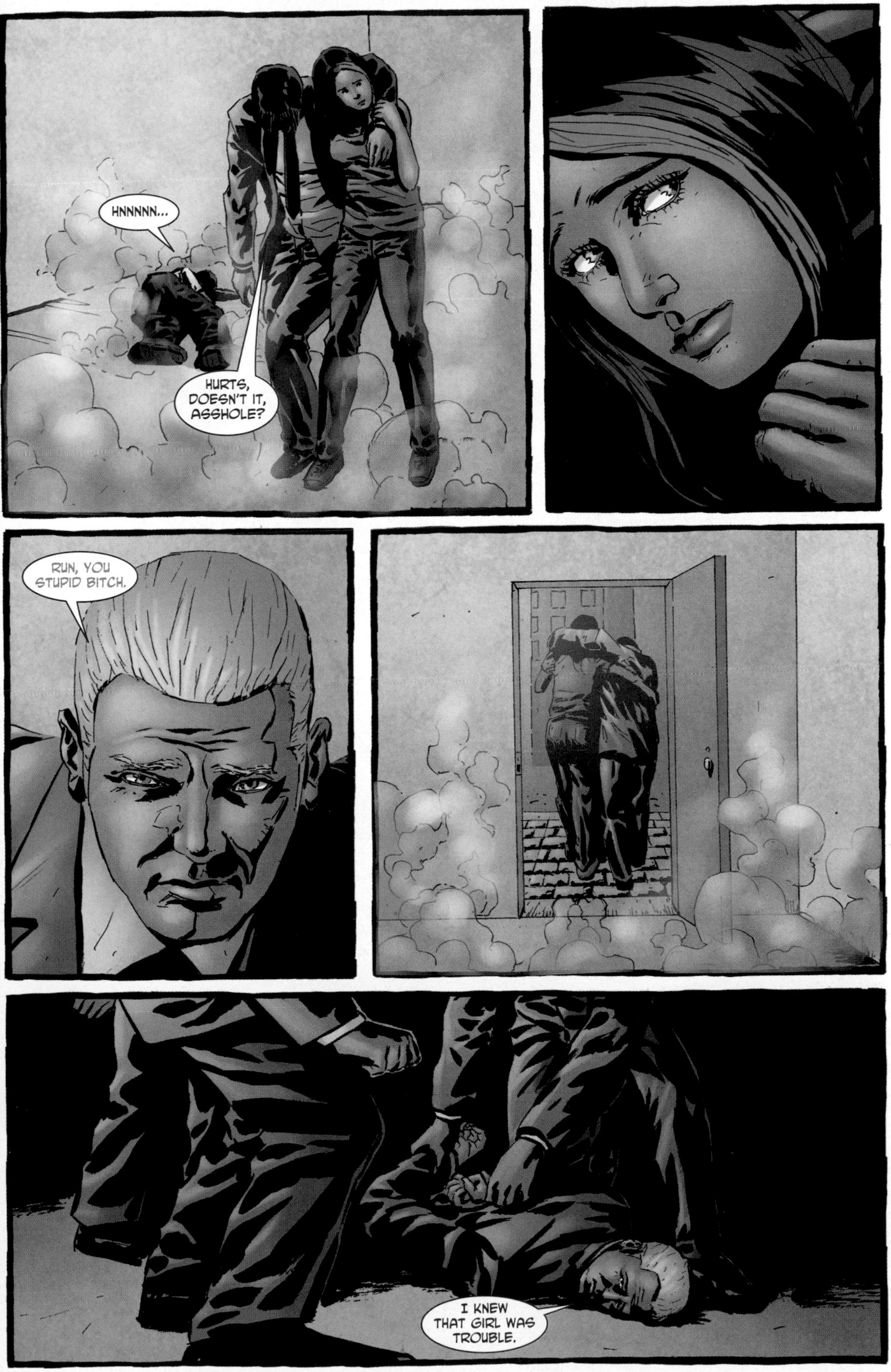
HNNNNN...
HURTS, DOESN'T IT, ASSHOLE?
RUN, YOU STUPID BITCH.
I KNEW THAT GIRL WAS TROUBLE.

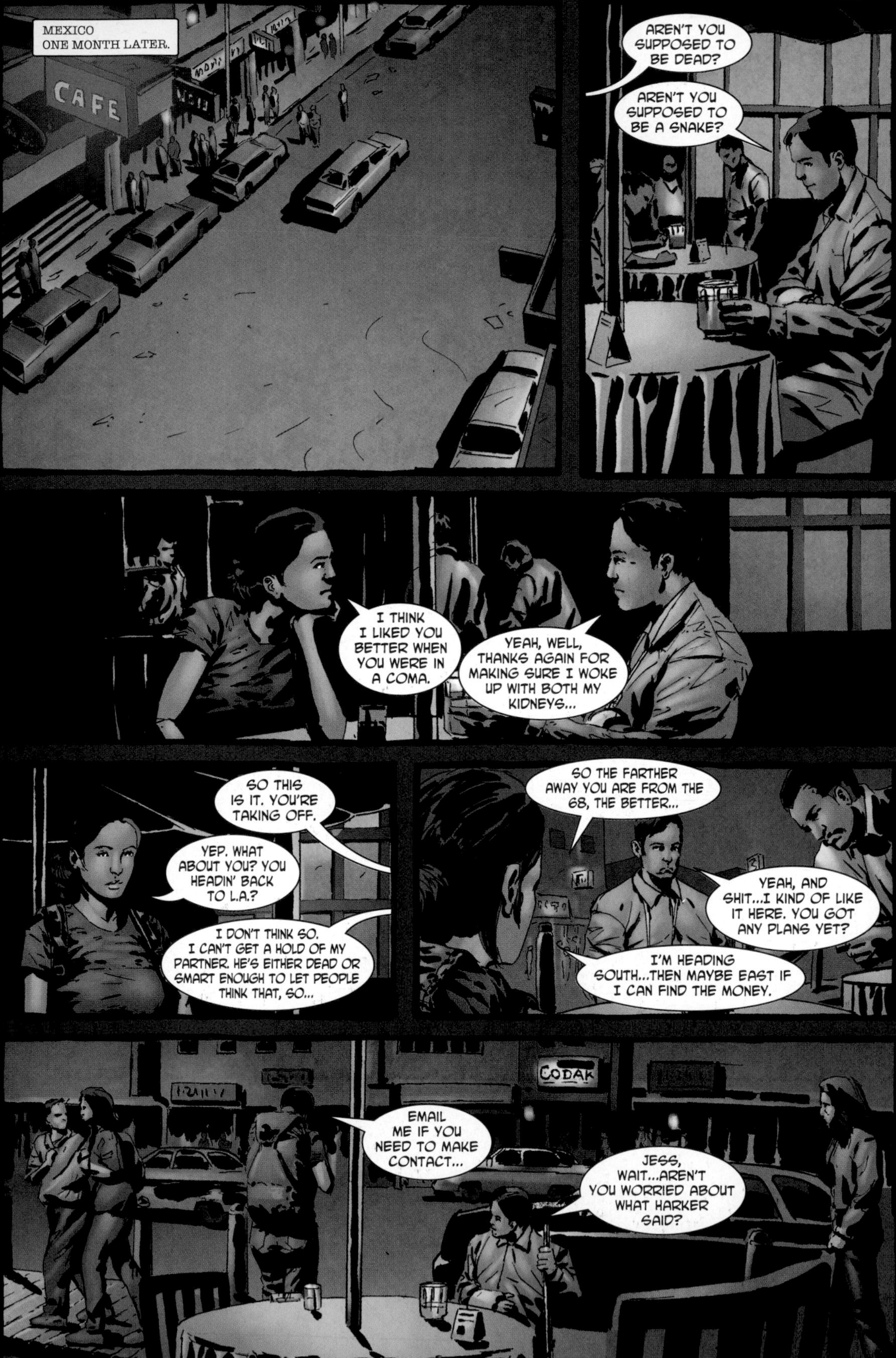
MEXICO
ONE MONTH LATER.
CAFE
AREN'T YOU SUPPOSED TO BE DEAD?
AREN'T YOU SUPPOSED TO BE A SNAKE?
I THINK I LIKED YOU BETTER WHEN YOU WERE IN A COMA.
YEAH, WELL, THANKS AGAIN FOR MAKING SURE I WOKE UP WITH BOTH MY KIDNEYS...
SO THIS IS IT. YOU'RE TAKING OFF.
YEP. WHAT ABOUT YOU? YOU HEADIN' BACK TO L.A.?
I DON'T THINK SO. I CAN'T GET A HOLD OF MY PARTNER. HE'S EITHER DEAD OR SMART ENOUGH TO LET PEOPLE THINK THAT, SO...
SO THE FARTHER AWAY YOU ARE FROM THE 68, THE BETTER...
YEAH, AND SHIT...I KIND OF LIKE IT HERE. YOU GOT ANY PLANS YET?
I'M HEADING SOUTH...THEN MAYBE EAST IF I CAN FIND THE MONEY.
CODAK
EMAIL ME IF YOU NEED TO MAKE CONTACT...
JESS, WAIT...AREN'T YOU WORRIED ABOUT WHAT HARKER SAID?

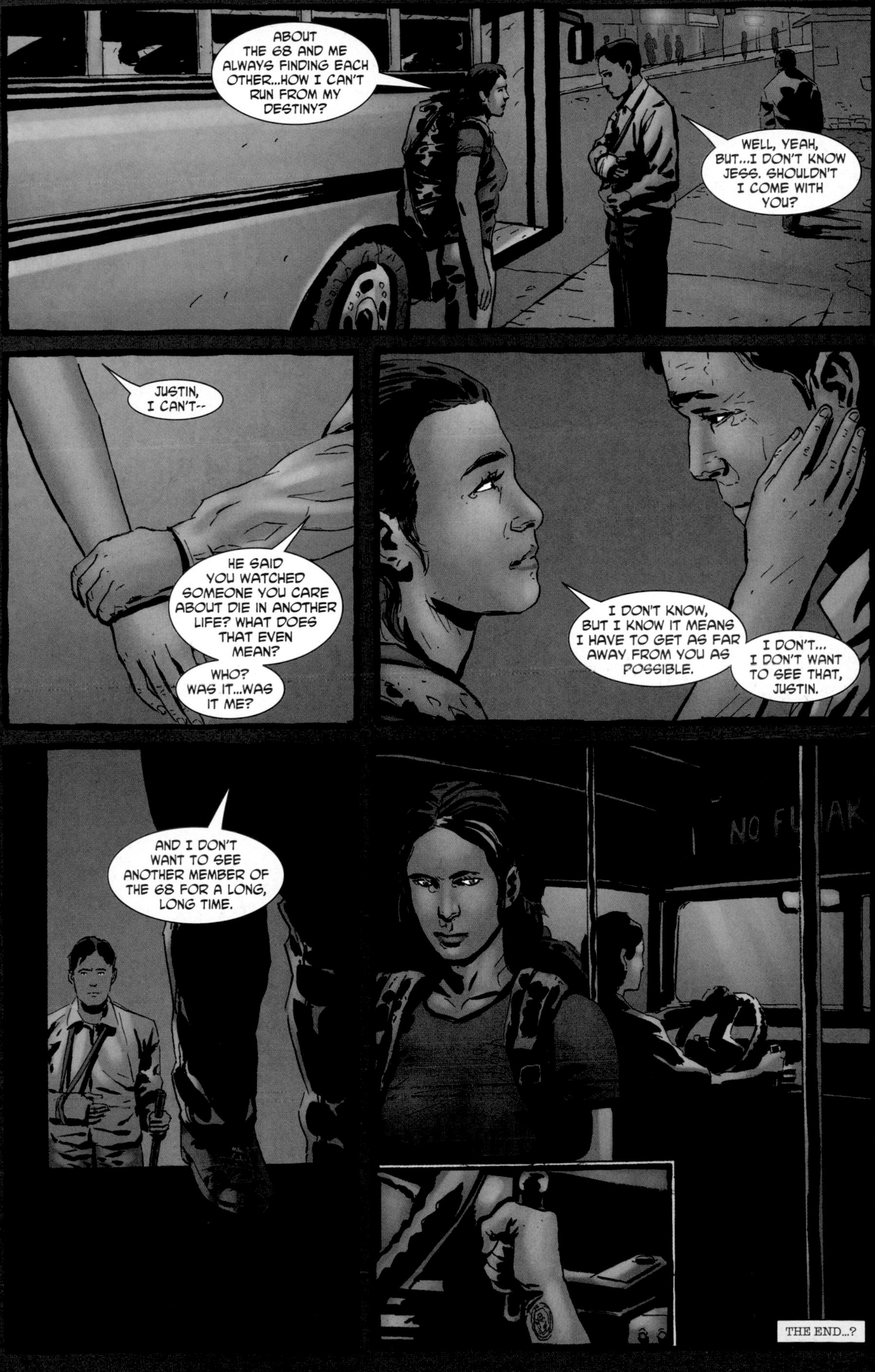
ABOUT THE 68 AND ME ALWAYS FINDING EACH OTHER...HOW I CAN'T RUN FROM MY DESTINY?
WELL, YEAH, BUT...I DON'T KNOW JESS. SHOULDN'T I COME WITH YOU?
JUSTIN, I CAN'T--
HE SAID YOU WATCHED SOMEONE YOU CARE ABOUT DIE IN ANOTHER LIFE? WHAT DOES THAT EVEN MEAN?
WHO? WAS IT...WAS IT ME?
I DON'T KNOW, BUT I KNOW IT MEANS I HAVE TO GET AS FAR AWAY FROM YOU AS POSSIBLE.
I DON'T... I DON'T WANT TO SEE THAT, JUSTIN.
AND I DON'T WANT TO SEE ANOTHER MEMBER OF THE 68 FOR A LONG, LONG TIME.
NO F
THE END...?

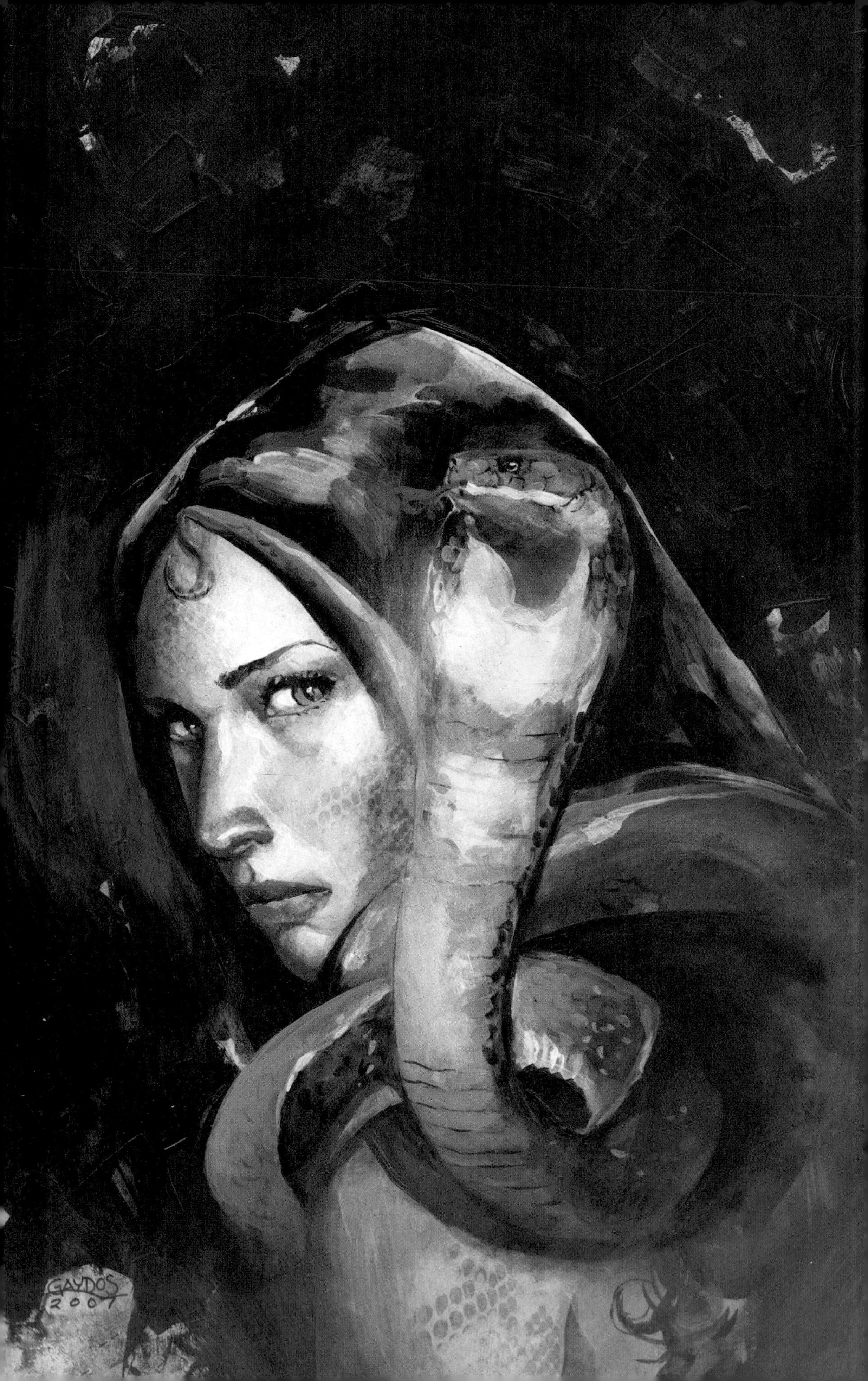
GAYDOS
2007

Los Angeles. 2006.
Jessica Peterson learns that she is
different, deadly... destined.

The story that she has become a part of, however,
is much older than she knows. In some ways, it is the
story of a Snake Goddess, enraged, seeking revenge for wrongs
perpetrated centuries ago. It is also the story of sixty-eight
greedy, prideful men, trapped in a cycle of reincarnation,
destined to be hunted by the various incarnations of the
Goddess until she successfully kills all of them
within a single lifetime.

But, in other ways, it is a story that begins
before time itself...

The Snake Woman Origin Tale

BY ZEB WELLS & MICHAEL GAYDOS

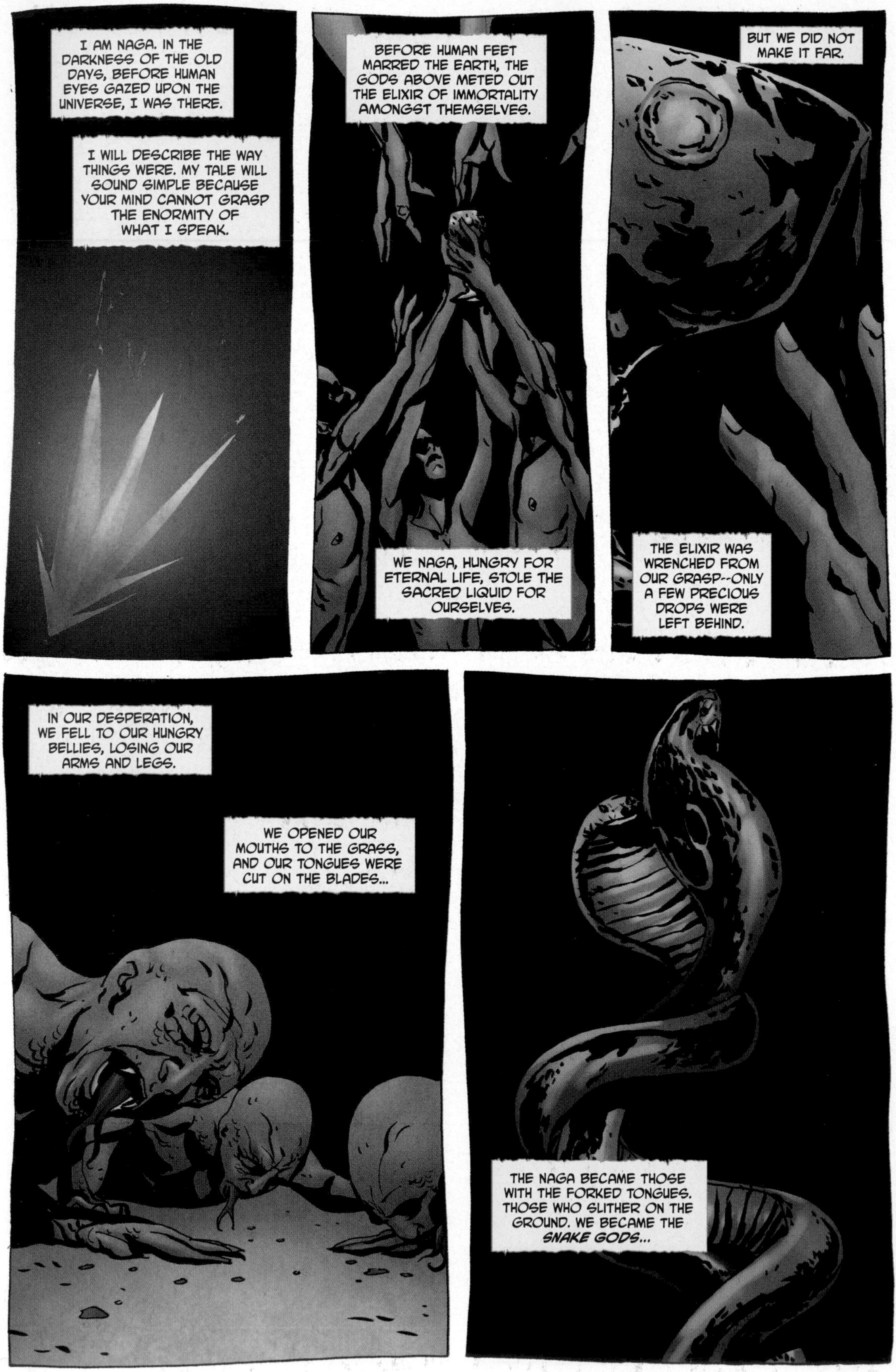
I AM NAGA. IN THE DARKNESS OF THE OLD DAYS, BEFORE HUMAN EYES GAZED UPON THE UNIVERSE, I WAS THERE.
I WILL DESCRIBE THE WAY THINGS WERE. MY TALE WILL SOUND SIMPLE BECAUSE YOUR MIND CANNOT GRASP THE ENORMITY OF WHAT I SPEAK.
BEFORE HUMAN FEET MARRED THE EARTH, THE GODS ABOVE METED OUT THE ELIXIR OF IMMORTALITY AMONGST THEMSELVES.
WE NAGA, HUNGRY FOR ETERNAL LIFE, STOLE THE SACRED LIQUID FOR OURSELVES.
BUT WE DID NOT MAKE IT FAR.
THE ELIXIR WAS WRENCHED FROM OUR GRASP--ONLY A FEW PRECIOUS DROPS WERE LEFT BEHIND.
IN OUR DESPERATION, WE FELL TO OUR HUNGRY BELLIES, LOSING OUR ARMS AND LEGS.
WE OPENED OUR MOUTHS TO THE GRASS, AND OUR TONGUES WERE CUT ON THE BLADES...
THE NAGA BECAME THOSE WITH THE FORKED TONGUES. THOSE WHO SLITHER ON THE GROUND. WE BECAME THE *SNAKE GODS*...

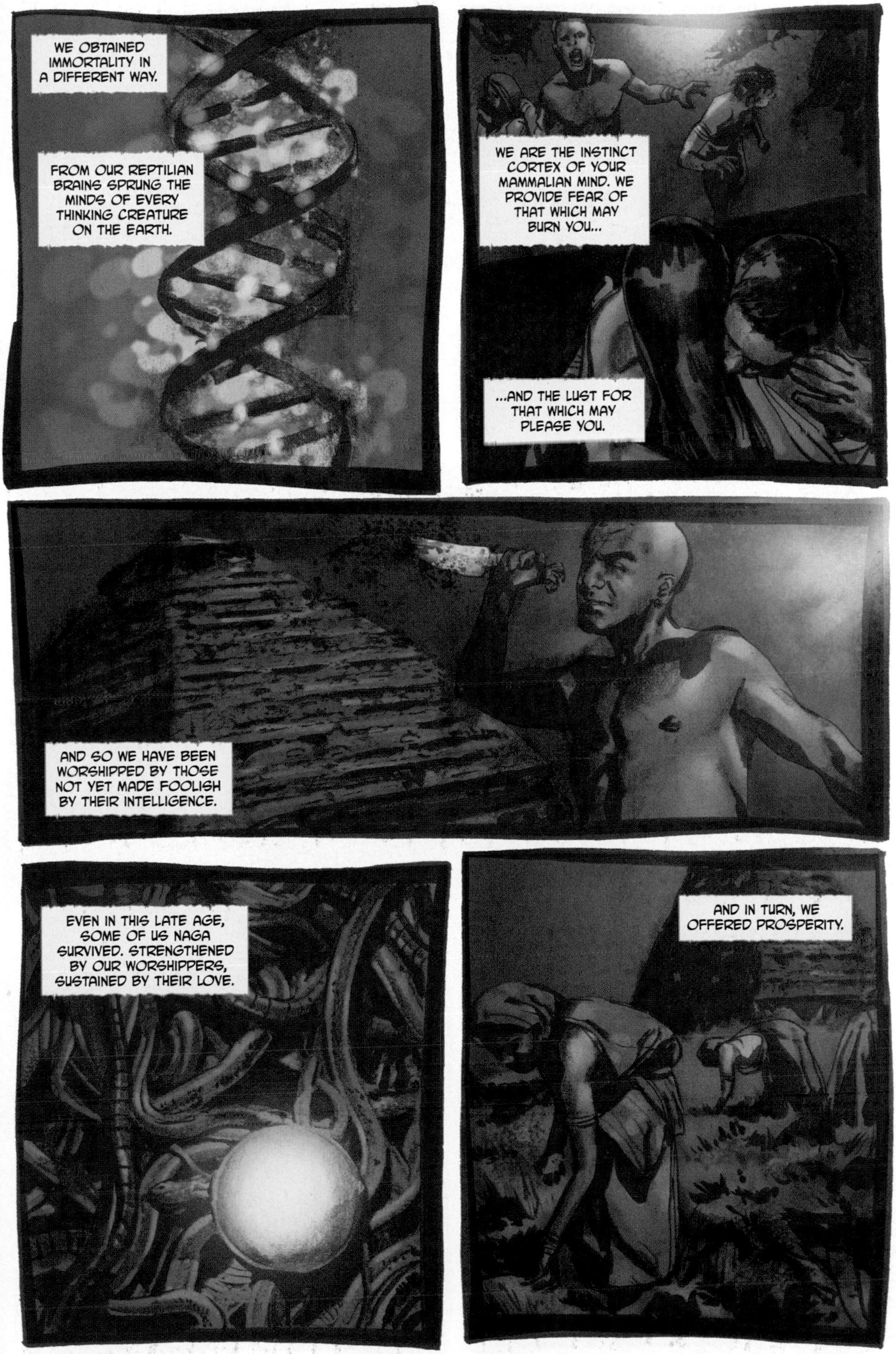
WE OBTAINED IMMORTALITY IN A DIFFERENT WAY.
FROM OUR REPTILIAN BRAINS SPRUNG THE MINDS OF EVERY THINKING CREATURE ON THE EARTH.
WE ARE THE INSTINCT CORTEX OF YOUR MAMMALIAN MIND. WE PROVIDE FEAR OF THAT WHICH MAY BURN YOU...
...AND THE LUST FOR THAT WHICH MAY PLEASE YOU.
AND SO WE HAVE BEEN WORSHIPPED BY THOSE NOT YET MADE FOOLISH BY THEIR INTELLIGENCE.
EVEN IN THIS LATE AGE, SOME OF US NAGA SURVIVED. STRENGTHENED BY OUR WORSHIPPERS, SUSTAINED BY THEIR LOVE.
AND IN TURN, WE OFFERED PROSPERITY.

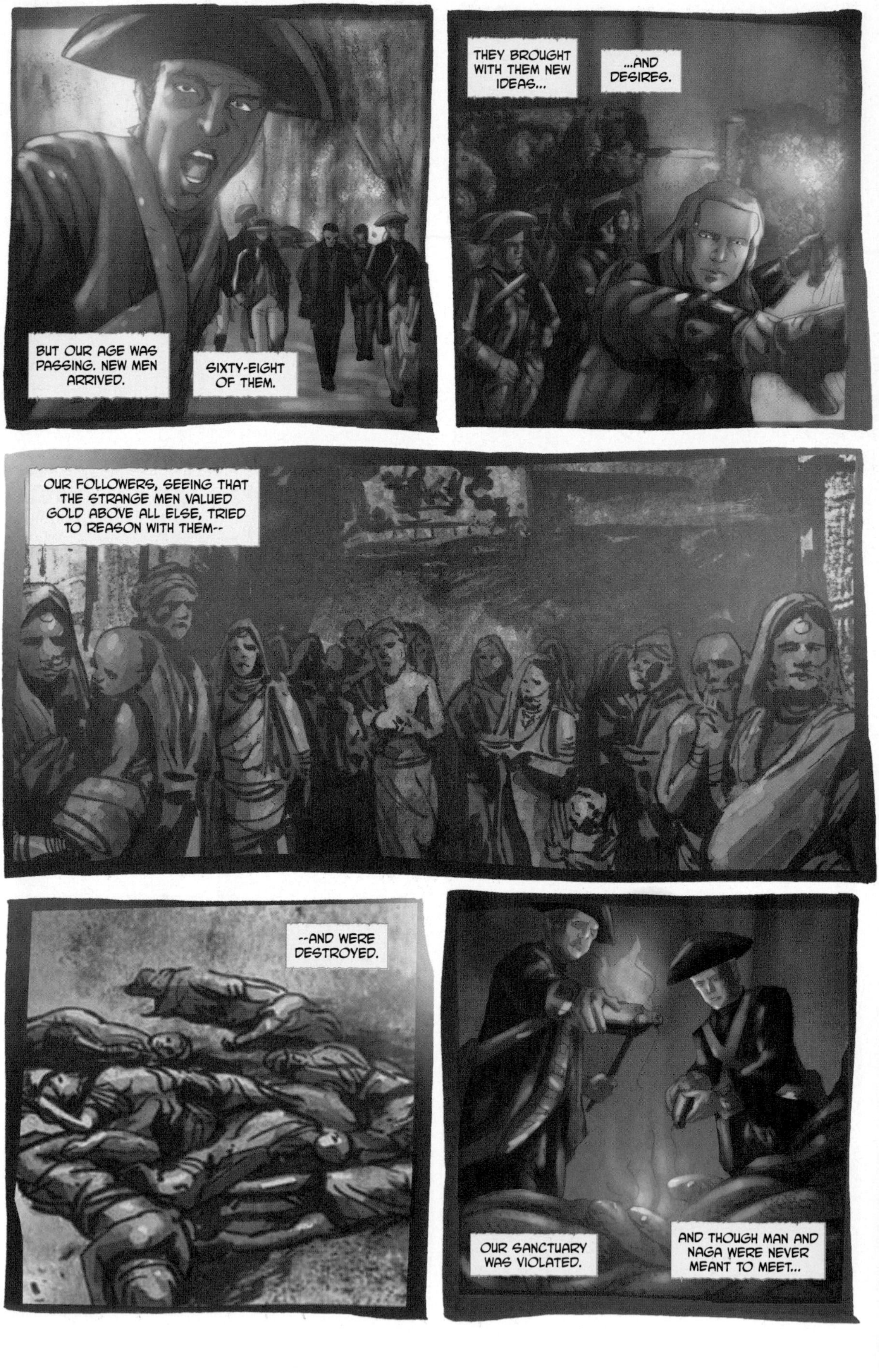
BUT OUR AGE WAS PASSING. NEW MEN ARRIVED.
SIXTY-EIGHT OF THEM.
THEY BROUGHT WITH THEM NEW IDEAS...
...AND DESIRES.
OUR FOLLOWERS, SEEING THAT THE STRANGE MEN VALUED GOLD ABOVE ALL ELSE, TRIED TO REASON WITH THEM--
--AND WERE DESTROYED.
OUR SANCTUARY WAS VIOLATED.
AND THOUGH MAN AND NAGA WERE NEVER MEANT TO MEET...

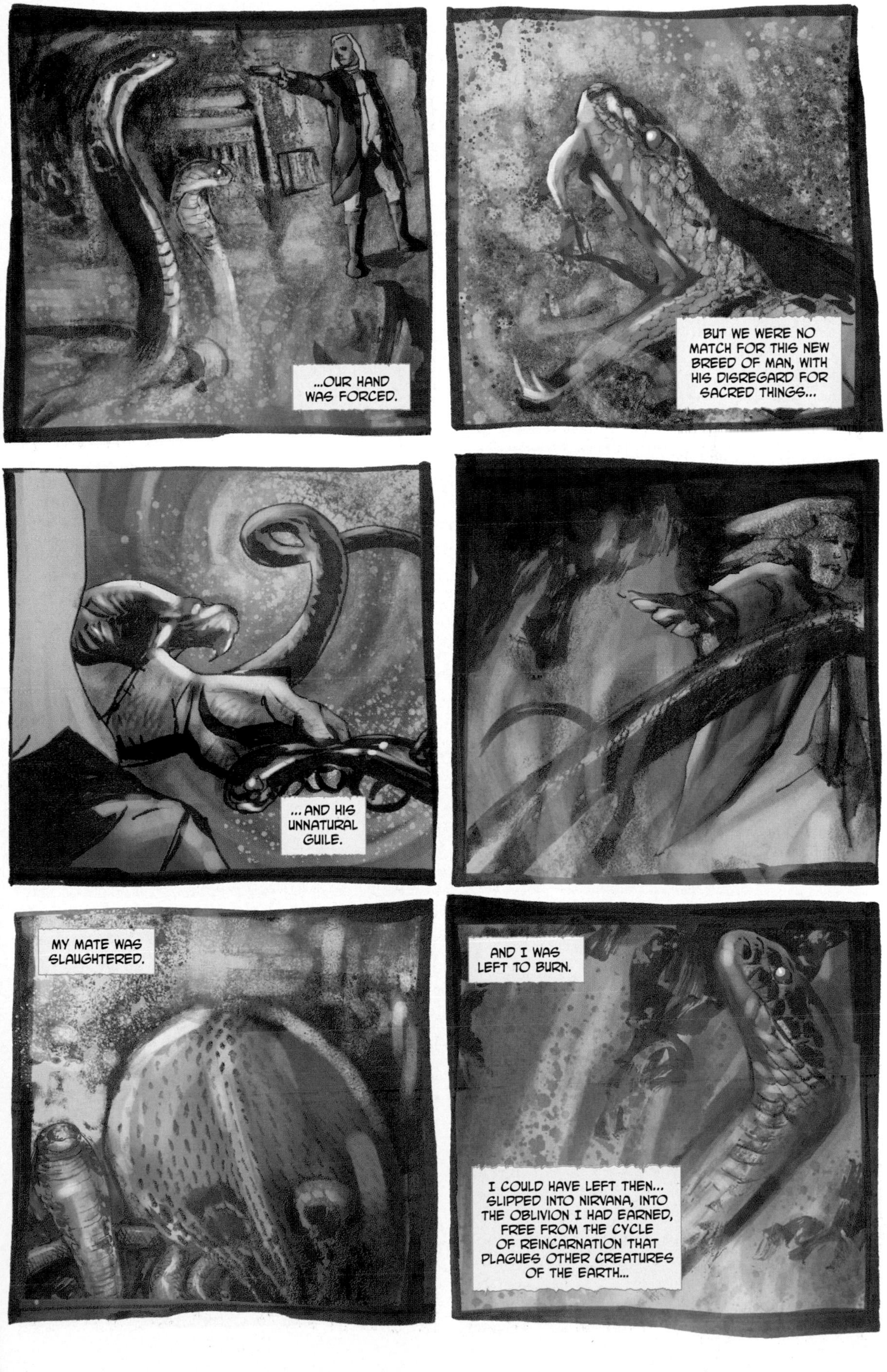
...OUR HAND WAS FORCED.
BUT WE WERE NO MATCH FOR THIS NEW BREED OF MAN, WITH HIS DISREGARD FOR SACRED THINGS...
...AND HIS UNNATURAL GUILE.
MY MATE WAS SLAUGHTERED.
AND I WAS LEFT TO BURN.
I COULD HAVE LEFT THEN... SLIPPED INTO NIRVANA, INTO THE OBLIVION I HAD EARNED, FREE FROM THE CYCLE OF REINCARNATION THAT PLAGUES OTHER CREATURES OF THE EARTH...

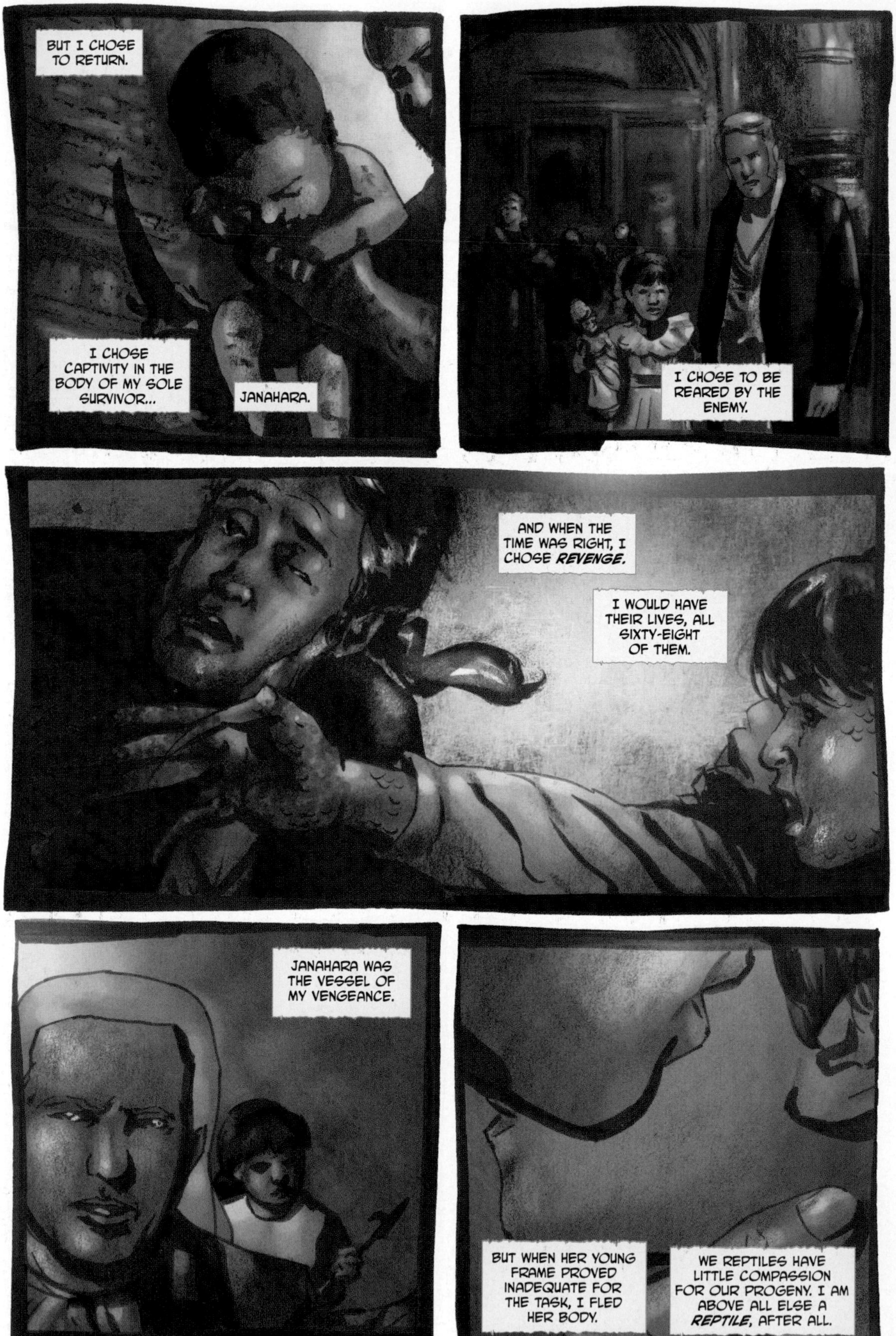

BUT I CHOSE TO RETURN.
I CHOSE CAPTIVITY IN THE BODY OF MY SOLE SURVIVOR...
JANAHARA.
I CHOSE TO BE REARED BY THE ENEMY.
AND WHEN THE TIME WAS RIGHT, I CHOSE *REVENGE.*
I WOULD HAVE THEIR LIVES, ALL SIXTY-EIGHT OF THEM.
JANAHARA WAS THE VESSEL OF MY VENGEANCE.
BUT WHEN HER YOUNG FRAME PROVED INADEQUATE FOR THE TASK, I FLED HER BODY.
WE REPTILES HAVE LITTLE COMPASSION FOR OUR PROGENY. I AM ABOVE ALL ELSE A *REPTILE*, AFTER ALL.

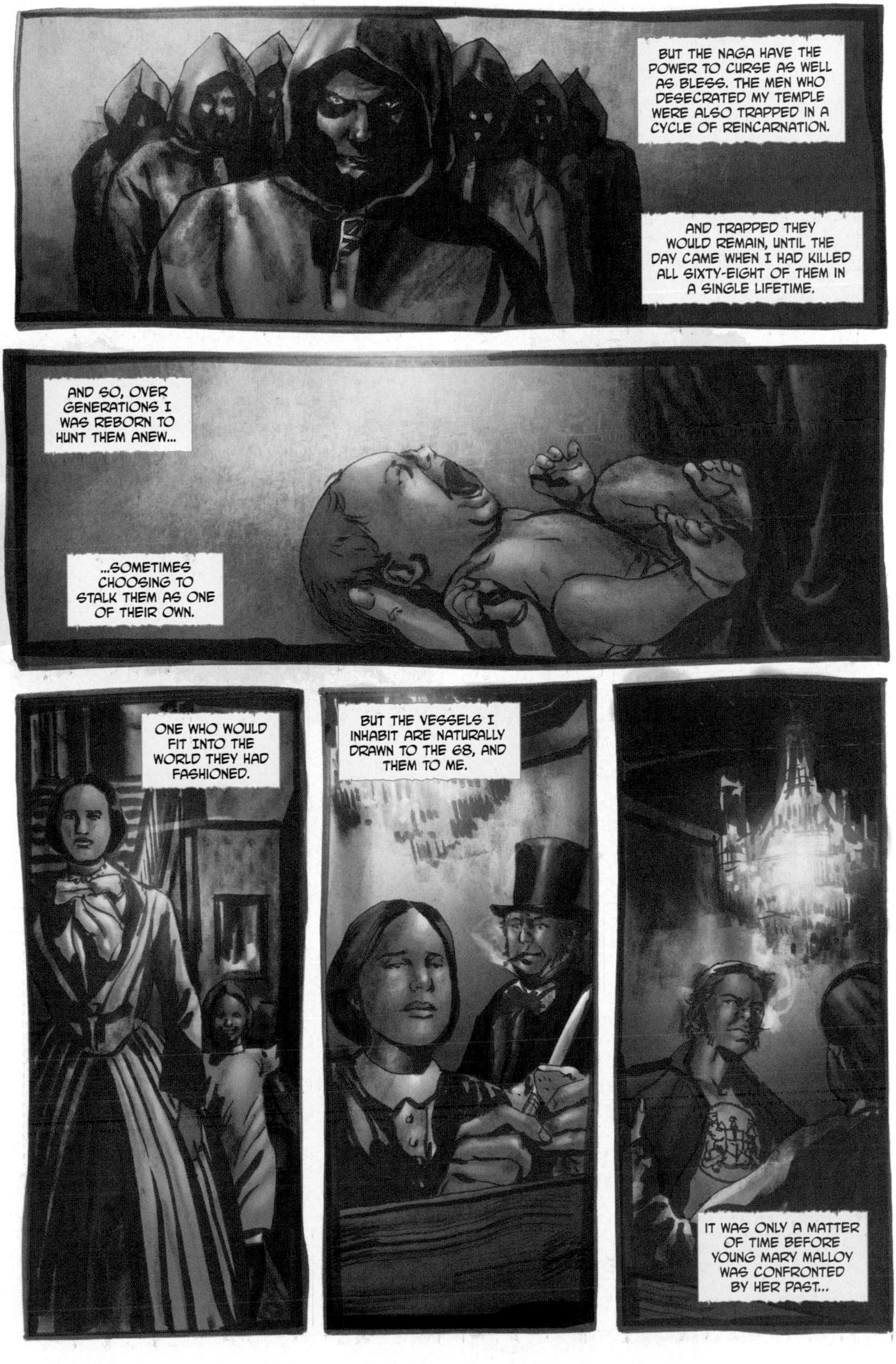
BUT THE NAGA HAVE THE POWER TO CURSE AS WELL AS BLESS. THE MEN WHO DESECRATED MY TEMPLE WERE ALSO TRAPPED IN A CYCLE OF REINCARNATION.
AND TRAPPED THEY WOULD REMAIN, UNTIL THE DAY CAME WHEN I HAD KILLED ALL SIXTY-EIGHT OF THEM IN A SINGLE LIFETIME.
AND SO, OVER GENERATIONS I WAS REBORN TO HUNT THEM ANEW...
...SOMETIMES CHOOSING TO STALK THEM AS ONE OF THEIR OWN.
ONE WHO WOULD FIT INTO THE WORLD THEY HAD FASHIONED.
BUT THE VESSELS I INHABIT ARE NATURALLY DRAWN TO THE 68, AND THEM TO ME.
IT WAS ONLY A MATTER OF TIME BEFORE YOUNG MARY MALLOY WAS CONFRONTED BY HER PAST...

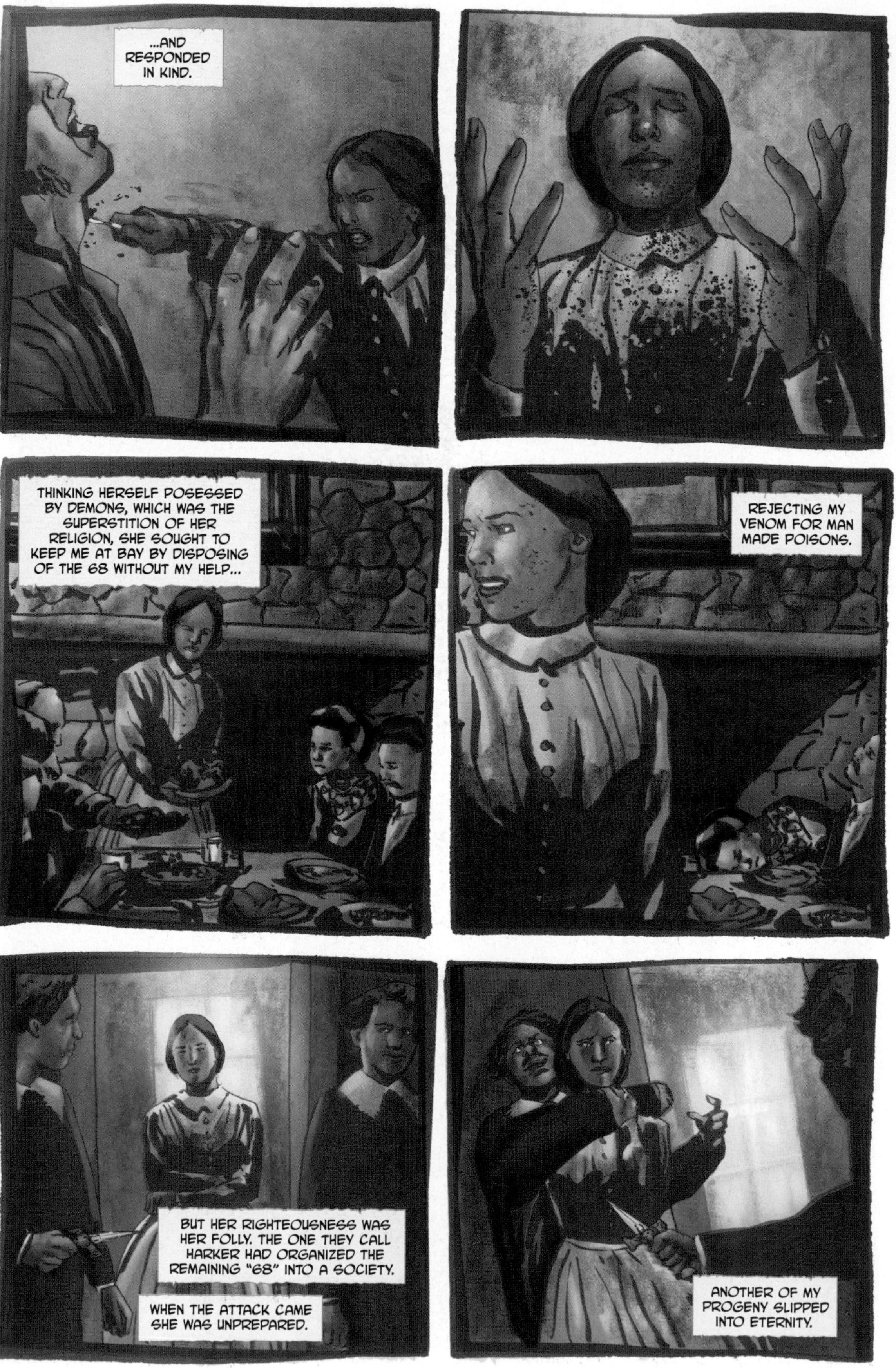
...AND RESPONDED IN KIND.
THINKING HERSELF POSESSED BY DEMONS, WHICH WAS THE SUPERSTITION OF HER RELIGION, SHE SOUGHT TO KEEP ME AT BAY BY DISPOSING OF THE 68 WITHOUT MY HELP...
REJECTING MY VENOM FOR MAN MADE POISONS.
BUT HER RIGHTEOUSNESS WAS HER FOLLY. THE ONE THEY CALL HARKER HAD ORGANIZED THE REMAINING "68" INTO A SOCIETY.
WHEN THE ATTACK CAME SHE WAS UNPREPARED.
ANOTHER OF MY PROGENY SLIPPED INTO ETERNITY.

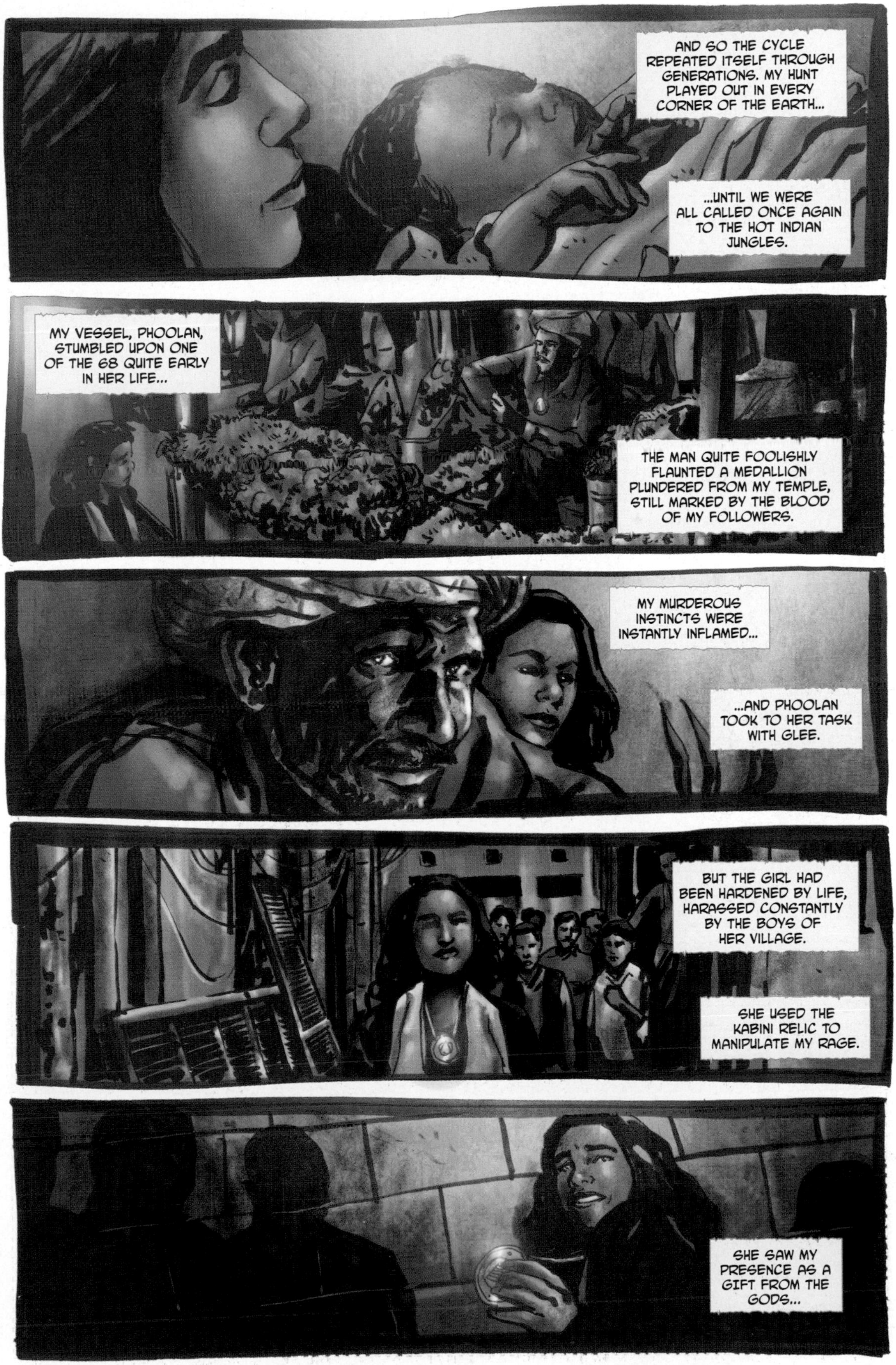
AND SO THE CYCLE REPEATED ITSELF THROUGH GENERATIONS. MY HUNT PLAYED OUT IN EVERY CORNER OF THE EARTH...
...UNTIL WE WERE ALL CALLED ONCE AGAIN TO THE HOT INDIAN JUNGLES.
MY VESSEL, PHOOLAN, STUMBLED UPON ONE OF THE 68 QUITE EARLY IN HER LIFE...
THE MAN QUITE FOOLISHLY FLAUNTED A MEDALLION PLUNDERED FROM MY TEMPLE, STILL MARKED BY THE BLOOD OF MY FOLLOWERS.
MY MURDEROUS INSTINCTS WERE INSTANTLY INFLAMED...
...AND PHOOLAN TOOK TO HER TASK WITH GLEE.
BUT THE GIRL HAD BEEN HARDENED BY LIFE, HARASSED CONSTANTLY BY THE BOYS OF HER VILLAGE.
SHE USED THE KABINI RELIC TO MANIPULATE MY RAGE.
SHE SAW MY PRESENCE AS A GIFT FROM THE GODS...

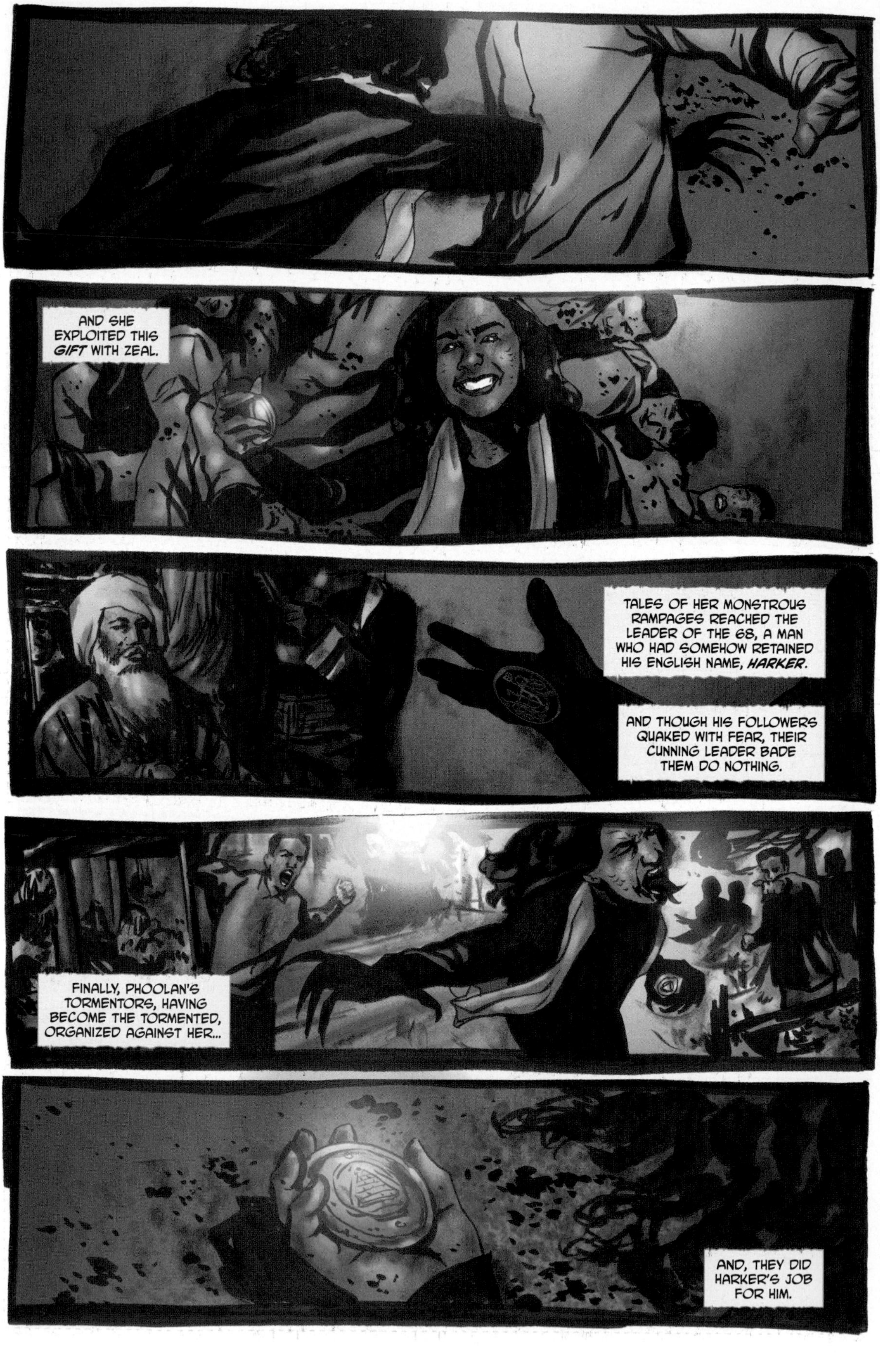
AND SHE EXPLOITED THIS GIFT WITH ZEAL.
TALES OF HER MONSTROUS RAMPAGES REACHED THE LEADER OF THE 68, A MAN WHO HAD SOMEHOW RETAINED HIS ENGLISH NAME, HARKER.
AND THOUGH HIS FOLLOWERS QUAKED WITH FEAR, THEIR CUNNING LEADER BADE THEM DO NOTHING.
FINALLY, PHOOLAN'S TORMENTORS, HAVING BECOME THE TORMENTED, ORGANIZED AGAINST HER...
AND, THEY DID HARKER'S JOB FOR HIM.

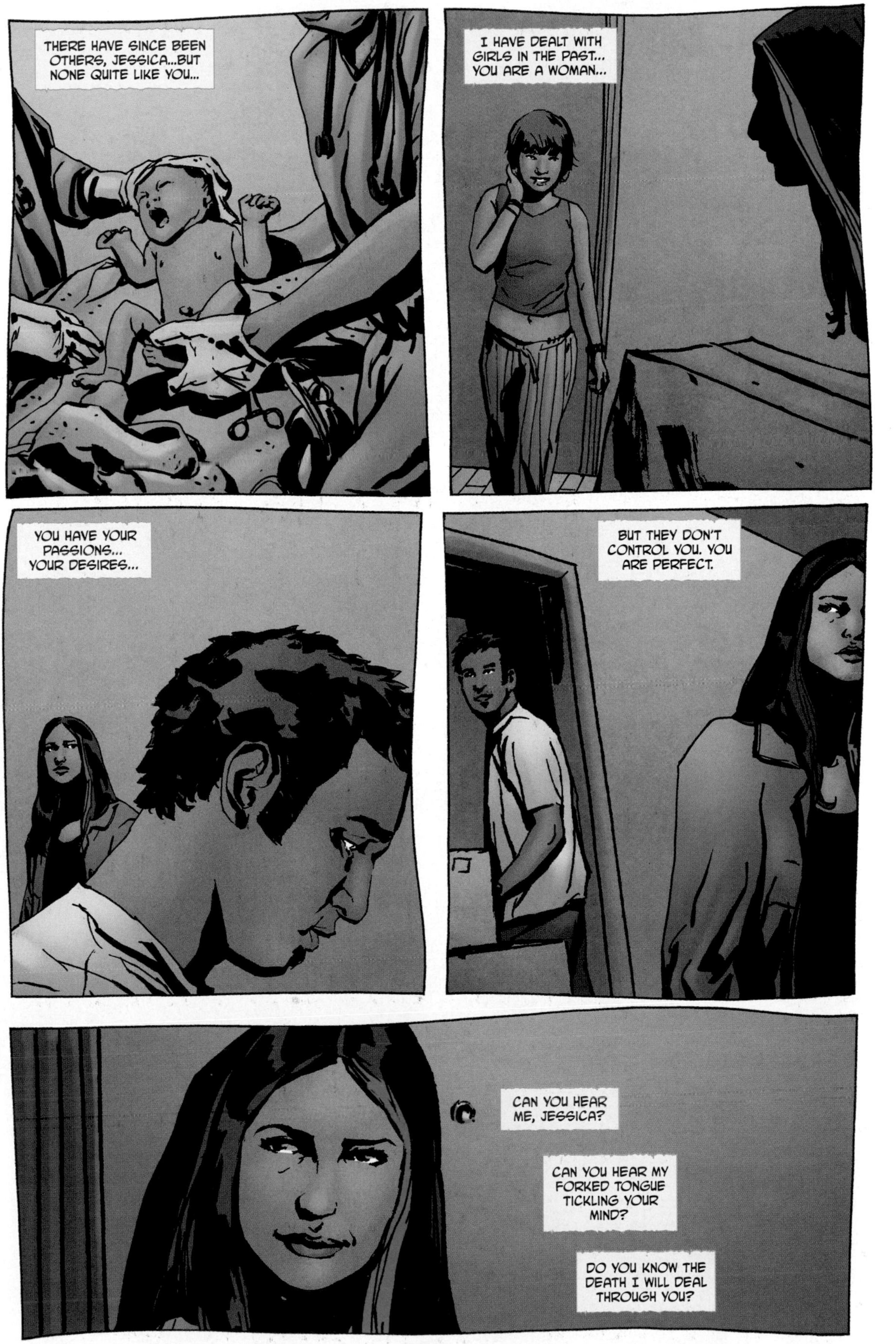
THERE HAVE SINCE BEEN OTHERS, JESSICA...BUT NONE QUITE LIKE YOU...
I HAVE DEALT WITH GIRLS IN THE PAST... YOU ARE A WOMAN...
YOU HAVE YOUR PASSIONS... YOUR DESIRES...
BUT THEY DON'T CONTROL YOU. YOU ARE PERFECT.
CAN YOU HEAR ME, JESSICA?
CAN YOU HEAR MY FORKED TONGUE TICKLING YOUR MIND?
DO YOU KNOW THE DEATH I WILL DEAL THROUGH YOU?

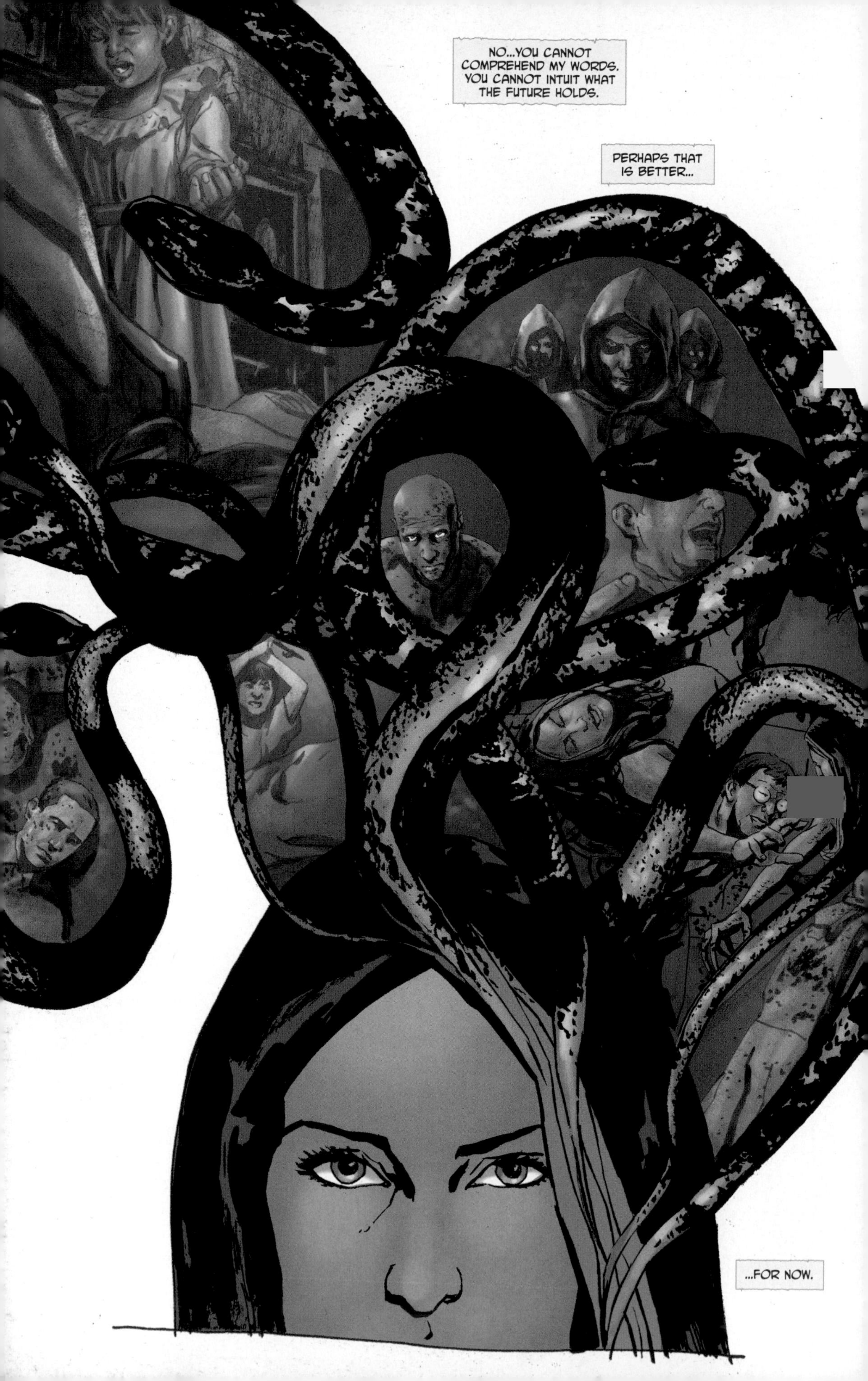
NO...YOU CANNOT COMPREHEND MY WORDS. YOU CANNOT INTUIT WHAT THE FUTURE HOLDS.
PERHAPS THAT IS BETTER...
...FOR NOW.

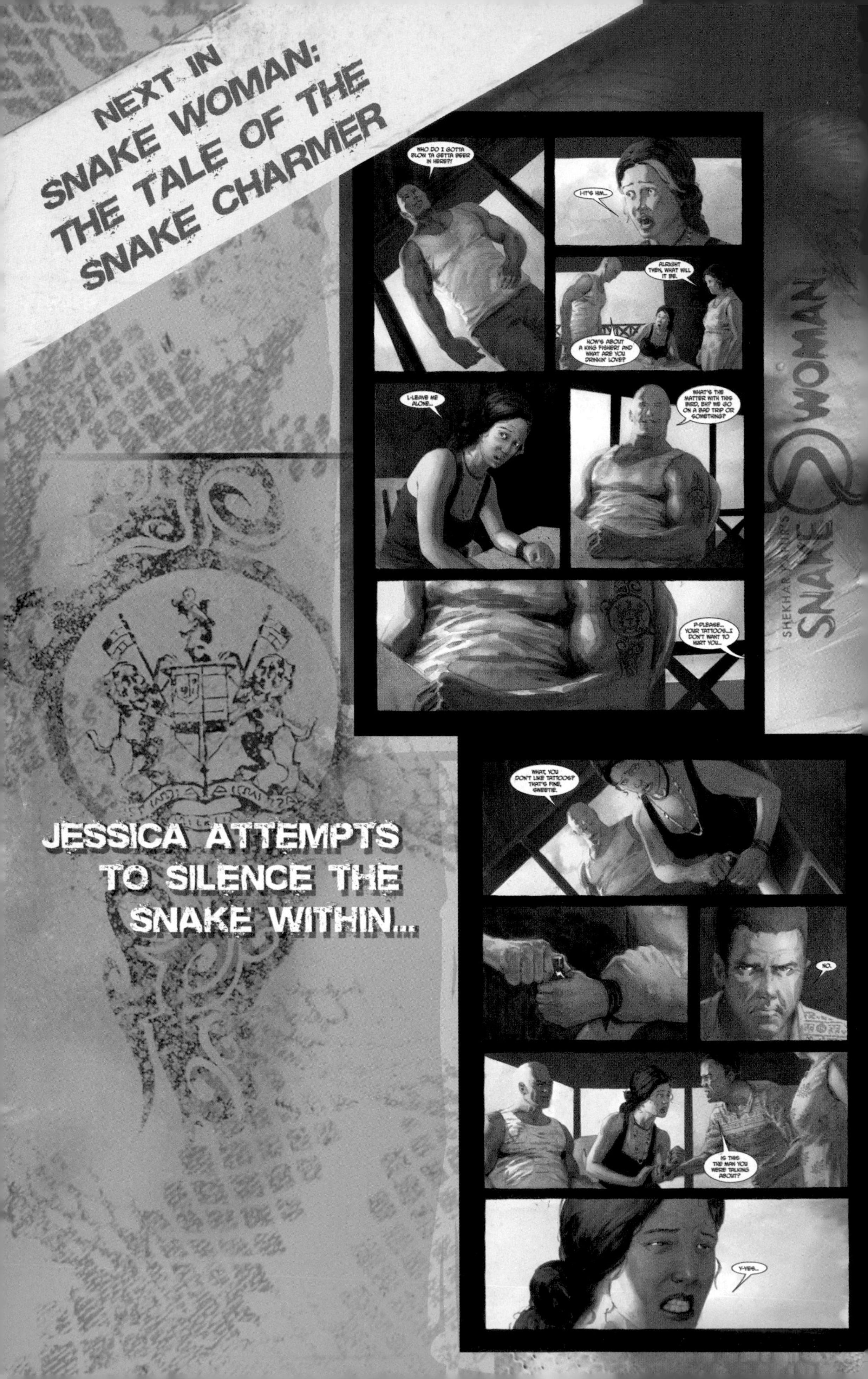

NEXT IN
SNAKE WOMAN:
THE TALE OF THE
SNAKE CHARMER
WHO DO I GOTTA BLOW TA GETTA BEER IN HERE?!
I-IT'S HIM...
ALRIGHT THEN, WHAT WILL IT BE.
HOW'S ABOUT A KING FISHER! AND WHAT ARE YOU DRINKIN' LOVE?
L-LEAVE ME ALONE...
WHAT'S THE MATTER WITH THIS BIRD, EH? WE GO ON A BAD TRIP OR SOMETHING?
P-PLEASE... YOUR TATTOOS...I DON'T WANT TO HURT YOU...
SNAKE WOMAN
WHAT, YOU DON'T LIKE TATTOOS? THAT'S FINE, SWEETIE.
NO.
IS THIS THE MAN YOU WERE TALKING ABOUT?
Y-YES...
JESSICA ATTEMPTS
TO SILENCE THE
SNAKE WITHIN...

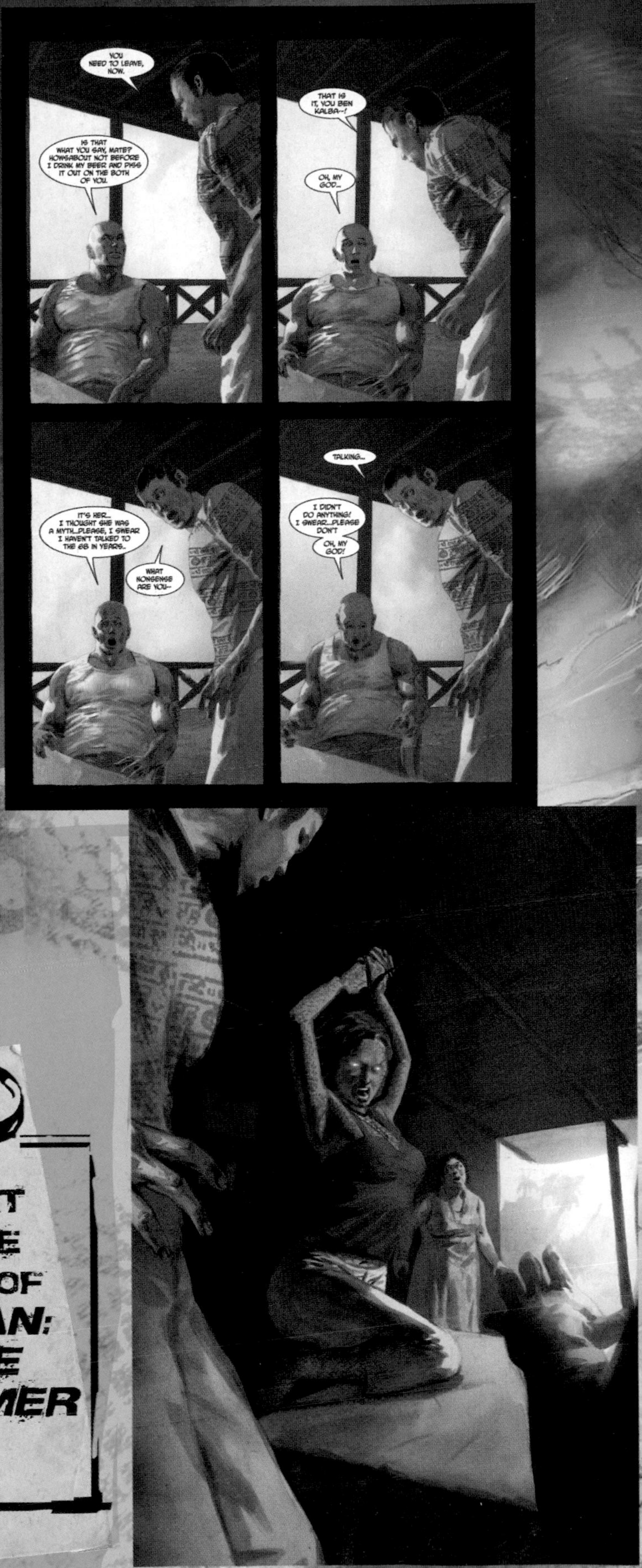
YOU NEED TO LEAVE, NOW.
IS THAT WHAT YOU SAY, MATE? HOWSABOUT NOT BEFORE I DRINK MY BEER AND PISS IT OUT ON THE BOTH OF YOU.
THAT IS IT, YOU BEN KALBA--!
OH, MY GOD...
IT'S HER... I THOUGHT SHE WAS A MYTH...PLEASE, I SWEAR I HAVEN'T TALKED TO THE 6B IN YEARS...
WHAT NONSENSE ARE YOU--
TALKING...
I DIDN'T DO ANYTHING! I SWEAR...PLEASE DON'T
OH, MY GOD!

BUT SOME REPTILES ARE JUST TOO DIFFICULT TO TAME...

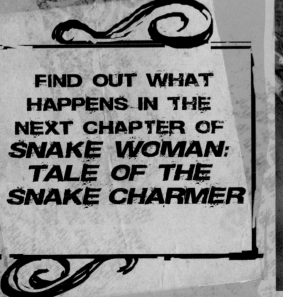

FIND OUT WHAT HAPPENS IN THE NEXT CHAPTER OF *SNAKE WOMAN: TALE OF THE SNAKE CHARMER*

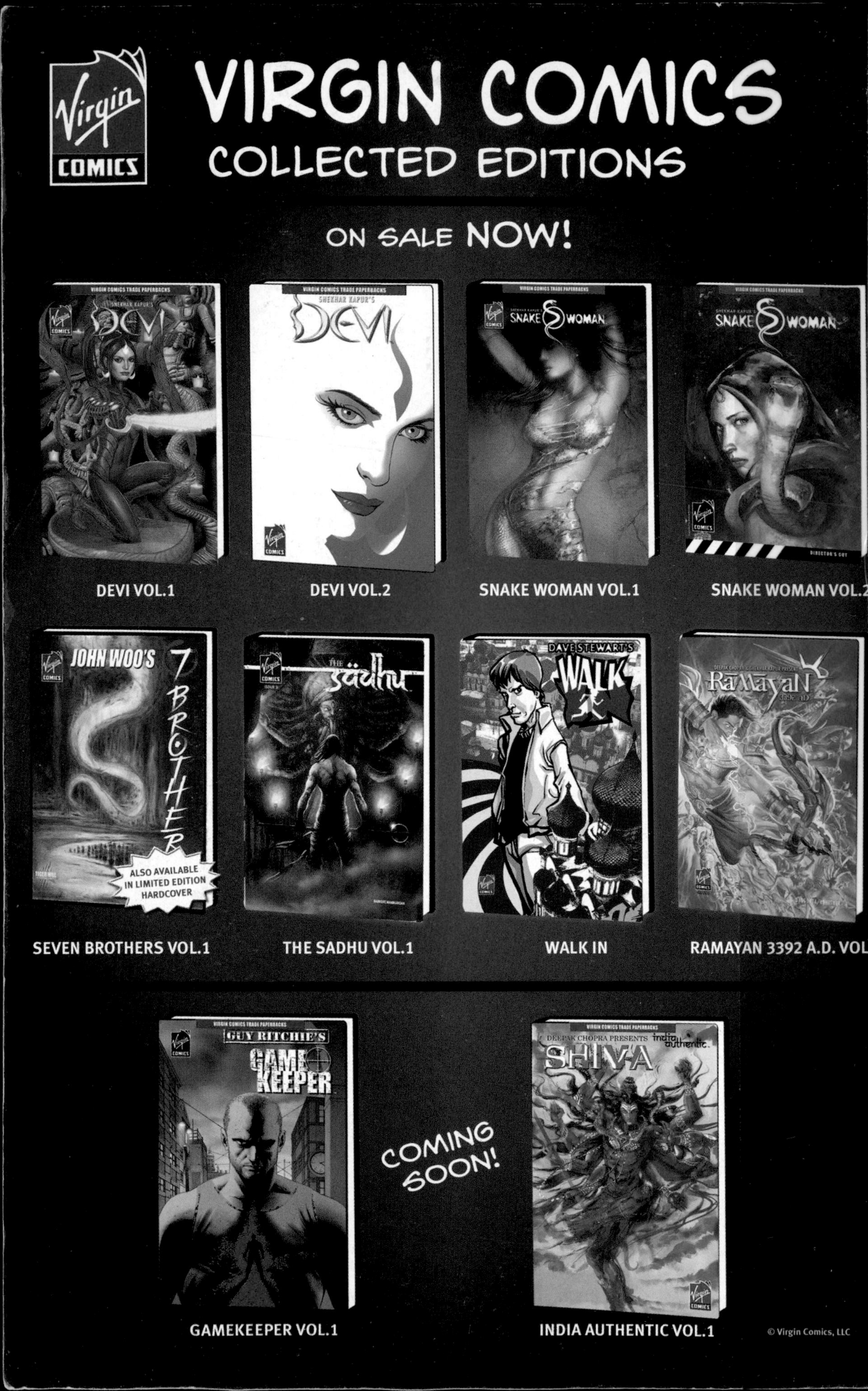

Virgin COMICS
VIRGIN COMICS
COLLECTED EDITIONS
ON SALE NOW!
DEVI VOL.1
DEVI VOL.2
SNAKE WOMAN VOL.1
SNAKE WOMAN VOL.2
JOHN WOO'S 7 BROTHERS
ALSO AVAILABLE IN LIMITED EDITION HARDCOVER
SEVEN BROTHERS VOL.1
THE SADHU VOL.1
DAVE STEWART'S WALK IN
WALK IN
RAMAYAN 3392 A.D. VOL
GUY RITCHIE'S GAMEKEEPER
GAMEKEEPER VOL.1
COMING SOON!
DEEPAK CHOPRA PRESENTS india authentic SHIVA
INDIA AUTHENTIC VOL.1
© Virgin Comics, LLC